Margaret Atwood

Genre Fiction and Film Companions

Series Editor: Simon Bacon

MARGARET

ATWOOD

A New Companion

Edited by Gina Wisker

PETER LANG

Oxford · Berlin · Bruxelles · Chennai · New York · Lausanne

Bibliographic information published by the Deutsche Nationalbibliothek.
The German National Library lists this publication in the German National Bibliography;
detailed bibliographic data is available on the Internet at http://dnb.d-nb.de.

A catalogue record for this book is available from the British Library.

Library of Congress Cataloging-in-Publication Data
Names: Wisker, Gina, 1951- editor
Title: Margaret Atwood : A New Companion / edited by Gina Wisker.
Description: Oxford ; New York : Peter Lang, [2026] | Series: Genre fiction
    and film companions, 26318725 ; 18 | Includes bibliographical references
    and index.
Identifiers: LCCN 2025023768 (print) | LCCN 2025023769 (ebook) |
    ISBN 9781800798618 paperback | ISBN 9781800798625 pdf |
    ISBN 9781800798632 epub
Subjects: LCSH: Atwood, Margaret, 1939—Criticism and interpretation |
    LCGFT: Literary criticism | Essays
Classification: LCC PR9199.3.A8 Z7477 2025 (print) | LCC PR9199.3.A8 (ebook) |
    DDC 813/.54–dc23/eng/20250528
LC record available at https://lccn.loc.gov/2025023768
LC ebook record available at https://lccn.loc.gov/2025023769

Cover image: Tracy/stock.adobe.com.

ISSN 2631-8725
ISBN 978-1-80079-861-8 (Print)
ISBN 978-1-80079-862-5 (E-PDF)
ISBN 978-1-80079-863-2 (E-PUB)
DOI 10.3726/b19711

© 2026 Peter Lang Group AG, Lausanne, Switzerland
Published by Peter Lang Ltd, Oxford, United Kingdom
info@peterlang.com – www.peterlang.com

This publication has been peer reviewed.

Contents

Contents

Acknowledgements

Many thanks as ever to Michelle Bernard for sensitive and focused engagement with sourcing critical reading, so much local editing and sorting the book out at every stage.

Thanks to Simon Bacon for enthusiasm, patience and support for the whole venture.

Thanks to Laurel Plapp at Peter Lang for patience and guidance throughout.

Thanks to all the contributors for great new takes on Atwood's work and for working with edits and re-writes when needed.

Final thanks to Calypso the poodle for accompanying me at each step both round the park to clear my head, and as the book gradually came together in my overcrowded little room.

Cambridge April 2025

Gina Wisker

Introduction

Margaret Atwood is always engaged with ways in which we understand, can story and challenge the versions of life which might control, curtail and silence us. She deals in exposing ways in which a materialistic consumer society could turn us all into disposable objects – whether in an everyday context of the family, where a mother can undermine and body shame her daughter (*Lady Oracle* 1981a) even beyond death, or a future-set fascistic, patriarchal society that can pervert relationships and enforce compliance and silence, particularly in women (*The Handmaid's Tale* 1985; *The Testaments* 2019). Imagining otherwise and somehow speaking out critically and creatively are tactics she and her characters use throughout her work, even if the word is long hidden in an archive or a coded record/testament. Talking back and taking back gendered power without despairing or hectoring, and active respect for diversity, are values and actions which run their course through the range of Margaret Atwood's works, particularly *The Handmaid's Tale*, novel, film and TV series through to *The Testaments* and the whole *MaddAddam* trilogy (2003–2013), alongside her interviews and letters, emphasising the power of reimagining, rethinking and acting with agency.

For several decades, Margaret Atwood has been and still remains a consistent, insightful, wry, concerned and utterly engaged voice for our varying times. A skilled weaver of words – a fount of powerful, insightful, practical knowledge about the importance of language in action, of carefully and deliberately choosing, speaking and sharing words – she enacts the magic of language, speaking truth to power. Starting with the domestic images of her daughter learning to speak and write, arranging words, Atwood's poem 'Spelling' reminds us that

A word after a word
after a word is power. (Atwood 1981b)

Her work deals (among much else) with the everyday terrors of internalised, socially embedded fascistic gender oppression, the insidious dangers of fundamentalism and other politically and psychologically reinforced forms of life denying bullying, as seen in *Lady Oracle* (1976), *The Edible Woman* (1969), *The Handmaid's Tale* (1985) and *The Testaments* (2019). It questions the trustworthiness of both received and silenced cultural and personal histories, revealing each to be versions of legitimated or unsanctioned fictions – for example, in *Cat's Eye* (1988) and *Alias Grace* (1996). An active voice for sustainability, ecological and human diversity, and for feminism, creativity and the worldviews of Indigenous people, she is rarely hectoring, always wise, wry and well-informed. Margaret Atwood puts her extraordinary imagination to work through the Gothic (*The Robber Bride* 1993), dystopian science fiction (*The MaddAddam* trilogy 2003–2013) (though she denied the definition for a while), short fiction/in memoir form (*Moral Disorder* 2006), the comic and much else in long and short fiction. Her early recognition came for her poetry and, after eighteen volumes, her most recent, *Dearly* (2020), enables a familiar, tightly controlled, personal, mythical, politically engaged voice that has as much space for family losses, gaps, hauntings, the beloved cat with dementia wondering what to do part way up the stairs at night, as for the daily escalating threats to the planet.

This book is a new Companion to Margaret Atwood's work, which does not intend to merely replicate the rich array of publications critically appraising her writing that is already available. Rather, it aims to do two things: to lay down critical engagements with her varied output, which offer sound yet new and updated discussions on those fundamental concerns of her work, on the major texts, and to explore relatively less visited, and/ or now highly topical issues and texts, and/or utterly new perspectives for 2025 and beyond. We always live in interesting times, and as we began this book, the apposite, all-seeing, ironic, satiric, critical and imaginatively constructive vision of Atwood's works, and of her interviews and public statements, felt like a report from a rebuilding moment, where irony and satire – specifically the forms and expression of liberated views in her books, TV series and films – could be rewarded with insightful responses, perhaps fewer school shootings, fewer toxic, misogynistic power games and even ways of tackling climate change. But continuing through 2025, it feels much darker again, which is when we need the outspoken, creative and critical voice of Atwood even more. Writing this, I sought an analogy for the moment and remember Wilfred Owen's 'Strange Meeting' (1918), thinking, first that the enemy the speaker killed, who now talks to the speaker as a ghost, could have been a friend under other circumstances, but more, the terrible predictiveness of the line 'when nations trek from progress'. I then discovered Jennifer Senior's interview with Atwood in *The Atlantic* (February 18, 2022) even a couple of years before the rapid slide backwards into another era of violence, divisiveness and misogyny in the US. They are talking here about Wilfrid Owen's poem, 'Strange Meeting', where Atwood notes the line 'I am the enemy you killed (my friend)', while the line I have in mind comes just a little earlier, noting the awareness of the poisoned future – the poisoned wells that the lies and hostilities will leave even when they might seem at least to cease, which damage will be difficult to resist and reject: 'none will break ranks, though nations trek from progress' (Owen 1918).

It is the role of the writer to expose such problematic behaviours even as they also, as Atwood can, write about the domestic version of facing the messy past and intending to do something more recuperative, filled with new life, and comparing the first steps to cleaning out the fridge, with multiple jars leaking in the domestic fridge:

Why are these jars still here?
They're full of old tom, green, brown and yellow and red, long overdue for the tossout
time going stale, tired, growing
Tiny gray spores, tiny poisons.

The little words of 'sadness and of tears', are discovered, are being cleared out. (Atwood 'Cleaning out the fridge' *Paper Boat*, 2023)

Atwood is aware of the constraints and possibilities for women under everyday misogynist and strong regimes – *The Handmaid's Tale* never ages and is always pertinent. Second-wave feminism is not only in her background but also a part of her DNA. She is remarkably both of the moment and, beyond that, worryingly prescient – she is personal and she is political, and all of this combines in her wry, absolutely accurate perspective on the world and on the individual life. Her presence, sensitivity and vast expert creative range is celebrated in the essays in this volume. As we were completing the volume, Margaret Atwood's collection *Paper Boat: New and Selected Poems 1961–2023* (2023) came out, which contained messages and fine writing that could not be overlooked.

Contributors in this collection write about her novels, short stories, her illustrated stories for children and the films and TV series that have developed from, and further develop, her work and arguments. There are discussions of her poetry and her engagements with music, and throughout the book, there is attention to the many ways in which, through her troubling, entertaining, thought-provoking writing, Margaret Atwood makes us see differently and question embedded power and urges us to act in a courageous and creative manner.

Speaking truth to power is one of Margaret Atwood's great consistent achievements, whether she is writing strongly worded letters about not polluting lakes and waterways; whimsically yet respectfully mourning and celebrating the fading and the favoured dead; or reprising and exposing stark, dystopian, misogynistic threats to the future of humanity. Given the terrifying and bizarre politics of 2024 onwards, both globally and in North America, we should expect she will have little rest and much to say to help her readership think through and articulate our own responses.

There is a great deal of critical work on Margaret Atwood, as indeed there should be, and although the call for contributions to this volume made suggestions about what could be covered, our contributors focused on both consistent and new issues in her work and chose to do so by concentrating less on the earlier than on the later work, which explains the brevity of the first part.

The book is divided into four parts. The first part, 'Early Work', looks at two of her novels, *The Edible Woman* and *Alias Grace*, each dealing with ways in which women are socially constructed yet can avoid, or challenge these constructions.

In her chapter, 'You look delicious', Lorna Piatti Farnell focuses on the gender politics, alimentary disturbances and consumerist media in *The Edible Woman*, especially where Marion (who, significantly, works in marketing and advertising) realises that marrying Peter would cause her to lose her identity. Her mental health declines, charted symptomatically through her relationship with eating, which becomes increasingly difficult. At one moment, she refuses to eat a juicy steak, horrified to realise this was a living being. The possibility of eating it reminds her of cannibalism and causes her to problematise her own body, but her response goes beyond a form of anorexia. It is a reaction against being consumed. When a self-silenced Marion suddenly realises that in constantly passing even simple choices and responsibilities on to Peter, she is losing her identity and power, she bakes a cake, an image, an effigy of herself, which Lorna Piatti-Farnell points out echoes ancient mythic rituals of sacrifice and power. And Marion is taking the power here. No longer the hunted or human consumable in this highly materialistic marketing world, where body image is aligned with selling and consuming goods and the married woman is a silenced, consumed item, she offers up the cake to be consumed instead of herself, a freeing, celebratory move and a revolt against both 'patriarchal and capitalist oppression in the Western societies of the Cold War era'.

In 'Channelling Women's Rage for Adult Audiences in the Twenty-First Century', Shannon Scott continues a focus on rightfully angry women, viewing Grace Marks in *Alias Grace* as a Victorian, Canadian female killer· akin to Lizzie Borden with her axe and Mary Ann Cotton with poison in her tea kettle. These fictionalised historical cases powerfully engage with social and gendered issues. Atwood's use of historical records and newspaper articles is aligned with Susanna Moodie's contemporary *Life in the Clearing versus the Bush* (1853), containing accounts of Moodie's visits to Marks in the penitentiary and the asylum, and acts like a police procedural. Marks, an Irish immigrant and female servant, is a product of her time and place, and Atwood grants her agency by bringing back to life, literally, through records and interviews, leading the reader to wonder about who is guilty / more guilty, and the relationship between her situation, her gender and the treatment of her guilt. This is an exploration of crimes committed by women in the Victorian era and of the treatment of insanity, rather than of 'true' guilt and the guilt associated with pregnancy out of wedlock. As Shannon Scott notes, the other women in service – i.e. Grace's close friend, Mary Whitney, and Nancy, the probably murdered housekeeper – both became pregnant after sex with their employers. Scott brings this up to date, considering pregnancy as still a litmus test of sorts in the twenty-first century, particularly for recent immigrants and the working classes.

Part II looks at *The Handmaid's Tale* (1985) and the *MaddAddam* trilogy: *Oryx and Crake* (2003), *The Year of The Flood* (2009) and *MaddAddam* (2013).

Gina Wisker's 'Salvaging Revisited' links all four of these novels with Atwood's writing on climate change and Indigenous knowledge. Salvaging, which normally suggests rescuing – a tricky word like many others in Gilead, where initially positive meanings are reversed – is a ritual battering to death of men accused of rape. In *The Handmaid's Tale* (Hulu TV) the Handmaids refuse to stone wayward Janine, in an act of rescue and agency. She is salvaged and rescued. The essay focuses on Atwood's imagining of the end of days – the results of the Anthropocene and man-made disasters – and links this to Atwood's upbringing in the bush, where her father was a forest entomologist; her research on climate change; respect for Indigenous knowledges; and her activist writings for the literal salvaging of the living planet. The essay ends with *The Testaments* (2019) reprising the need for testimony, free speech and positive action in a repressive world, even in what Agnes and Nicole define as a 'festering shit heap'(2019: 379), their own country.

Laura-Jane Devanny, in focusing on the Crakers in *Oryx and Crake* in 'Possibilities and Pitfalls of the Literal Posthuman', points out that these hybridised, cyborgian creatures, a product of both technology and nature, could not only be seen as workable, harmonious posthuman models, but also are an example of the logic of advanced capitalism, biotechnology, bio-capitalism and the commodification of life. There are no easy solutions here. These perfect creatures are unnatural, placid and scary, leaving the protagonist, Jimmy, concerned. However, as storytelling is a characteristic of humanity and part of the evolution of human consciousness along with language, so the figure of the boy Blackbeard allows continued hope for imagination among the new generation of these cross-species subjects.

In 'Memory, Mourning and Nostalgia in *Oryx and Crake*', Sarah Wagstaffe picks up where the previous essay left off, with Jimmy / Snowman wishing to lead the newly invented humanoid Crakers out of their birthplace in the Paradise Dome, into the world. This essay builds on work by Brooks

Bouson (2004) and Coral Ann Howells (2006), identifying a split narrative and enabling a kind of double consciousness, represented by Jimmy himself as he embraces challenge and joy through creating stories for the creative Crakers. Atwood's insistence on an emotional and imaginative context for human sexuality, love and nostalgia informs Jimmy's gift to the Crakers of his own history, and storying, which offer comfort and guidance, thereby ending on a positive note.

Sarah Worgan's 'Surplus Life in Margaret Atwood's *Oryx and Crake*' next considers the development of what have been called 'control societies' and the importance of the biotech company in the field of genetics, where corporations gain control over life systems – as Crake recognizes, a 'financialization of life and death'. There is a topical exploration of the relationship between economies and life sciences in this text, theorised through Foucault.

After the two slightly more positive endings of the previous two readings of *Oryx and Crake*, to quote Crake, 'we're in deep trouble' (Atwood 2004: 347). Future life is envisaged in a liminal space as humanity consumes itself in excess.

The Testaments, the focus of the third part, attracted the most contributions (four) probably because of the collection's timing during and towards the end of the main COVID-19 pandemic wave.

In 'How Gilead Fell: An Ecocultural Reading of *The Testaments*', Coral Ann Howells engages with the novel's positioning, offering an ecocultural reading based on Atwood's feminist and ecological concerns, underpinning the novel's interactive relationships between ecology and human agency. Atwood stages a dialogue between totalitarian and regeneration narratives in *The Testaments*, identifying Gilead as paradigm of the totalitarian state thriving on misogyny, bodily abuse and denial of basic kinship relations, perverting what it means to be human. Aunt Lydia is seen here as a dangerous figure, one of Atwood's 'spotty-handed villainesses', with her role as a prime agent of women's oppression, 'unforgiving witness' and 'implacable enemy', as her secretly written Ardua Hall Holograph reveals. The testament is a counter-narrative. She is a double agent working for May Day, and particularly in the more rounded TV version, Aunt Lydia manages versions of events through the many files under her control, including those of bloodlines. The essay emphasises the damage that Gilead does to mothers, daughters and all females under totalitarian order, while sisterhood becomes a problematic concept. It offers an astute reading of the calculating nature of Aunt Lydia, who sees the young women as instruments for revenge, her 'destroying angels'. An open ending could signal the potential for regeneration and renewal in the intertwined expression of individual and collective resistance to tyranny, or at least its beginning.

In her chapter 'Childhood Rites and Rights in *The Testaments*', Blanka Grzegorczyk builds on Atwood's obituary for Angela Carter (Atwood 2005), which notes how Carter, 'born subversive', remade history by focusing on the underbelly of life, and decides that this applies to Atwood and her 'playful' and 'rebellious' young female characters in *The Testaments*, using this term, as Foucault would, to show how they recover subjugated knowledge – eroded by dominant histories in Gilead – indicating ways in which they can reclaim or claim power. For Atwood's young women, this is a grassroots reaction against Gilead and its oppressive modes of upbringing and silencing. Central here is the passing on of news vital to women's survival in Gilead and dependent on acts of collective solidarity, which includes both the girls and Aunt Lydia, with her control over versions of recorded knowledge and her obsession with whether she can trust her implied reader to pass it on to fuel change. Sally McLuckie's illustrated chapter 'Embracing the Witch: The Influence of Spiritual Feminism in Aunt Lydia's Transformation from Witch to Goddess', explores Aunt Lydia as a goddess symbol moving between Hecate and Venus, embracing the witch and imbued with mystical and sacred qualities. McLuckie challenges historical, negative views of women's energies and spiritual powers and shows how the novel offers reclamation of a women's form of spirituality. She argues that Aunt Lydia is not aligned with Western Judeo-Christianity but rather in opposition and as a replacement. Aunt Lydia, then, is a witch, a 'political revolutionary', who critiques and attacks the authority of Commander Judd, the Divine Order, and the foundations of Gilead society.

The next chapter, Jade Hinchliffe's 'Reading Atwood's Feminist Dystopian Fiction Alongside Feminist Surveillance Studies', develops an unusual approach in explaining surveillance studies and its relationship with scholarship on speculative fiction, largely focused on both *The*

Handmaid's Tale and *The Testaments*, to consider how Atwood's feminist dystopias contribute to our understanding of surveillance and gender. Feminist theory, dystopian studies and surveillance studies are combined to develop a completely new focus on the gaze, on surveillance of bodies as well as sexualized identities. There is an exploration of how women navigate spaces differently because of their gender, relating surveillance, gender and embodiment in a dystopian society. Self-surveillance is also important in *The Handmaid's Tale*, and medical surveillance, another form of control, is linked to exploring how the World Health Organization invests in health education, forcing compliance on women. This essay mentions work from the Global South and explores adaptations using the focus and effects of current technologies, in which ordinary citizens expose injustice.

The fourth part of the book explores the diversity of Atwood's writing and focuses on her less widely explored work. Australians Jessica Gildersleeve and Laurie Johnson look at the abuses of Shakespeare in *Hag-Seed*, Atwood's revision of *The Tempest*. Here Felix, a teacher of theatre in a men's prison, reprises Prospero's role in *The Tempest*, exploring Atwood's relationship between literature and responsibility, asking what is revenge and what is justice, particularly through the arts and the interactive audience, using Shakespeare's words as curse (as does Caliban). *Hag-Seed*, they argue, observes the chaotic ethics of literature and its potential, not only for improvement, but also for destruction. These authors extend their exploration beyond *The Tempest* to consider other texts, including Oscar Wilde's *The Portrait of Dorian Gray*, which alludes to the play. In discussing adaptations that take different elements of the play to explore further — for example, Ariel's torture and Prospero's calling up a storm — they note that *Hag-Seed* prompts questions about the role of literature, the morality or otherwise of writing, and even 'the paradoxical purposelessness of literature'.

Also a rarity is University of Toronto Professor of Musicology Robin Elliott's chapter on Margaret Atwood's engagement with the broader arts and music, examining Atwood's own libretti in which composers set her words to music and Canadian composers set her poems to music for voice and instrumental accompaniment. Others have adapted her novels to create musical stage works and soundtracks. Her interests are diverse, and music appears in the short stories, ranging from classical to folk, country and pop, and she's made selections on Desert Island Discs. Toronto is a city of music and the arts, and Elliott's essay opens up an area of Atwood's work that has received little attention to date, including *The Handmaid's Tale* as an opera and *MaddAddam* as a ballet (commissioned by the National Ballet of Canada, in association with Britain's Royal Ballet).

Surprisingly few opted to explore Atwood's rich range of short stories; however, in her chapter, Dunja M. Mohr looks at fairy tale politics, focusing on an Atwood story and exploring the role of storytelling as a bearer of truth, revelation of multiple meanings, voice doubling and mirror imagery. Each of Atwood's texts is open to a myriad of different interpretations, and this essay looks at what has worked with the Brothers Grimm fairy tales compilation, with their stock characters and settings and their oral roots. The history of metamorphosis, ambiguities, stereotypes and inequalities are toyed with in Atwood's short story, 'Impatient Griselda', which comes right up to date, reprinted in *Old Babes in the Wood* (2023), her most recent short story collection at the time of writing, topical with its pandemic narrative frame, parodic scifi and feminist fairy tale rewriting of 'Patient Griselda'. Thus, there is intertextuality, dark humour and a comic science fiction setting (Atwood does toy with science fiction despite earlier refusals). This tale has unreliable narrators and an alien entertainer mimicking fairy tale dissemination.

The next chapter is by Fiona Tolan on feminist killjoys, happiness, feminism and troublemaking, drawing on Atwood's 2010 *The Heart Goes Last* with its focus on sex bots and Elvis impersonators and set initially in post–economic crash America. Fiona Tolan uses, among others, Sarah Ahmed's critical work looking at second-wave feminism's construction of the white, middle class domestic sphere as a site of incarceration. Atwood's fiction typically speaks to this feminist view, undercutting the notion that objects and certain life trajectories promise happiness. Fiona Tolan's chapter takes us right back to the beginning of this book, mentioning Marion in the *Edible Woman* (1969), who rejects Peter's marriage proposal, having constructed a version of self as a cake to be devoured, and other revolutionary women such as Agnes in *The Testaments*, who resists an arranged marriage. Atwood has many troublesome young and older female characters resisting social pressures to be silent, submissive or happy with their lot, specifically feminist activists in *The Handmaid's Tale*, and in the *Cat's Eye*, compared here to Doris Lessing's work. Charmaine adopts the happy housewife heroine role, celebrating her home and washer dryer, and 'signs away her liberties'. This is a politically astute essay, and in comparing her to Aunt Lydia, Atwood asks readers to consider what they would do in Charmaine's situation: collude, or not, in a failing capitalist system that does not protect Charmaine's job in Positron, which, as part of the Consilience project, involves administering lethal injections to troublemakers, thus supporting a violent, oppressive system to remain safe herself. A range of critics are brought in to explore issues of resistance and collusion in this well-theorised, crucial piece which goes to the heart of questions about what you can do as a woman – once you have pointed out inequalities in humanity, can you be anything more than a feminist killjoy? And is that enough? Tolan ends with asserting the significance of the feminist killjoy, with the final defiance of the mother figure in Gilead.

Helene Staveley, in 'Empowering the Inner Nitwit', focuses on Margaret Atwood's work for kids. The chapter first mentions children in a range of Atwood's novels and then examines her writing for children, enabling us to see similar themes throughout her work. *Up in the Tree* (1978), *Princess Prunella and the Purple Peanut* (1995), *Rude Ramsey and the Roaring Radishes* (2003) and *Bashful Bob and Doleful Dorinda* (2004) all emerged at times when Atwood was writing stories for adults, involving posthuman dystopias, and Helene Staveley argues that they act as the kind of match to the tougher work. In these children's picture books, children and animals coexist productively, and Atwood playfully reconfigures core ideas about humanity and survival. Staveley makes a cogent argument for ways in which the picture books for children engage in posthumanist philosophies, relationships between child and animal, cross-species friendships and what it means to be fully human. Atwood herself talks about writing for young people in terms of release, a recuperation of playfulness and energy. Effective strategies are explored here through each of the books, filled with fable, fairy tale dimensions, child protagonists and friendly animal helpers, accompanied by artwork from prominent children's illustrators to give a sense of the interaction between the image and the words. At one point, Staveley notes that Atwood is 'playfully needling her loyal adult fan base by bringing them to stutter and stumble while reading her books to their kids', which exposes her sense of humour. These are socially critical as well as entertaining tales.

As this book came to a close, more relevant research was published and deserves a mention. Given the topicality of Atwood's work for our times, there will be much more before the book is published. An ecofeminist approach, in Lorna Piatti Farnell's chapter, is also engaged with in Daniella Irene Baker's 'From Enduring to Living: An Ecofeminist Reading of Margaret Atwood's *The Edible Woman* and Han Kang's *The Vegetarian*' (2025), which comments on body-image and societal pressures on women. For the chapters on *The Testaments* and the role played by Aunt Lydia, Peter Sabo and Rhiannon Graybill's work (2022) provides new insights and Ewelina Feldman-Kołodziejuk's (2025) article offers a re-evaluation of Aunt Lydia's earlier villainy (*The Handmaid's Tale*) by way of the lens of her undercover identity, revealed in the later *The Testaments*, thus encouraging re-reading, empathy and reinterpretation (a common practice with historical events and figures).

Margaret Atwood was first known as a poet and has continued to write poetry throughout her career. Gina Wisker's final chapter does not attempt to pull together all the themes and collections of Atwood's poetry, rather choosing to focus on some strands, mainly diversity and survival, between two collections: the most recent *Dearly* (2020) and *Morning in the Burned House* (1995). The chapter begins by noting that Atwood has an extraordinary way of sensing future loss in presence, a line we have seen throughout her work, particularly in her concern for ecology and human futures. It also considers ways in which her poetry deals with patriarchy and often uses the revisionist feminist mythology that appears throughout her work to do so. Margaret Atwood's poetry ranges from the domestic, often wry and gentle, recognising the everyday in homes, which might be subjected to nuclear war, or equally to family loss, each leading to empty spaces at kitchen tables. The poetry covers a whole range of emotions and contexts, emphasizing domestic interactions and warmth, survival or unease and signs of impending loss. In *Dearly*, lack, loss and some lingering traces of survival infuse almost everything, almost everywhere. Both these collections offer a sense of a lack of solidity and presence — the potential of emptiness.

One poem from *Dearly* sensitively domesticates dementia and family loss, focusing on the cat who is gradually losing her own mind, forgets where she is or what she should be doing. Loss is an issue that runs all the way through Atwood's work in terms of loss of ecological diversity, of humanity, of freedom and of personal futures, and this collection in particular is filled with ghosts. Nonetheless, there are also lively poems representing versions of women, for example, 'Pin Up Girl', in which Atwood revisits earlier territory. The disruption of the domestic is immediate in the Goldilocks story in *Morning in the Burned House*, while domestic loss is also very personal, because of the loss of her father, then her mother's dementia and loss. In *Dearly* Atwood's partner, Graeme Gibson is first pre-mourned because of his own dementia, followed by his death. The whole book, *Dearly*, is really an insightful and loving memory. One central poem in this is 'The Invisible Man', in which the presence of the man is seen as an absence. In line with her consistent equation of human lives and those of living beings and ecologies on the planet, the loss of individuals here is like the loss of the complex living ecology of the world. Her question emphasises potential loss and emptiness.

> oh, children,
> will you grow up in a world without birds?
> will there be crickets, where you are? ('The Invisible Man' Dearly, 2020)

Margaret Atwood's family and personal poetry is of a piece with care for the planet and living things, land, creatures and people. There are also echoes, reminders and continuities, and in her last poem, she talks of picking blackberries. 'The best ones grow in shadow', ('Blackberries' in *Dearly* (2020 :33) like her poems and the rest of her writing, waiting presumably for the right time.

Part I

Early Work: *The Edible Woman* and *Alias Grace*

Lorna Piatti-Farnell

'You look delicious': Consumerist Media, Gender Politics and Alimentary Disturbances in Margaret Atwood's *The Edible Woman*

References to food abound in the pages of Margaret Atwood's *The Edible Woman* (1969). The life of the novel's protagonist, Marian McAlpin, is traced through the metaphorical stencil of food imagery, whilst issues of taste and lifestyle, and power and ideological conflict, are repeatedly connected to the production and consumption of food and its representation. In the early stages of the novel, Marian is repeatedly shown enjoying and indulging her appetite, as she often consumes numerous snacks – from peanut butter to canned rice pudding – just before lunchtime. The catalyst to a change in her eating habits is an unexpected proposal of marriage from her boyfriend, Peter. Following her instinctive acceptance of the proposal, Marian soon discovers that marriage equals slipping away into socioeconomic obscurity, as she is expected to simply quit her job and become a homemaker. After this realisation, her mental health progressively declines, and her emotional and political situation is charted symptomatically through her relationship with eating, as food becomes – both literally and metaphorically – hard to stomach. Rather than an isolated instance of breakdown, Atwood offers Marian's story as emblematic of women of the main character's generation. Indeed, through food metaphors – in particular, the specific psychological frameworks around food avoidance – Atwood seems to be providing a reflection of the sociopolitical situation of the 1960s, which already carried the seeds of the next gendered revolution brought by second-wave feminism. This appears to confirm Erik Erikson's assertion that 'in all periods of history, mental disturbances of epidemiological significance or special fascination highlight a specific aspect of [human] nature in conflict with the times' (1975: 22).

Taking this as a critical starting point, this chapter explores how *The Edible Woman* portrays both consumption and the performance of gender as increasingly mediated by simulacral practices. Particularly, through the idea of 'dead meat', Atwood suggests that, in a consumer society, the idea of woman is also constructed by images to be 'consumed'. Pervasive links to advertising images of seemingly gendered consumables, from beer to filet mignon, are constructed throughout *The Edible Woman,* as the novel achieves a level of self-conscious interrogation of the fusion between political economy and gender politics that goes beyond simply portraying consumer identities as conflicted and liminal spaces. The narrative negotiates the possible displacement of material reality by the consumerist chimera of marketed needs, as consumption becomes a metaphor for both capitalist economies and complex gender relations. A famous passage in *The Edible Woman* offers us an image of a woman eating a heart-shaped Valentine's cake and feeling as though she is consuming herself: '[s]he cut into the cake. She put a forkful into her mouth and chewed it slowly; it felt spongy and cellular against her tongue, like the bursting of thousands of tiny lungs. She shuddered and spat the cake out' (Atwood 1969: 207). Openly unravelling a sub-text of cannibalism in the consumer world – embodied in the Valentine's cake – and exposing anxieties about gendered economies, Atwood's novel explores the intersections between food, commodity fetishism, representation and sexual politics. In this chapter, I will focus on how *The Edible Woman* tacitly renders concerns about 'cannibalised' consumers in capitalist economies, but voices a more polemical, analytical confidence. Atwood provides us with a gothic exploration of self-harm – in the form of food avoidance – in order to conjure anxieties about the gendered nature of consumption. *The Edible Woman* unveils how, in Westernised societies, consumption has long ceased to be solely about nourishment and food has become part of an increasingly dematerialised realm of representations, signs and images.

In the novel, Marian's life, unfolding in urban Canada in the 1960s, is implicitly proffered as representative: the protagonist is confronted by a pathway which Sarah Sceats describes as 'more or less that of any young educated woman of the time: university, work, marriage' (2004: 96).

Marian has a steady, yet tedious job in market research, a pleasant boyfriend and a select group of friends. Her eating habits appear to be 'healthy' (Atwood 1969: 11); she craves food and becomes annoyed when unable to eat properly: 'I didn't realise how late it was [...] I had to skip the egg and wash down a glass of milk and a bowl of cold cereal which I knew would leave me hungry before lunchtime. I chewed a piece of bread while Ainsley watched me' (Atwood 1969: 12). Indeed, Marian appears to have strong opinions about both her daily lifestyle, including the food she carefully selects and consumes. However, after her engagement to Peter becomes official, Marian seems content to fade into the background behind her strong-minded fiancé:

> I heard a soft flannelly voice that I barely recognised, saying "I'd rather have you decide that. I'd rather leave the big decisions to you". I was astounded at myself. I'd never said anything remotely like that to him before. The funny thing was I really meant it. (Atwood 1969: 90)

Although superficially it appears as though Marian has accepted a submissive and subordinate position, a dramatic change in her relation to food is symptomatic of underlying emotional and ideological conflict. As the novel progresses, Atwood uses food and eating metaphors in order to encapsulate the ambivalence of Marian's condition. Here, Atwood's sexual politics seem to be expressed with clarity. For instance, the repeated image of the egg functions as a mirror-image for Marian's feelings. The morning after Peter's proposal, Marian's breakfast egg breaks as it touches the boiling water, thus failing to achieve the perfect consistency she had intended: 'I manoeuvred the egg into the saucepan; it cracked immediately [...] I inspected my egg, which was sending out a white-semi-congealed feeler like an exploring oyster [...] I got my thumb stuck in it. It wasn't done after all' (Atwood 1969: 84). The egg, of course, is a traditional symbol for new life and rebirth, but here it also signifies something indecisive and investigative: the messy, broken egg plunged into hot water mirrors Marian's repressed anxiety regarding her fate as well as functioning as an allegorical signpost to her biological destiny as breeder rather than breadwinner. Peter clearly tells her that 'he considered it unfair to marry if you couldn't afford to support your wife' (Atwood 1969: 108).

Having established Atwood's desire to explore the interface between political economy and patriarchy, we can now proceed to explore the ways in which *The Edible Woman* portrays the practice of consumption and the performance of gender as increasingly mediated by simulacral images. Particularly, how Atwood suggests that, in a consumer society, the idea of woman is also constructed by images and consumed using the idea of 'dead meat'. An unconscious rebellion against her situation begins to ferment inside Marian and manifests itself in the development of food loathing. The triggering episode in this process takes place during a romantic dinner with her fiancé. At the table, wife-to-be Marian happily contemplates her image in a soup spoon, as if she were on the menu: 'Marian gazed down at the small silvery image reflected in the bowl of the spoon: herself upside down, with a huge torso narrowing to a pinhead at the handle end' (Atwood 1969: 146). The distorted and deformed features displayed in the cutlery clearly signify an anticipated destiny in which her intellectual abilities will be eclipsed by her biological functions. Whilst Marian drifts towards intellectual passivity, Peter takes control:

> She had fallen into the habit in the last month or so of letting him choose for her. It got rid of the vacillation she had found herself displaying when confronted with a menu: she never knew what she wanted to have. (Atwood 1969: 147)

When Peter's food choice – a juicy filet mignon – appears on his plate, Marian observes his skilful cutting of the steak. The activity's violent yet paradoxically neat nature reminds her of the adverts for Moose Beer, a popular beverage aimed at men, which was part of an advertising survey she had worked on. One can argue that Atwood foregrounds the integration of hegemonic gender codes with the workings of consumer capitalism. Advertising strategies are channelled as a system of external stimuli that aim to promote consumption whilst seemingly reinforcing dominant formulations of dichotomous gender identities. *The Edible Woman* achieves a clear level of self-conscious interrogation of the fusion between political economy, gender politics and consumer identity.

Watching Peter consume his meal, Marian is instinctively reminded of the images of hunters and fishermen – iconographic examples of 'manly' men – which accompany the advertising of the beer:

> The fisherman wading in the stream, scooping the trout in his net, was too tidy [...] the fish was so unreal; it had no slime, no teeth, no smell, it was a clever toy, metal and enamel. The hunter who had killed a deer stood posed and urbane, no twigs in his hair, his hands bloodless. (Atwood 1969: 150)

The images going through Marian's mind seem to have, on the one hand, violence, ruthlessness and death as a common denominator, and on the other, they appear to be objectifying the dead animals as willing victims, happy to be eaten. The Moose Beer adverts are as seductive as they are implausible and fictionalised. The absence of blood devitalises these creatures and implicitly robs them of a previous living existence. 'Of course, you didn't want anything in an advertisement to be ugly or upsetting; it wouldn't do, for instance, to have a deer with its tongue sticking out' (Atwood 1969: 150). The advertising imagery here resonates with Marian's instinctive and growing awareness of entrapment.

At the same time, in embryonic form here, one can witness a potentially politicised sensitivity to the way in which the reality of food itself is consumed through highly mediated images that belong to the representational regimes of gender identity. As Roger Haden argues, commercial enterprise exploits the fact that food, especially of animal origin, has 'the capacity to take on a plethora of meanings [that] pushes it beyond its role [...] into [...] being a language' (2005: 344). The 'language' of the Moose Beer advert attempts to translate the 'substance' of the fish – a dead animal which has now become food – into a functional 'signifier' of the fisherman's strength and technical proficiency. It is noteworthy in this respect that Marian describes the fish and the 'bloodless deer' as 'unreal' and 'incongruous' (Atwood 1969: 150). In the light of these descriptions, one might venture that the adverts Marian observes are *more than* 'unreal' and in fact belong to the realm of the 'hyper-real'. One year after the publication of *The Edible Woman*, Jean Baudrillard's critique in *The Consumer Society* (1970) proposed that visual media were supplanting material reality with inauthentic images, creating a world of pseudo-existence: 'the world of the pseudo-event, of pseudo-history, and of pseudo-culture [...] [is] produced [...] as artefacts from the technical manipulation of the medium and its coded elements [...] it is this and nothing else, which defies all signification whatsoever as consumable'

(1990: 92). Baudrillard's critique is also broadly consonant with that offered by Guy Debord. In his seminal study of *Society of the Spectacle* (1967), Debord proposes that Marx's prophecy – 'all that is solid melts into air' – has come to pass in contemporary consumer society: 'all that was once directly lived has become mere representation' (1994: 12). The explosive proliferation of images and representations of commodities produces 'moments of fervent exaltation' similar to 'convulsionary' and 'miraculous cures' of the 'old religious fetishism' (Debord 1994: 12). This process has also been described more recently, in Baudrillardean terms, by Haden: 'consumer understanding and appetites are continually exposed to recursive forms of mediation, which undermine any[thing] real' (Haden 2005: 351).

Indeed, Marian's sense of the 'unreal' quality – a 'metallic' and 'clever' look – of the dead fish and deer is, in a nascent form, a consciousness of the extent to which images of food are deployed in consumer society as a tool of artifice in the manufacture of gender and lifestyle. The image of the strong, food-providing man gestures towards an idealised and overdetermined concept that recalls Roland Barthes's idea of the commercial alibi. Barthes conceives the alibi in consumer society (especially as connected to food) as a 'representational form of truth' that, through systems of signification, lends the product an appealing idea of 'display' by 'transmitting a situation' and connoting some sense of historical or cultural 'truth' (1997: 21). The Moose Beer adverts seek legitimacy and appeal by echoing mythic, practically pre-historic archetypes of masculine identity. As a result, the experience of drinking beer is mediated through simulacral images of 'Fishers' and 'Hunters', which seemingly belong to the sphere of Barthes's commercial system. Clearly then, in this approach to product representation – defined by Pasi Falk (1994: 151) as a 'mode of transformation' – the beer as a product is largely eclipsed by images of models engaged in unrelated activities. It is through these images that the male consumer can potentially experience, through a 'mystical connection', and a Debordian moment of 'fervent exaltation' (Falk 1994: 151).

Marian's suspicion of a possible displacement of material reality by the consumerist chimera of marketed needs and imagery contextually recalls Raymond Williams's 1960s critique of advertising as a 'magic system'. Williams proposes that the clichéd assumption that contemporary society is 'too materialistic' detracts from the dematerialising force of consumer capitalism:

> If we were sensibly materialistic, in that part of living in which we use things, we should find most advertising to be of insane irrelevance. Beer would be enough for us, without the additional promise that in drinking it we show ourselves to be mainly young at heart or neighbourly. But if these associations sell beer [...] as some evidence suggests, it is clear that we have a cultural pattern in which the objects are not enough but must be validated, if only in fantasy, by association with personal and special meanings. (Williams 1962: 185)

Echoing Williams' critique of beer marketing, the Moose Beer adverts aim to relocate attention to the 'personal and special meanings' of 'fantasy': 'Any real man, on a real man's holiday – hunting, fishing or just plain old-fashioned relaxing – needs a beer with a healthy, hearty taste, a deep-down manly flavour' (Atwood 1969: 26). Despite its glossy surfaces of happiness and fulfilment, the prime objective of advertising and marketing is of course the creation of consumer subjectivities based on false needs and a profound sense of lack. In the Moose Beer adverts, a sense of lack is communicated to the consumer, a void that promises to be filled only by the consumption of the product: 'Moose Beer is just what you've always wanted for true beer enjoyment' (Atwood 1969: 26). The images of 'real' men and the suggestive jingle in the adverts – incanting words such as 'needs', 'real' and 'wanted', 'Moose, Moose, Moose, Moose BEER!' (Atwood 1969: 26) – imply that the failure to purchase the product will result in a failure to conform to hegemonic gender codes. As a representation of 'real' masculinity – and its association with some kind of ancestral 'want' – the image of the sportsman enjoying beer appeals to the male consumer as it promises, borrowing Falk's words, to offer a 'surplus good' (Falk 1994: 161). It becomes clear that the unknown thing the consumer had 'always wanted' – even without knowing – truly is the 'rough-and-ready' Moose Beer (Atwood 1969: 26). Attaching a name to the paradoxically fictional image of a 'real' man not only creates a representation of need, want and desire, but also allows that representation to become singularised and associated with a sense of wholeness, completion and certainty. As Falk argues, 'transformed into a representation, the product must stand clearly apart from other products [and] it will be individualised to the potential consumer as a party to a bilateral (albeit imaginary) relationship' (Falk 1994: 162).

Returning to Marian at the restaurant with her fiancé, one should notice how her nausea and visual disturbance, as Peter's filet mignon blends with the 'unreal' Moose Beer advert, is rooted in an instinctive sensitivity and firsthand experience of the mediation of food in consumerist society through image and text. Marian experiences an epiphanic insight into the reality and history of the product before her. The final realisation that the 'filet' used to be a living cow destroys her appetite and she finds herself totally unable to ingest it:

> She looked down at her own half-eaten steak and suddenly saw it as a chunk of muscle. Blood red. Part of a real cow that once moved and ate and was killed, knocked on the head as it stood in a queue [...] Of course everyone knew that [...] But now it was suddenly there in front of her [...] She set down her knife and fork'. (Atwood 1969 151–152)

Marian's rejection of the red meat also seems linked to a deeper sense of affinity with the prospect of bovine acquiescence. Her refusal to eat the red meat could be symptomatic of an identity-related process that Brett Silverstein explores in terms of 'gender ambivalence': a concept representing 'the conflict over femininity' in heterosexual relationships (1995: 85). The dead meat on Marian's plate embodies the expectations she feels gradually imposed on her; her expected feminine subordination to Peter seems exemplified in the meat, which he promptly and ruthlessly consumes. The different attitudes displayed by Marian and Peter towards the filet could be interpreted as an unconscious indication of their respective opinions towards gendered roles. This appears to echo Peter Blos' idea that gender ambivalence often 'denotes contradictory emotional attitudes toward the same object, either arising alternatively, or existing side by side' (1941: 57).

After the episode of the filet mignon, Marian's culinary refusal extends to a variety of foodstuffs, and her condition gradually presents itself as an eating disorder. One could argue that her sense of ambivalence about her gendered social position is internalised through food loathing. She becomes unable to eat eggs, meat and the majority of processed foods; she refuses to eat a heart-shaped Valentine's cake because its texture feels fleshy in her mouth: 'like the bursting of a thousand tiny lungs' (Atwood 1969: 207). Even carrots and other vegetables appear to turn Marian's stomach as she imagines them as sentient creatures that might experience pain:

> She became aware of the carrot. It's a root, she thought, it grows in the ground and sends up leaves. Then they come along and dig it up, maybe it even makes a sound, a scream too low for us to hear, but it doesn't die right away, it keeps on living, right now it's still alive. (Atwood 1969 178)

Whilst people around her attribute her incapacity to stomach most foods as 'bridal nerves' (Atwood 1969 206), Marian becomes increasingly aware of the demands and expectations associated with her marriage and the forthcoming wedding. Her symptoms become more severe as she finds herself in deep conflict with social expectation: 'they had probably been worried she would turn into a high-school teacher or a maiden aunt or a dope addict or a female executive [...] she could picture the anxious consultations over cups of tea' (Atwood 1969: 174). According to Hilde Bruch, food rejection is characterised by 'an all-pervasive sense of ineffectiveness, a feeling that one's actions, thoughts and feelings do not originate within the self but rather are passive reflections of external expectations and demands' (2000: 19) Since Marian's refusal of food is not consciously driven by a desire to lose weight, it would seem inappropriate to speak of it in terms of anorexia nervosa. However, aspects of her eating disorder do share significant similarities with this condition. A 'distorted body image', Bruch goes on to suggest, is an evident sign of anorexia (2000: 19). Indeed, one might recall here the image of Marian's bloated reflection in the spoon earlier in the novel, which acted as a precursor to her declining relationship with food.

Whilst she does not strive to be thin, it is still evident that Marian appears to have a difficulty conceptualising her own body. When, in preparation for a party, Peter requests that Marian improve on her 'mousy' appearance. (Atwood 1969: 228), she goes through great lengths to fulfil his request. Subsequently, however, she catches a glimpse of herself in the mirror and experiences disorientation: 'Her attention caught on the various details, the things she wasn't used to – to the fingernails, the heavy ear-rings, the hair [...] what was it lay beneath the surface these pieces were floating on, holding them altogether?'(Atwood 1969: 229). This objectified depiction of physical representation not only draws attention to the conflicted gendered politics in the novel, but also points to a general sense of dematerialisation that is suggested as proper to consumer culture: the melting of food, body and various commodities into images. It is possible here to draw a parallel between Marian's 'broken' appearance in the mirror and the image she recalled when examining the filet mignon: '[It] made her think of the diagram of the planned cow at the front of one of her cookbooks: the cow with lines on it and labels to show you from which part of the cow all the different cuts were taken' (Atwood 1969: 151). The textbook cow, divided into zones and pieces, speaks to Marian of objectification and the dissection of the body into discrete 'problem areas'. In seeing her reflected image as an agglomerate of different pieces, she seems to be sensing a connection between her body and the world of production-consumption. As Marian perceives these links as disciplines imposed on her body, Atwood arguably encourages the reader's recognition of the extent by which individual psychology is *socially* produced. According to this interpretation, eating disorders are not understood as an individual problem, but as part of a widespread psychopathology linked to consumer capitalism and the patriarchal gender system.

These connections between body image and the world of selling goods leads to the possibility that social and cultural stimuli can be the direct cause of particular alimentary pathologies. According to Sigmund Freud, 'one of the vicissitudes an instinctual impulse may undergo is to meet with resistances [...] under certain conditions, the impulse then passes into the state of repression' (1991: 523). The initial hesitations in Marian's mind are slowly substituted for the certainties of married life, as if her instinctual desires are being repressed in favour of a more 'rational' perspective on marriage. In Freudian terms, we might say that 'rejection based on judgement will be found to be a good method to adopt against an instinctual impulse' (Freud 1991: 523). It could be argued that the 'external stimuli' of the marriage proposal initiates a process of repression that will result in neurosis; the reaction to the external situation becomes a repressed instinct and, therefore, seemingly disappears from Marian's consciousness. That disappearance, however, proves to be only temporary. Indeed, as Freud suggests, 'it may happen that an external stimulus becomes internalised – for example, by eating into and destroying some bodily organ – so that a new source of constant excitation and increase of tension arises' (Freud 1991: 523). In similar terms, Marian's repressed reaction to external circumstances – to the desire to reject Peter's marriage offer – is quickly internalised, and her identity 'substitute' comes about, in an echo of Freudian analysis, 'by displacement along a chain of connections' (Freud 1991: 531). When witnessing Peter devouring his steak, Marian seems to make a unconscious association between the dead meat and his 'butchering' skills with knife and fork; this association, it would appear, becomes the basis for a dislike of any food that she considers 'alive'. In this way, Marian's anxieties about marriage are displaced onto foodstuffs. Her repulsion for 'live' foods can therefore be seen as an alimentary phobia generated by repressed anxieties associated with social stimuli.

As Atwood unveils connections between gendered divisions, political economies and alimentary disturbance, one could argue that Marian experiences a chain of substitutions and displacements. Firstly, she substitutes her career for her marriage; her anxieties about her place in the marriage economy are then substituted for a food phobia. Finally, she substitutes her repressed, anxious self for a cake-woman. As the end of the novel approaches – and after an episode of infidelity with her friend Duncan – Marian seeks resolution to her conflicts with Peter by confronting him. She decides to bake a cake in the shape of a woman and serve it to him as an ironic gesture. A lot of attention goes into the preparation of the cake, which is skilfully made to resemble Marian herself:

> With two forks she pulled it in half through the middle. One half she placed flat side down on the platter. She scooped out part of it and made a head with the section she had taken out [...] The spongy cake was pliable, easy to mould. She stuck all the separate members together with white icing [...] She set about clothing it, filling the cake-decorator with bright pink icing [...] She made a smiling lush-lipped pink mouth and pink shoes to match. (Atwood 1969: 269)

The woman-cake is clearly Marian's ironic self-objectification: "'You look delicious,' she told her. "Very appetizing. And that's what will happen to you; that's what you get for being food'" (Atwood 1969: 270). The accusations directed towards the woman-cake articulate Marian's anxieties that Peter will eventually 'eat' her. This is emphasised by the cake's nature as an edible object – 'delicious' – which inevitably inspires desires of appropriation and domination. The act of symbolic substitution is foregrounded by Marian's challenge to Peter:

> "You've been trying to destroy me, haven't you," she said. "You've been trying to assimilate me. But I've made you a substitute, something you'll like much better. This is what you really wanted all along, isn't it? I'll get you a fork," she added somewhat prosaically. (Atwood 1969: 271)

The woman-cake is served in order to be consumed in Marian's place, as the ideal, identity-deprived object that allows itself to be eaten without complaint.

The fact that Marian decides to accomplish liberation through the use of an effigy echoes mythic rituals of social power. According to Freud, 'one of the most widespread magical procedures for injuring an enemy is by making an effigy of him [...] whatever is done to the effigy, the same thing happens to the detested original' (1991: 92). As an offering to Peter which is meant to satisfy his desire for assimilation – '[t]his is what you wanted all along' – the effigy cake can be seen as sacrificial. This interpretation becomes particularly persuasive if one considers that, earlier in the novel, Atwood describes Peter's control over Marian in terms of a 'deity' (Atwood 1968: 84). Initially, Freud contends, the sacrificial meal was meant to signify 'an act of fellowship between the deity and his worshippers' (1991: 92). The material offered as sacrifice would be of an edible nature, and the exchange would be interpreted as an act of kinship. In *The Edible Woman*, however, the offering of the woman-cake seems to have the opposite effect. Whilst still sacrificing to a 'deity', it could be argued that Marian uses the offering as a substitute for her devotion, so that the bond of fellowship between herself and Peter can be severed by the serving. The sacrificial function of the effigy cake bestows upon it the power to end both corporeal and psychic ties between the one who made it and the 'enemies' that must be banished. As the culinary embodiment of a female nature that allows itself to be assimilated, the effigy cake represents an 'enemy within' that Marian is trying to defeat and embodies her fulfilled political clarity.

There is one final symbolic function that can be attributed to the presentation of the effigy cake, which takes us back to political economy by establishing a link between the female totem, commodities and capitalism. As a consumable commodity in itself, the woman-cake epitomises the workings of capitalism that, in the novel, seem to want to maintain women in the lower levels of the labour market. The connection is provided here when Marian describes her workplace at Seymour Surveys as an 'ice-cream sandwich':

> The company is layered like an ice-cream sandwich, with three floors: the upper crust, the lower crust, and our department, the gooey layer in the middle. On the floor above are the executives and the psychologists – referred to as the men upstairs, since they are all men [...]. Below us are the machines – mimeo machines, I.B.M. machines for counting and sorting and tabulating the information [...]. Our department is the link between the two: we are supposed to take care of the human element, the interviewers themselves. (Atwood 1969: 13)

At Seymour Surveys, women are meant to remain in the middle, unable to rise to executive positions that are held exclusively by 'the men upstairs'. When married, women are then expected to leave the workplace and produce the next generation of consumers. This situation was particularly common in the 1960s, when women in the workforce composed what Judith Ann describes as the 'Secretarial Proletariat': 'The work itself was completely routinised, mindless toil [...] Isolation by hierarchy of the different levels of female clerical labour was a very potent tool in the hands of management' (Ann 1970: 89; see also Hobgood 2002). Thus, when Marian offers Peter a literally consumable version of her commodity self, she is symbolically renouncing, in a secular ritual, the layer-cake power structures of white-collar labour and the 'dead meat' 'de-vivification' of marriage. The fact that the cake is a fabricated image – created specifically with Peter's male-orientated desire in mind – offers an ironic counterpart to the fictitious nature of the Moose Beer adverts which proliferate in the novel as a warning about gender and power relations in consumerist society. David Harvey argues that 'the interweaving of simulacra in daily life [...] conceal[s] [...] the social relations implicated in their production' (1989: 9). The 'cannibalisation' of the woman-cake – much like the deer and the fish in the adverts – is used as a sign which highlights the ephemeral character of goods and foregrounds the layer-cake imbrications of capitalist and patriarchal structures.

One can see here how, in presenting people – particularly women – as consumable commodities, Atwood explores the possibility of being 'cannibalised' by a burgeoning desire to 'consume' in patriarchal and capitalist societies. Atwood offers a lucid critique of consumer tendencies in everyday existence. *The Edible Woman* proposes an eloquent reflection on the gendered cannibalisation of the woman as a wife and mother in a consumer society. Advertising images within the food industry are exposed as a testament to the part played by consumption in the construction of a social identity. The unequivocal totemisation of the 'consumable' body in the novel underpins political influences beneath the surface of social life. Maintaining a pervasive self-conscious approach to gender politics, as mirrored in alimentary disturbances, Atwood does propose, however, a relatively hopeful resolution to consumer cannibalisation, encouraging a deliberate revolt against patriarchal and capitalist oppression in the Western societies of the Cold War era.

Shannon Scott

Channelling Women's Rage for Audiences in the Twenty-First Century

Lizzie Borden with her axe. Mary Ann Cotton with poison in her tea kettle. Grace Marks with her handkerchief. In historical biofiction, female killers can become demonized, eroticized, or feminist heroes for contemporary audiences. While this essay will primarily examine *Alias Grace* (1996) by Margaret Atwood, there are many fictionalized texts that engage with nineteenth century female killers as readers/audiences remain fascinated with these historical cases.[1]

Situating Atwood's novel within the context of other works examining Victorian murderesses reveals connections between the nineteenth and twenty-first centuries, such as *Lady Killers* (2022–), one of the most popular podcasts from the BBC. In each episode, Lucy Worsley and Rosalind Crone connect a 'lady killer' from the past with issues that women in the twenty-first century continue to face: '[...] we have curated a collection of cases representative of female killing and living in the past, all of which have continued relevance to the present' (Green 2024: n.p.). In neo-Victorian fictionalized texts featuring historical female killers, the grisly details of the crimes certainly play a factor in their allure, as with all murder stories, but it's the emphasis on justice issues, specifically those involving class and gender, that holds the strongest appeal.

---

1 Agnes McVee in *Agnes, Murderess* (2019) by Sarah Leavitt; Lizzie Borden in Sarah Schmidt's *See What I have Done* (2017); Mary Ann Cotton in the series *Dark Angel* (2016) by Gwyneth Hughes; Belle Gunness in Victoria Kielland's *My Men* (2021); Belle Gunness in Camilla Brice's *In the Garden of Spite* (2021); Agnes Magnúsdóttir in *Burial Rites* (2013) by Hannah Kent; Jane Toppan in Mary Kay McBrayer's *America's First Female Serial Killer: Jane Toppan and the Making of a Monster* (2020).

We look to the past to understand the present, since justice issues from the nineteenth century still haunt our society today: reproductive rights, healthcare, pay equity, childrearing and caregiving, education, incarceration, racial prejudice, and sexual and domestic violence. Unfortunately, while some things have changed significantly in terms of class and gender rights since the nineteenth century, the changes might not be as progressive or systemic as one would hope. It is my contention that the continued interest in nineteenth-century female killers by contemporary female authors and audiences reveals not just an avid curiosity about why women committed murder in a previous era, but also why women today contemplate or commit murder as a solution to injustice, poverty, and abuse. Because these historical killers were often maids, mothers, or cowed daughters of cruel and controlling fathers, fictionalized accounts of their lives are often sympathetic and frequently elicit identification and catharsis from their predominantly female audiences.

Margaret Atwood's *Alias Grace* (1996) is one of the first and most compelling texts to portray the real-life case of a Victorian murderess, Grace Marks. While Atwood's mesmerising depiction of Grace pulls readers in, the novel is simultaneously an exploration of issues in Victorian Canadian society. Jackie Shead points out that *Alias Grace* highlights 'the exploitation of immigrant labour and power politics of its class and gender relations' (Shead 2016: 88). Atwood recaptures marginalized Victorian voices through careful research of her subject, Grace Marks, situated within her historical context. *Alias Grace* continues to resonate with contemporary audiences because its world reflects our own, engaging in an ongoing discourse about violence, crime and punishment, then and now.

Grace Marks immigrated from Northern Ireland to Canada, where she worked as a domestic servant in several households. In 1843, she was sixteen years old and employed as a housemaid for Thomas Kinnear in Richmond Hill, Ontario. Kinnear was a prosperous farmer and a bachelor. He was romantically involved with his housekeeper, Nancy Montgomery, who was pregnant at the time of her murder, likely with Kinnear's child. James McDermott, who ran the stables at Kinnear's estate, was accused, along with Grace, of killing Thomas Kinnear, who was found in his cellar with a fatal bullet wound. Nancy Montgomery was also murdered. She was hit in the head with an axe, dumped into the cellar, and strangled to death, her body stuffed beneath the washtub. McDermott and Marks fled together after the murders, making it to Lewiston, New York, before being caught and deported back to Toronto for trial.

There are conflicting confessions from Grace Marks and James McDermott, each blaming the other for the crimes. Grace claimed McDermott threatened and kidnapped her and that she had no part in either murder. However, Grace stood trial wearing Nancy Montgomery's dress and bonnet, which she had taken before absconding from Kinnear's home. Her attire did not help her case. Since Grace Marks and James McDermott were both convicted of the murder of Thomas Kinnear, there was never a trial for Nancy Montgomery's murder. Though both received a death sentence, only McDermott was hanged. The jury recommended mercy for Grace, who was young and attractive and came across more sympathetically than McDermott. Instead, Grace Marks was sentenced to life in Kingston Penitentiary, where she remained, except for a brief stay in an asylum, until 1872 when she was released. Grace, then in her forties, moved to America to work as a domestic servant, and once there, all records of her disappeared.

Margaret Atwood uses historical records to resurrect Grace Marks, from Marks's multiple confessions, to newspaper articles printed during the trial, to Susanna Moodie's *Life in the Clearings versus the Bush* (1853), which contains accounts of Moodie's visits with Marks, both in the penitentiary and in the asylum; in short, all the paraphernalia of Marks's life, all bones Atwood uses to flesh out a captivating portrait of a teenage girl who may or may not have been a murderess, but who was indisputably a product of her time and place, a female working-class immigrant in nineteenth-century Toronto. Ariella Van Luyn claims that historical biofiction like *Alias Grace* 'can ascribe motives to their female characters, allowing a critique of the social and economic power structures that regulate women's behaviour and enact punishment on their bodies while at the same time rendering them powerless' (2019: 70). Marks's status as an Irish immigrant and female servant, as well her subsequent life as a convict, all expose much about Victorian Canadian society and become as relevant as whether or not Grace is guilty of murder. Atwood avoids negative accusations made against much criminal biofiction that emphasizes the criminals' personal lives 'as opposed to a repressive Victorian social order' through her meticulous research, knowledge of the past, and an awareness of how that past affects the present (Napolitano 2020: 357). Atwood's *Alias Grace* shows that all inner lives are altered by the outer circumstances of a larger society, where women, immigrants, and the working class are seen as subordinate or even subhuman by those who are monied, established, and hold positions of power and authority. As a result, personal trauma and the Victorian social order are not mutually exclusive but utterly interconnected.

And yet Grace Marks cannot be written off as simply a victim of circumstance or a repressive social order. Atwood grants her protagonist agency. As Anne Schwan writes, 'Atwood refuses to oversimplify class and gender discrimination or to present women such as Grace as a silent, helpless victim of social circumstance' (2014: 186). Atwood does this by holding Grace accountable not for the murder of Thomas Kinnear, but for the murder of fellow female servant, Nancy Montgomery. In *Alias Grace*, the mystery of Grace's guilt or innocence mainly revolves around her role, be it active participant or complicit bystander, in Nancy's murder. Nancy died not from the axe wound to her head, or the fall down the cellar stairs, but from being strangled by a handkerchief that allegedly belonged to Grace. Did Grace supply McDermott with the handkerchief that ended Nancy's life? Did she help McDermott do it? Did she do it herself? The focus on Nancy's murder in Atwood's novel becomes like the trial Nancy's murder never received in the nineteenth century. As a domestic servant, like Grace, and as a 'fallen woman' impregnated by her employer, Nancy's murder was not given the same magnitude of attention as Kinnear's murder. Atwood's neo-Victorian text addresses and zeroes in on that omission.[2]

In the miniseries *Alias Grace*, based on Atwood's novel and released in 2017, writer Sarah Polley likewise emphasizes Nancy's murder and Grace's possible role in it. Atwood and Polley, who worked together extensively

---

2   In *See What I have Done*, Sara Schmidt similarly calls attention to the female victim Abby Borden, as opposed to Andrew Borden, perhaps because Abby's murder was treated with such minimal importance compared to Andrew's murder during much of Lizzie Borden's trial.

on the adaptation, agreed to maintain ambiguity regarding Grace's guilt. They also agreed not to overly focus on the personal titbits known about Marks's life, but to instead highlight the society in which she lived, the society that informed her choices or lack of choices, where being a young female immigrant, away from her family and working in the homes of strangers, could become fraught, if not downright dangerous.

The first episode begins with a monologue, recited in voiceover by Grace, played by Sarah Gordon, taken primarily from Atwood's novel about what it means to be a 'celebrated murderess.' The speech, given as Grace stares into a mirror, is unsettling, yet it is the smash cuts, the almost subliminal flashbacks to Nancy's murder, that are far more disturbing in their suddenness, vividness, and repetition, occurring at least six times in the first episode. Director Mary Harron, who also directed *American Psycho* (2000), claims she didn't want to 'prettify' the crime or the era but to create a sort of 'anti-Downton Abbey' (Ostad 2017: n.p.) Consequently, there is nothing sentimental, romanticized, or nostalgic in the series, which accurately mirrors Atwood's tone in the novel.

Nancy's body is thrown down the cellar stairs like a rag doll, landing dazed and blinking and bloodied, over and over and over. Yet the violence doesn't come across as gratuitous, due to the briefness of the flashbacks. In one blink of flashback, an axe is sharpened. In another, a gash opens on Nancy's forehead as she picks peonies. In another, Nancy's body is dismembered by James McDermott. In another, Nancy's body is pulled by the arm, dragged across the dirt floor of the cellar. In the final fall of the first episode, Nancy crashes down the stairs, sprawling half dead amongst broken preserves, her blood mingling with stored root vegetables. Scholar Juanita Marie Tenorio notes that due to the recurrence and obscuring of these brief flashbacks to Nancy's body, 'one might be tempted to conclude that Grace is such an accomplished liar that she does not flinch at the violence of her memories' (2021: 197). And indeed, Grace's face during these flashbacks is placid, making the effect even more unnerving to the viewer. All the flashbacks of Nancy's murder put together probably equal less than a minute of screen time, yet the impact is jarring. And the body gore is not overdone or campy. Instead, it feels entirely real, as if Grace's memories, truthful or imagined, work like intrusive thoughts, becoming ours, so the violence becomes shared too. In contrast, Thomas Kinnear's murder, with his body thrown into the cellar, is given only one flashback in Episode One and not brought in again until the fifth episode. The fate of the female servants, both Nancy and Grace, victim and perpetrator, is highlighted in the series as it is in the novel.

In the first episode, Grace discusses two other murders that she considers but ultimately chooses not to commit. Grace is the daughter of an abusive and alcoholic father. He's shown backhanding Grace's mother as they board the ship for America. After her mother's death, there are scenes in Toronto where Grace's father calls her 'a stupid ugly whore,' then grabs her and throws her against a wall, where she crumples, unconscious, to the floor. This scene appears in Atwood's text as well as in Polley's translation, except Grace's concern about the incident is articulated clearly in the former: I 'feared that he might someday break my spine or make a cripple out of me' (Atwood 1996: 129). This is a legitimate fear for Grace. If she became disabled, what would she do? She couldn't raise her siblings. She couldn't work. She probably couldn't marry. All the avenues out of poverty, or at least maintaining subsistence living, would be closed.

In the series, Grace's father later apologizes for his violence, kissing her while she recovers on a straw mattress. He then attempts to rape her. In the following scene, Grace cleans ashes from the hearth as her father sleeps on the same straw mattress. Grace gazes thoughtfully at a heavy iron pot of ashes and back at her father. Struggling with the weight of the pot, she manages to stagger closer to him, lifting it high to drop it on his head, but she stops herself. In Atwood's novel, the scene reads,

> I had begun to have thoughts about the iron cooking pot, and how heavy it was; and if it should happen to drop on him while he was asleep, it could smash his skull open, and kill him dead, and I would say it was an accident; and I did not want to be led into a grave sin of that kind, though I was afraid that the fiery red anger that was in my heart against him would drive me to it. (Atwood 1996: 129)

Grace recounts this experience to Dr. Jordan, a psychiatrist deciding whether to write a recommendation for her early release from prison, so perhaps she creates a scenario where she once contemplated murder, but her conscience kept her from it. However, if the story were true, she thought it out well. If Grace managed to kill her father with the iron pot, with the biggest risk being a failure to kill him on the first attempt, she could have made it look like an accident. It would, despite Grace's admission of a 'fiery red anger', be a crime of practicality, not passion. When one's choices are limited, the consequences of a crime no longer outweigh the consequences of not committing that crime, so murder becomes a viable option. In this case, law enforcement would have investigated, but perhaps not too closely. Her father was a well-known drunk, unlikeable and impoverished. He was certainly no wealthy landowner like Thomas Kinnear. And Grace was the oldest child of nine; who would take her away from the children? It would likely be considered a tragic accident, especially if it had occurred in Ireland before Grace left for Canada.

In nineteenth-century Ireland, before a rise in domestic abuse cases in the late 1880s, spousal homicide rates were lower than anywhere else in the United Kingdom (Conley 2007: 128). This is largely considered a result of intervention from sources outside the law, such as priests, neighbours, and extended family that 'offered shelter to women who left abusive husbands, as well as retaliation against abusers' (Conley 2007: 128). In contrast, for abused wives in Victorian England, the rates of spousal homicide were higher since women typically relied on the law to intervene (Conley 2007: 125–126). Domestic violence is an example of an issue from the nineteenth century that continues in the twenty-first century. The year 2022 was one of the worst years for domestic violence homicides in Ireland in over a decade. According to the Garda, 52% of murders in Ireland in 2022 were a result of domestic violence, with cases of domestic violence that resulted in women's deaths following an upward trend globally ('2022 Deadliest Year' 2022: n.p). Grace's instinct to kill her father, and in doing save herself, would be one she had to follow because family, friends, and neighbours were not in Toronto to step in and remove the threat when society (i.e. the law) failed.

The second contemplation of murder also occurs when Grace looks at her younger siblings on the boat to Canada. In both the series and novel, she says,

> I will confess to having a wicked thought, when I had all the young ones lined up on the dock, with their little bare legs dangling down. I thought, I might just push one or two of them over, and then there would not be so many to feed, nor so many clothes to wash. [...] But it was only a thought, put into my head by the Devil, no doubt. Or more likely by my father, for at that age I was still trying to please him. (Atwood 1996: 108)

Again, she illustrates to Dr. Jordan that she thought about committing murder but did not follow through, distinguishing between thought and action. Yet Ana Sentov notes that this 'morbid example can be read as an insight into the mind of a future murderer, but also as evidence that ethics and morals may hold little meaning for those who struggle to make ends meet' (2019: 112). In other words, without sentiment, Grace weighs the benefit of fewer mouths to feed. Simultaneously, readers and viewers question how much we should judge Grace's thoughts when she's unable to properly care for those she becomes responsible for, with little to no assistance from extended family or society.

The most prevalent crimes women committed in the Victorian era were abortion, infanticide, and prostitution, which reveals a lot about the era in terms of women's choices and legal rights. But today, the statistics are not much different. In the US, in 2021, most murders were still committed by men, roughly 88%, while women committed about 11%; however, most women killed family members, not strangers (FBI 2022: n.p.). Furthermore, two-thirds of infanticides were perpetuated by women, with women responsible for 80% of homicides where the victim was under a year old (Fox 2020: n.p.). The motives, as in the nineteenth century, may be economic, as they were with Grace, but usually such crimes committed by women were and are attributed to temporary insanity or postpartum psychosis. Certainly, insanity can be the fallout of such a crime. As Grace recalls, during her period in the Asylum, a patient 'had killed her child, and it followed her around everywhere [...]' (Atwood 1996: 31). However, dismissing the economic aspect of infanticide, and making it solely about a woman's mental instability, absolves society, then and now, of its role in creating conditions that can lead to such tragic choices. Grace's thoughts about her father and her siblings show that statistics and motives concerning *why* women commit homicide are much the same today as they were in the nineteenth century.[3]

Before she meets Mary Whitney, pregnancy is primarily an economic fear for Grace. It begins with Grace's mother in Northern Ireland, who

---

3   This is also portrayed much more ghoulishly in *Dark Angel*, where Mary Ann Cotton murders her children to collect insurance money.

has nine living children and three dead children during her marriage to Grace's father. Besides the challenges of pregnancy and postpartum care, the main hardship for Grace's mother, and indeed the entire Marks family, is financial. There isn't enough money to buy adequate food, clothing, or shelter. Grace's father, who is frequently unemployed or squandering their meagre resources on alcohol and gambling, exacerbates the situation by repeatedly and cruelly condemning his wife for her incessant breeding as if he has no responsibility in the situation. Grace claims,

> I cannot remember my mother when she wasn't in what they call a delicate condition; although there is nothing delicate about it that I can see. They also call it an unhappy condition, and that is closer to the truth—an unhappy condition followed by a happy event, although the event is by no means always happy. (Atwood 1996: 107)

Grace quickly backtracks on the idea that a birth is always a happy event, because in her experience as the eldest girl of nine children, it isn't. Instead, each time her mother gives birth, Grace's father threatens infanticide, claiming that he will drown the baby 'like a kitten in a sack' or 'knock the new baby on the head and shove it into a hole in the cabbage patch' (Atwood 1996: 108, 110). This would not have been an unprecedented reaction to extreme poverty and a lack of access to contraception or abortion. For example, in Belfast in 1861, nineteen-year-old Ann Boyd and her mother Jane Boyd were tried for the murder of Ann's baby, which was born out of wedlock. Though the Boyds claimed the baby girl was born dead, according to witnesses as well as the coroner, the baby was born alive and was killed before being buried in the backyard cabbage patch. Rosalind Crone, citing the work of historian Elaine Farrell and official criminal statistics, discovered that infanticide in Ireland in the second half of the nineteenth century was a weekly occurrence, though many cases likely went unreported, and for women who registered their marital status in the criminal record, more than 60% of the women who committed infanticide were unmarried (Worsley 2024: n.p.). In these situations, women who were caught for the crime of infanticide often pleaded guilty to 'concealment of birth' as an alternative to 'murder' in order to receive lighter sentences (Worsley 2024: n.p.). In contrast, in Atwood's novel, Grace's mother never considers infanticide to control her growing and destitute family, though her husband certainly does, and so does Grace.

Although Grace's Aunt Pauline helps the Marks family with money and childcare, when Pauline becomes pregnant after many years of trying to conceive, her husband insists on putting his nuclear family first. For Pauline and her husband, this birth will be a 'happy event,' but for Grace, it means her aunt can no longer help them, so they must leave Ireland and emigrate to Canada. On the miserable voyage across the Atlantic, Grace's mother passes away, her body thrown into the sea. Although Grace mourns her mother, she also feels anger toward her, which is Grace's default emotional reaction to the loss of all the pregnant women she cares for during the novel. While Grace refuses to view pregnancy as a 'delicate condition,' she does view her mother as 'delicate,' a delicacy that fills Grace with resentment and loathing: 'She was a timid creature, hesitating and weak and delicate, which used to anger me. I wanted her to be stronger so I would not have to be so strong myself' (Atwood 1996: 105). Her mother's weakness forces Grace to grow up and take charge too early. Delicacy becomes synonymous with weakness as Grace inherits the responsibility for caring and providing for her siblings and handling her father's drunken rages.

This anger returns with two other women who experience the 'unhappy condition': Mary and Nancy. Grace claims,

> I had a rage in my heart for many years, against Mary Whitney, and especially against Nancy Montgomery; against the two of them both, for letting themselves be done to death in the way that they did, and for leaving me behind with the full weight of it. (Atwood 1996: 457)

Both Mary and Nancy experience pregnancies out of wedlock as a result of sex with their employers. For Mary, the pregnancy means not only the loss of her position at the Alderman Parkinson house but also disgrace and destitution since she has no family to help her. Instead, Mary knows that 'now no decent man would marry her, and she would have to go on the streets, and become a sailors' drab as she would have no other way of feeding herself and the baby' (Atwood 1996: 173). This isn't an exaggeration but a reality, especially since the father of Mary's baby, when asked to honour his ring of engagement, tells Mary to drown herself. The best option seems to be spending all her money and all of Grace's money to obtain an abortion from a doctor who treats her like a beggar, even as she hands him the hefty payment. The resulting botched abortion leads to

Mary's horrific death, witnessed by Grace, as Mary painfully bleeds out in the bed they share in the attic. She begs Grace not to get help for fear of shame and punishment. The violent death of her friend scars Grace even more than her mother's death at sea. It is also a death that Grace blames on Mary for letting herself get into that condition to begin with. The loss is devastating and life-changing, and it arguably leads to the death of Nancy Montgomery.

Grieving, Grace accepts the offer to work for Kinnear not because the pay is higher but because Nancy 'resembled Mary Whitney' (Atwood 1996: 202). However, Grace soon discovers the two women are nothing alike in personality. Grace doesn't love or even like Nancy. Still, she doesn't actively dislike Nancy, or lose respect for her, until she learns about Nancy's two pregnancies. First, Grace discovers Nancy's current 'unhappy condition' is the result of her relationship with their employer, Thomas Kinnear. François Couturier-Storey and Jeffrey Storey argue that Nancy may have harboured 'ambitions to move upward in society, ambitions that were criticized by the lower class (Grace and McDermott) [...]' (2011: 55). While this claim is likely true, Grace is even angrier to discover that Nancy has been pregnant previously: it's 'common knowledge that Nancy had a baby when she was working over at the Wrights,' by a young layabout who ran off and left her, only the baby died' (Atwood 1996: 255). Mackenzie, Grace's lawyer, hints at infanticide: 'She'd had a baby previously, you know—which died, I presume of midwives' mercy' (Atwood 1996: 374).

Unlike Mary, whose one mistake led to her death, Nancy received a second chance and didn't learn from the past. Instead, she made the same mistake again. This carelessness, paired with the fact that Nancy faced no consequences or punishment, infuriates Grace. While Susanna Moodie contended that Grace's motive for the murder of Nancy Montgomery was jealousy over Nancy's better treatment as a servant in the Kinnear household, Atwood's novel suggests a different motive. On her first visit to Grace Marks in the penitentiary, Moodie claimed, 'Grace was very jealous of the difference made between her and the housekeeper, whom she hated, and to whom she was very insolent and saucy' (Moodie 1989: 197). Moodie added that Grace complained, 'What is she better than us? [...] that she is to be treated like a lady, and eat and drink the best. She is not better born than we are, or better educated' (Moodie 1989: 197). If this remark is accurate, which is highly contentious, it suggests Grace's jealousy of Nancy's attempt to climb the social ladder could be the motive, if not for the murder, then for allowing McDermott to deploy his murderous plan while she stood aside. But in *Alias Grace*, this 'better treatment' is not what bothers Grace about Nancy Montgomery. Grace simply cannot accept that Nancy survived, and Mary didn't. The horror of Mary's death and the fact that Nancy (in Grace's perception) faced no consequences for either pregnancy grinds at Grace: '[...] it would not be fair and just that she should end up a respectable married lady with a ring on her finger, and rich in the bargain. It would not be right at all' (Atwood 1996: 276). A ring on Nancy's finger is an injustice Grace cannot reconcile. It brings to mind the gold ring that Mary was given by her fickle lover, the same gold ring Grace had to sell in order to buy Mary's tombstone. The unfairness is unbearable for Grace: 'Mary Whitney had done the same as her, and had gone to her death. Why should one be rewarded and the other punished, for the same sin?' (Atwood 1996: 276). Nancy's violent death becomes a way of righting the scales.

Grace often recalls Mary Whitney, her words, her face, her death, and what Mary might do if she were in Grace's situation. This happens at a pivotal moment in Grace's life when Jeremiah offers to take her away with him, away from the bloody storm brewing at Thomas Kinnear's estate. Grace is more than tempted; in fact, she wants to leave. Life on the road with Jeremiah would mean a life away from household drudgery and the perils of female servitude. But she doesn't leave with Jeremiah, despite her desire or instinct. Instead, Grace remembers what happened to Mary Whitney and worries that Jeremiah might impregnate and abandon her. As unlikely as these misfortunes seem knowing Jeremiah's character, and as fearful as Grace is about McDermott's threat of violence at the Kinnear estate, she remains more fearful of pregnancy. Grace is stymied by the trauma of Mary's death, so much so that she cannot take an escape route when it's offered.

In the last pages of the novel, Grace thinks that she might be pregnant after her marriage to Jamie Walsh. It is neither an illegitimate pregnancy nor one that would cause financial hardship, yet Grace does not view it as a 'happy event.' Instead, her response is subdued.[4] As Grace ponders this potential pregnancy from the comfort and safety of her veranda, enjoying her new freedom in America, she also wonders if the 'heaviness' and cessation of her menstrual cycle 'might as easily be a tumour' (549). The reader gets the impression that Grace might even prefer the latter. Throughout the novel, Grace fears pregnancy more than anything else, even being hanged, because it reveals female vulnerability in Victorian society more than any other condition. If a woman has little money, it reveals just how little money. If she breaks the social norms and has sex before marriage, it reveals her looseness. And the consequences are steep. Women lose their jobs, their health, their freedom if they seek abortion in a place where it is illegal, and sometimes their lives.[5] For Grace, to become pregnant means to become prey: to rich sons who won't honour their promises, to prison guards and doctors who abuse their authority, to husbands that cannot be easily escaped. It means that an unhappy condition will most likely lead to an unhappy event. And while rights and conditions have improved since the nineteenth century, pregnancy remains a litmus test of sorts for how our twenty-first century society treats women, particularly recent immigrants and the working classes.

4   This subdued response could also be because this is Grace's second pregnancy since Reverend Verringer believes and Atwood's research suggests that Grace's stay at the asylum led to an unwanted pregnancy, the result of rape. However, this possible pregnancy is not explored or discussed by Grace in Atwood's novel.

5   The attempted murder of Belle Gunness while she is pregnant occurs in both Camilla Bruce's *In the Garden of Spite* and Victoria Kielland's *My Men*. The incident in both texts becomes the motive for her subsequent crimes. The murder and assault of pregnant women by intimate partners was high in the nineteenth century and remains one of the leading causes of death for pregnant women today.

Part II

The Handmaid's Tale and the *MaddAddam* Trilogy

Gina Wisker

Salvaging Revisited: Margaret Atwood's Feminist Eco-Gothic Challenges to the Anthropocene and her Writing on Climate Change and Indigenous Knowledge

Walking into a Margaret Atwood novel is like being in a grimmer, Eco-Gothic, parallel universe to our own where most things are worryingly familiar, taken a few steps further than you would want, into the darkness.

In a terrifying moment in the TV series *The Handmaid's Tale* (Hulu 2017–), the red-cloaked, white-wimpled Gilead Handmaids comply (some eagerly) with 'salvaging', the ritual battering to death of men accused of rape. Latterly, however, they claim agency, refusing to stone the wayward Janine in a 'particicution'. Atwood is fond of worldbuilding and wordplay, both of which expose word-warping and silencing which stifle life. Instead of the lies and silence, she engages with positive powers of repurposing words, invention, writing and reimaginings, dredging active hope from end-of-the-world scenarios. Salvaging also means rescuing from destruction. Beginning with her poem 'Frogless' (1990), which imagines a future in which rivers and lakes have been so poisoned that there are no more frogs, only disfigured, sick fish and consequently disfigured, sick people, she develops her predictions of ecological disaster across her range of writings, from activist letters to short stories and novels. This essay focuses mainly on exploring Atwood's imagining of the end of days, the devastating results of the Anthropocene, man-made disasters, in *The Handmaid's Tale* (1985), the *MaddAddam* trilogy (2003, 2009, 2013) and then *The Testaments* (2019). Most of the disasters are indeed shown to be created by men, but many are perpetuated by women as well as men – women who collude with disrespect for life and its diversity, such as the Aunts in *The Handmaid's Tale*, for example. We look here at how Atwood brings gender and sustainability issues to the fore using the (feminist) Eco-Gothic (Smith and Hughes 2013), warning of the results of reductive worldviews and destructive actions. Margaret Atwood's dystopian Eco-Gothic fiction works and her accompanying research work on climate change and Indigenous knowledge, immerse us in worlds recognisable as our own but badly damaged by the results of the Anthropocene, with its selfish, violent, hypocritical controls, thefts, and its deliberate destruction of ecological and human diversity. Fundamentally ecological, Atwood's works enacts threats and positive possibilities, arguing for the importance of diversity, healthy connectedness between everything: humans, animals and nature. In this current and/or recent moment (up to and including COVID-19 and beyond) of a real waterless flood, she celebrates ecological richness, simultaneously insisting on the importance of articulation, speaking out, testifying and doing so with a diversity of voices. In her work, salvaging can be used productively, not as that ironic 'newspeak' version of a purge, but rather rescuing diversity and ecological balance, initiated through engaged activism of writing, and imagining possibilities, in these otherwise dark future worlds. This old/new wisdom is based on ecological worldviews and practices influenced by Indigenous people in harmony with, rather than brutal control over, the living world.

Margaret Atwood (1939–) was born in Ottawa, Ontario, and it should not be surprising that her work resonates with a real understanding and respect for the natural world, as much of her upbringing took place in the wild, in nature, first in the bush outside Ottawa. Latterly from age seven, when the family moved to Toronto, they oscillated between both the edges of Toronto and the bush because of her father's work as a forest entomologist – he and his students researched and lived in these wild natural areas each summer. She could see all around her then, as now, how human carelessness was destroying nature and any form of natural balance. In her poem 'Frogless' (1990), Atwood focuses on a single example of a future of ecological disaster – a shrivelled, near-future world, where any evidence of wildlife and nature are only deformed animals and plants – nature betrayed, and a broken chain of existence affecting everything.

> The sore trees cast their leaves
> too early. Each twig pinching shut
> like a jabbed clam. (Atwood 'Frogless' *The Paris Review* 117: 1990 n.p.)

There is 'booze' in the spring water run-off, and 'pure antifreeze' refers possibly both to that used in cars but also to an unnatural, heated burning which leads to a halt in the natural seasons, the changes in the weather, so that the worms in the stream are /the stream as it worms along is 'drunk and burning'. Everything is deformed. An eel has an eye growing from its cheek. The fish are 'sick' and the people who eat them, because they are the only fish left, are then equally contaminated and 'wrecked', 'Then they get born wrong'(Atwood 1990: n.p). The threat of climate change, toxicity and death in life is immediate in this poem from 1990 and casts a dark shadow over the future:

> This is home.
> Travel anywhere in a year, five years,
> And you'll end up here. ('Frogless' in *The Paris Review* 117: 1990 n.p.)

The effect on the next generation is deadly. In this poem, nothing is salvaged. The warning is stark.

> The people eat sick fish
> because there are no others.
> Then they get born wrong. ('Frogless' in *The Paris Review* 117: 1990 n.p.)

Atwood uses such Eco-Gothic images of the wrecked everyday in this poem, and throughout her writing career, as she imagines such scenarios of human-originated disasters whether through ignorance or, as in the *MaddAddam* trilogy, through deliberate, careless, amoral play which culpably ignores the delicate and necessary balance of the interdependency of all living things on the planet. Her writing in many different formats, from poetry and fiction to her activist letters, shows her consistent engagement with ecological balance, sustainability and survival. Coral Ann Howells notes that Atwood's work prompts a 'shared recognition of complicity in her strong warning against global pollution as wilderness relates to myth' (2006: 48). Margaret Atwood's warnings about the destructive carelessness of humans and her active interest in the importance of nature, biodiversity, ecology and sustainability are informed by her learning from her upbringing and also from the experience and wisdom of Indigenous people on her visits to Australian Aboriginal elders and communities, and through her engagements with Canadian

First Nations people. Details of her interactions and subsequent activism and statements and letters are to be found in among the huge collection of her papers in the Thomas Fisher Rare Book Library at the University of Toronto, in 'The Brown Box'.

The Brown Box

Atwood's Eco-Gothic speculative works are influenced by interest in ecology, sustainability, biodiversity and Indigenous knowledge. She uses the powers of her writing to be heard through letters, journalism and public appearances. Brooks Bouson (2004) notes Atwood 'draws openly on the discourse of environmentalism as she emphasizes the effects of global warming on the future world' (Brooks Bouson 2004: 140) in which land turns arid, rivers and seas dry up, and animals and fish disappear, leaving humans with little sustenance. Atwood turns to ecologically balanced, complex and diverse thinking and eco-diversity, with extensive influence from Canadian First Nations and Australian Aboriginal Indigenous knowledge. The Brown Box in the University of Toronto's Thomas Fisher Rare Book Library contains evidence of her readings and her active responses to climate change and the damage caused by human selfishness and carelessness, both to the environment and other species. Works she responds to include *Biomimicry: Innovation Inspired by Nature* (Benyus 1997), and *North of Caution: A Journey through the Conservation Economy on the Northwest Coast of British Columbia* (Gill 2001). In the latter, the Nisga'a tribe explain unity between human and animal, light and dark, berating the young who needlessly kill animals and fish (known to have supernatural powers), ignoring the warnings of their elders who lived in a form of constant dread of an inevitable catastrophe. Such knowledge offering insights and terrible warnings enables speculation, and thus salvaging, beyond 'Extinctathon', which is the endgame of *Oryx and Crake* (Wisker 2017).

When considering Atwood's engagement with sustainable development, ecology and diversity across the full range of her writing and activism, we might wonder whether this is a temporary focus and what a writer is able to do to engage imaginations so that some active rethinking can lead to rebalancing and a chance of survival. We can ask why sustainable development and ecology matter; how can literature engage with issues of sustainable development and ecology; and why should it do this. And for Atwood, as for many other writers now, is this just a fad?

Eco-Gothic enables the exploration and expression of both the darkness and death, of ignoring and destroying difference, and insights into survival, many of which are fundamental to the ways in which Indigenous people think and act. Atwood's work seeks out and respectfully shares, basing her own arguments on such Indigenous knowledges which celebrate diversity and ecological richness.

She writes in a wide variety of forms, from poetry concerned with the effects of toxic waste on the whole ecosystem, for example, in 'Frogless', to letters arguing for the maintenance of the health of a lake. Her dystopian fictions identify the destruction of the planet as a result of ignoring a holistic view of humankind and nature, instead living for the present, using up resources and ignoring and marginalizing variety and difference. The critique enabled through character and story in Eco-Gothic exposes abjection, marginalization, Otherising, and destruction and denial of difference, of variety and potential, all of which leads to atrophy, entropy – i.e. running down – and extinction. Eco-Gothic also has a positive developmental drive, as it can imagine the ways forward. Speculative or fantasy fiction is both theorised and immensely practical. It can imagine and enact both the horrific results of such wilful ignorance and the potential for a more positive future. The underpinning drive is that of survival, diversity and thriving.

Without history, and without testimony of different experiences in history, there can be no memory and no movement forward. The next step beyond understanding how we got to such a mess – and what could happen – is to speculate and then embody positive creative diversity in human actions in the works of fiction. It involves taking responsibility for the future through acting in a fashion that is aware and encourages diversification and sustainability. In *The Handmaid's Tale*, the *MaddAddam* trilogy and *The Testaments*, there are slivers of creativity and alternative arguments against reductive and oppressive worldviews and behaviours.

Turning around the most oppressive character in *The Handmaid's Tale*, Aunt Lydia, and showing her using the power of written testimony to reveal secrets suggest alternative ways of acting and is a very hopeful, creative and future-focused creation that is also ecologically sound.

Atwood notes 'with alarm that trends derided ten years ago as paranoid fantasies had become possibilities, then actualities' (Atwood 2005). 'Perhaps we'll have some breathing room – a chance to re-evaluate our goals and to take stock of our relationship to the living planet from which we derive all our nourishment, and without which debt finally won't matter' (Atwood 2008). Her narratives suggest, even from the jaws of extinction through ignorance, misplaced power and a refusal of diversity, human agency survives, and we evolve through lessons learned from nature and Indigenous knowledge. Two of her statements in 2012 show her close engagement with and concern for the future of life on the planet. In an interview 'Fiction, future, environment', Atwood (2012) highlights the deadly link between the de-oxygenation of the world's oceans and its consequences for the planet. In her Introduction to a new 2012 edition of *Survival* (1972), she comments on the wisdom of the First Nations people: 'I was talking recently to a Canadian First Nations man who sells whitefish at a local farmers' market, I mentioned Zebra mussels, an invasive species that is now a large and destructive presence in the Great Lakes, what did he think should be done about this problem? I asked him. "Nature will take care of it" he said' (2012).

The Gothic and Eco-Gothic

Steve Bruhm points out that 'the Gothic itself is a narrative of trauma' (2006: 268). A Gothic perspective reminds us of dark secrets, and it hints at repercussions and revenge. It is often an ironic, cruel, and astute revelation of contradictory behaviours and their resulting damage, which, in Atwood's work, is combined with an ecological and a gendered, feminist perspective, with Eco-Gothic and ecofeminism, to produce what might be called the Feminist Eco-Gothic.

Eco-Gothic (Smith and Hughes 2013; Carr 2013; Alder and Bavidge 2020) uses characteristics of the literary Gothic to expose belief systems and contexts as entrapping, resulting in physical, psychical and psychological control and destruction of ecological balance and human life. Ecofeminism 'occurs at the intersection of gender justice, animal rights, environmental conservation' (Carr 2013: 160). Atwood's vision and versions of the world are dark, exposing destructive hierarchies of power, ignorant, wilful undermining and erasure of others, of animal, human and natural lives. Much of her work focusing on climate change and Indigenous lives and practices and on a need to find sustainable equitable ways of living. It is influenced by Eco-Gothic and Ecofeminism to articulate, i.e. express, and also put into action what we might call here a feminist Eco-Gothic. Feminist Eco-Gothic offers a theorised lens on gender, ecological balance and imbalance, and power and politics, dramatising and exposing monstrous damage wrought by culpable meddling with natural processes, the future of the planet and its life forms, and human lives and reproduction. Atwood's feminist Eco-Gothic emphasizes toxic misuse and misrepresentations of technology and science, posing problems for balanced human and natural co-existence and continuity of life. Denial of human rights is the deadly context for communities surviving in constricted worlds fatally damaged by the selfish human-dominated values and acts of the Anthropocene and climate change. In her activist writings, Atwood exposes ignorant and selfish ecological damage, the erasure of diversity of species and human behaviours, and the imposition of a constrained conformity and uniformity. Articulating and dramatising in her range of writing the problems, their sources and effects brings to light arguments about the importance of diversity, generosity, constant evolution and learning from difference. Offred's resistance and record in *The Handmaid's Tale*, the hybridity of Jimmy and the Crakers in the *MaddAddam* trilogy and the alternative perspective and survival of women in *The Testaments* offers some hope for humanity's future, something salvaged.

The Handmaid's Tale

Global pollution lies behind *The Handmaid's Tale*, emphasizing the terrible consequences of destroying balance in nature and amongst people. In *The Handmaid's Tale*, post bio-disaster, social structures and artificial power-based relationships are maintained by military rule, silencing and brutal punishment. The defamiliarisation and disruption, exposed by Eco-Gothic, emphasise local and global warnings, evidencing damaged relationships among the environment, animals and humans. In Gilead, women's roles are stratified to reflect social use: hostess wives; Marthas doing housework; and Handmaids procreating, though often bearing 'unbabies' to their owners/masters. For those dying in the 'Colonies', which are toxic wastelands, and for Handmaids forced into childbearing, there is no imaginable way forward or out. Historical proven knowledge, free speech and debate are denied, exemplified in the emblematic use of the walls of Harvard University, now a fortress of unknowing, and of lies, on which are hung the hooded bodies of detractors of Gilead's fundamentalist, tyrannical control and policed survival. In this totalitarian state based on survival and procreation, the silencing of women and their managed fertility is of utmost concern, as they are to Atwood and decades of readers considering reproductive technologies, fundamentalist controls and tyrannies and the disempowerment of women. *The Handmaid's Tale* presents a monstrous future that could wipe everything out and render the world sterile. Atwood points out that it is only in some sense a work of pure fiction (dystopian fiction, even science fiction) since its horrors are based in history: group executions, sumptuary laws, book burnings, the Lebensborn program of the SS and child-stealing by the Argentine generals, the history of slavery and the history of American polygamy.

> Offred records her story as best she can; then she hides it, trusting that it may be discovered later, by someone who is free to understand it and share it. This is an act of hope. [...] Roméo Daillaire, [...] chronicled both the Rwandan genocide and the world's indifference to it. So did Anne Frank, hidden in her secret annex. (Atwood 2017)

However, even though we are unsure of Offred's survival once she escapes at the end of the novel, the narrative emphasises agency, the importance of control over one's body and voice and refusal of enforced language and behaviours of misdirected power. Diversity, fertility, witness, testimony and agency are the only hope for the future.

Atwood continues to write speculatively and darkly, using Eco-Gothic and imagining a deadly future with the *MaddAddam* trilogy (*Oryx and Crake*, 2003; *The Year of the Flood*, 2009; *MaddAddam*, 2013).

The *MaddAddam* trilogy

The trilogy opens with *Oryx and Crake* and an end-of-the-world toxic wasteland in which possibly the very last human is barely surviving. Jimmy/Snowman sits up against a tree, the dead and dying world all around him:

> Snowman wakes before dawn. He lies unmoving, listening to the tide coming in, wave after wave sloshing over the various barricades, wish wash, wish wash, the rhythm of heartbeat. He would like to believe he is still asleep.
>
> On the eastern horizon there's a greyish haze, lit now with a rosy, deadly glow. Strange how the colour still seems tender, the offshore towers standout in dark silhouette against it, rising improbably out of the pink and pale blue of the lagoon, The shrieks of the birds that nest out there and the distant ocean grinding against the ersatz reefs of rusted car parts and jumbled bricks and assorted rubble sound almost like holiday traffic. (Atwood 2003: 3)

The mixture of beauty: a 'rosy glow'; intended leisure fun: 'holiday traffic'; and utter destruction here brings into sharp relief the loss of humanity, the ecosystem and the world's future. Jimmy seems initially to be the only human salvaged from the disaster of almost total extinction. Luckily, as it emerges, there is a new form of being: the colourful, somewhat childlike Crakers, named for Crake, whose amoral game-oriented carelessness about life is enacted through his creation of the sterilizing Blyssplus pill and his end-of-world games with everything living. Each novel in the trilogy outlines the steps to and from these destructive acts; in *The Year of the Flood*, human life is cheap and brutal gangs roam what's left of the post-apocalyptic world as some begin to try to start to cultivate edible foods again and restart some forms of life. When the pandemic in Atwood's work took over, nothing normally trusted in (God, tight family units, isolation) could actually save the vast majority of the population.

The Year of the Flood takes us into a different space in this post-apocalyptic world: 'Then all of them had left, once the trouble hit. They'd gone home to be with their families, believing love could save them' (Atwood, 2003:7). The extent is global and the ways of treating it unknown since all previous solutions, life changes and cures fail. The parallel with the constantly developing and endless mutating COVID-19 virus strains in the recent global pandemic are unignorable.

> This was not an ordinary pandemic: it wouldn't be contained after a few hundred thousand deaths, obliterated with biotools and bleach. This was the Waterless Flood the Gardeners so often had warned about. It had all the signs: it travelled through the air as if on wings, it burned through the cities like fire, spreading germ-ridden mobs, terror, and butchery. (*The Year of the Flood,* 2003:20)

Atwood recognizes the potential for destruction and end of the world due to carelessness, lack of values, and deadly habits of waste. The prediction of a waterless flood in *The Year of the Flood* in particular seems very prescient. Something is salvaged at the end of the trilogy: at the end of *MaddAddam,* the Crakers and what remains of the humans are to live together and even to interbreed. Exactly what will develop is as yet unknown.

The key drivers for any kind of survival in the Eco-Gothic trilogy *Oryx and Crake, The Year of the Flood* and *MaddAddam* are sustainable development, respect for and enabling of difference, diversity, versatility and metamorphosis.

The Testaments (2019)

With so much continued focus on *The Handmaid's Tale,* with the terrifying Hulu TV version (2017–present) and the parallels of inhumane behaviour against women in recent and current history, particularly in Iran and Afghanistan, we might ask what can be salvaged from *The Handmaid's Tale* except a caution – a warning. Atwood's follow-up, her alternative reading of the past of *The Handmaid's Tale* and the future for Gilead and for women, appeared with *The Testaments* in 2019.

The power of writing and language are crucial in *The Testaments,* where oppositional voices and variants of perspective and history are deemed so potentially damaging that, as in *The Handmaid's Tale*, they are forbidden and punished. In the context of Atwood's feminist, ecocritical work, women are silenced and prevented from reading and writing, defined as too complex for their meagre intelligence. But silencing, like enabling, thinking, speaking and writing, is all about power, and those considered others – women, Indigenous people, migrants or any opposing critical voices, through being silenced, cannot offer creative alternative views and ways forward. Here women cannot read 'the dangerous works of world literature' (*The Testaments* 2019: 300). Only those with 'strong mind and steadfast character could be trusted with them,' (Atwood 2019:302). For women: 'Our minds were too weak for reading. We would crumble, we would fall apart under the contradictions' (Atwood 2019:304). This silencing, refusal of access to alternative views and skewed views of the contemporary experience of the future and past dams up any criticism and blocks ways of seeing problems and futures from different points of view, thereby perhaps finding ways to solve them. 'First-hand narratives from Gilead are vanishingly rare— especially any concerning the lives of girls and women. It is hard for those deprived of literacy to leave such records' (Atwood: 2019: 412).

Atwood aligns the right to different perspectives, thought and speech with validation of diversity, thereby challenging the closing down and life denial of everyday constrained existence in Gilead.

The Testaments uses a more comic than tragic or horror structure. There are three clear alternative voices and three women's stories: Daisy/Baby Nicole /('Jade'), Offred/June's child by Nick the chauffeur who escaped to Canada; her half-sister Agnes, Offred/June's first child, learning to be an Aunt to escape a brutal marriage; and Aunt Lydia, once sadistic and controlling, now secretly working for justice and a mole for the activist group Mayday. Lydia, with her semi-worshippers and recruiters, the Pearl Girls, and her many written hidden secrets (slipped inside a copy of Cardinal Newman's *Apologia Pro Vita Sua*), has the power of insider information and history, upholds the world of Gilead yet undermines it, is the controlling voice in *The Testaments*, the keeper of secrets, and the one who can, in the end, direct what survives, what is salvaged and how it can be understood.

Atwood (2019) insists the novel contains 'tons of hope – lots and lots of hope' while Kakutani (2019) contrasts writing (first person) testimony with the satirical epilogues of *The Handmaid's Tale* and *The Testaments* produced by Piexoto and his pompous colleagues.

Three perspectives and voices create an immediate sense of creative alternatives, boding well for the future and for the survival of the girls. Although there is a harsh, brutal past to be reckoned with and an uncertain present and future, the tone is not relentlessly distressing. Although attacked and on the brink of being shut down, there is also notable resistance, as evidenced by the Mayday group. Aunt Lydia in her testament, the Ardua Hall Holograph, is critical, amused, wry and ironic. Testaments are records: if other voices are allowed and can survive, so there can be contention, disagreement and creative thinking, and escapes from and solutions to straitjacketed ways of behaving and thinking. Diversity and life can begin to flourish. Speaking to us, under oppression, violence and deception, the three narrators of *The Testaments* enable varied perspectives and histories, alternatives and life. Writing and speaking out, even if coded initially and hidden, offer testimony. Towards the end, Lydia addresses us directly, mentioning access to secrets:

> The collective memory is notoriously faulty, and much of the past sinks into the ocean of time to be drowned forever; but once in a while the waters part, allowing us to glimpse a flash of hidden treasure. (Atwood 2019: 415)

Agnes and 'Baby Nicole' have the last word:

> 'You think that festering shitheap can be renewed?' I said. 'Burn it all down!' 'Why would you want to harm so many people?' she asked gently. 'It's my country. It's where I grew up. It's being ruined by the leaders. I want it to be better.' 'Yeah, okay,' I said. 'I get it. Sorry. I didn't mean you. You're my sister.' (Atwood 2019: 379)
> 'Politics is complex as it's a place. People. Not everyone is awful'. (Atwood 2019: 379)

Feminist Eco-Gothic acts as a useful critical lens to explore how Margaret Atwood engages with and critiques the culpable ignorance, carelessness and dehumanization with which people treat other people, other animals and the environment. Crake and Jimmy play with creatures and humans at a remove, through videogames. Crake, in particular, experiments without ethics or morals, lacking engagement with others and with the real, the diverse and the future. It is such carelessness and dehumanization that leads to entropy and death and to the running down of life forms and of life. Much of what we read in Atwood's work might seem initially to be far-fetched, but as she notes herself, there is very little she is making up; much of it has already happened or is on the brink of happening. What her work argues for is a balanced biodiversity and some actual active care for others and the planet. The treasure is other histories, readings, possibilities, diversity, and ways forward. Something vital is salvaged. Not everything should be wiped away.

Laura-Jane Devanny

Possibilities and Pitfalls of the Literal Posthuman: Atwood's Paradice Project

The concept of the posthuman is a fascination within contemporary culture, with the various impacts of technological and scientific advances giving way to questions about the type of subject that will inherit and inhabit the consequences of these developments. Through her depiction of the Crakers within her *MaddAddam* trilogy, Margaret Atwood utilises speculative fiction as a site of critical engagement to interrogate the social consequences of projected technologies, particularly genetic engineering and biotechnology (Defalco 2017: 432–51). In *Bodies of Tomorrow: Technology, Subjectivity, Science Fiction* (2007), Sheryll Vint argues that these technologies have put existing boundaries between human, machine and animal into crisis, with changes to the body being one of the spaces where 'the posthuman may be literally made' (Vint 2007: 8). As one such literal creation of a posthuman body, the Crakers address some of the more urgent questions posed by posthumanism and the possibilities of changing embodiment. Considering how these bodies are constructed and imagined demonstrates how Atwood initially positions the Crakers merely as the logical conclusion of an unquestioned corporate and commercial ethos; however, the ending of the *MaddAddam* novel, which marks the ending of the *MaddAddam* trilogy, reveals the Crakers as a symbol of hope for the future of post/humankind.

In her influential work *How We Became Posthuman: Virtual Bodies in Cybernetics, Literature and Informatics* (1999), N. Katherine Hayles defines the posthuman as 'an informational-material entity' (Hayles 1999a: 11), where the posthuman ground of being is computation and humans are envisioned as information (Hayles 1999a: 246). Ultimately, this understanding of the posthuman involves the seamless articulation of humans with intelligent machines (Hayles 1999a: 34). This 'seamless articulation' serves to blur the boundary lines of demarcation between human, machine, nature and technology, reworking and expanding the current human subject to the point that there is no definitive 'human' subject. Dismantling binarisms in such a manner has the potential to be radically liberating, but Hayles notes there is an accompanying tendency to devalue the relevance of embodiment within the sphere of the posthuman (Hayles 1999a: 48) due to the emphasis placed upon information technologies. Such a disregard for materiality is similarly argued by Vint to result in the posthuman being marked by a culture of individualism and isolation (Vint 2007: 13). Like Hayles, Vint worries that prioritising information technologies could lead to an acceptance of the self as something separate from physicality; this would mean losing oneself and becoming something less than (rather than beyond) human (Vint 2007: 124–5). She therefore puts forward a call for 'an embodied posthumanism' (Vint 2007: 182). Rosi Braidotti's *The Posthuman* (2013) reaffirms this call for an embodied posthumanism through the notion of a vital materialism, or 'matter-realism' (Braidotti 2013: 67) – a concept of posthuman subjectivity that is 'embodied and embedded, firmly located somewhere' (Braidotti 2013: 51). To counter any essentialist implications that may arise from the perception of human identity as rooted in the material realms of corporeality, Braidotti promotes a rhizomatic approach that encourages awareness of these binary categories as processes, therefore involving movement and fluidity. This movement takes place via the 'posthuman nomadic subject' (Braidotti 2013: 93, 188), fluid and constantly shifting yet firmly located in its material surroundings. The model of the nomadic subject facilitates mediation of the binary categories within posthumanism through its flexibility and interconnectedness.

One possible vision for a posthuman nomadic subject is provided through Atwood's literary conception of the Crakers, introduced within the first novel of the *MaddAddam* trilogy, *Oryx and Crake* (2003). The Crakers are a new species of human that have been biologically engineered by genius scientist Crake to inhabit the post-apocalyptic world of the novels following the near-obliteration of humanity. As the 'evolutionary heir' (Hayles 1999b: 157) to the human race, they are a literal creation of a *post*human life form. In conducting his experiments to modify human genetic material, Crake initiates evolutionary developments akin to those found naturally in the rest of the animal kingdom – 'As Crake used to say, *Think of an adaptation, any adaptation, and some animal somewhere will have thought of it first*' (Atwood 2004: 194) – by utilising technology to duplicate and enhance already-existing biological developments within the natural world. Through merging natural with technological processes, Crake is simply speeding up the evolution of humans to allow them to more efficiently adapt to their natural habitat, effecting a transition from humans to their evolutionary heirs. Crake's Paradice Project is the ultimate example of the engineering, modification and exploitation of genetic material, being an example of what Amelia Defalco terms as a type of 'transhumanist biotechnology' that sees 'biotechnology employed in the pursuit of human perfection, control, and transcendence of ecological interdependence' (Defalco 2017: 432–51). However, rather than an attempt at independence from ecology, the Crakers have been modified to rely upon, and thrive within, their natural environment. As strict vegetarians they can digest roots, grass and leaves, topping up this diet with their own caecotrophs; their luminescent green eyes enable vision in the dark; their citrus scent wards off mosquitoes; they have regulated mating rituals based on the females' reproductive cycles; their speeded-up growth rate enables optimization of their life cycle (which ends at thirty years of age); and they even possess the ability to physically heal themselves through an in-built purring mechanism. Without the emphasis on information technologies, the Crakers experience none of the accompanying individualism and isolation as aforementioned by Hayles and Vint, instead acting very much as an interdependent collective whose existence is rooted in nature, biology and materiality with a return to a state of ecological harmony. In many ways, the posthuman figures of the Crakers are the perfect blueprint for the future.

Ironically, the narrative flashbacks of *Oryx and Crake*'s sole human survivor, Jimmy (a.k.a. Snowman), to the conception and design of the Crakers and their engineered origins provide constant reminders that it is, in fact, technology that has enabled such a synthesis between these posthumans and the environment around them. In positioning them as hybridized cyborgian creatures that are the product of both technology and nature, it becomes possible to recognize the Crakers as examples of Hayles' concept of the posthuman as material-informational entities, and Atwood initially appears to portray this posthuman model as one of harmony and one that works. However, the discourse of consumerism and advertising used throughout the novel to describe the design of the Crakers situates them within the surroundings of an increasing globalized commercialization, representing a realization of what Braidotti describes as 'opportunistic trans-species commodification of Life that is the logic of advanced capitalism' (Braidotti 2013: 60). As Crake says, when describing the results of his aptly named Paradice Project, 'These are the floor models. They represent the art of the possible' (Atwood 2004: 359). The Crakers have also been designed to meet societal measures of desirability, with smooth skin, no fat, no bulges, no cellulite and no body hair: 'They look like retouched fashion photos, or ads for a high-priced workout program' (Atwood 2004: 115). This commercialized perfection is presented as less than, rather than more than, human[1] – 'Maybe this is the reason that these women arouse in Snowman not even the faintest stirrings of lust. It was the thumbprints of human imperfection that used to move him' (Vint 2007: 8) – and there are several mentions of the Crakers' unnatural, inhuman nature by Jimmy, who describes them as 'placid, like animated statues. They leave him chilled' (Atwood 2004: 115). Through Jimmy's narrative viewpoint, the reader subsequently comes to understand that the perfection the Crakers embody is simply an extreme form of regulation that is the product of a neo/hyper-capitalism combined with biogenetic technology, or a form of biocapitalism through which biological life becomes the central commodity (Defalco 2017: 432–51). This reflects Braidotti's concerns over the consequences of a form of posthumanism produced within late modernity, whereby '[a]dvanced capitalism and its bio-genetic technologies engender a perverse form of the posthuman' (Braidotti 2013: 7).

Further reminders of the capitalist ethos that influenced the design and creation of the Crakers are given within the third and final novel, *MaddAddam* (2013), where the growing community of survivors consists

---

1   A worry expressed earlier by Vint (2007). However, rather than being due to a posthuman emphasis on information technologies and an acceptance of the self as something separate from embodiment, the Crakers are here presented as less than human because of the perfected nature of their embodiment.

partly of some of the scientists who were commissioned to work on Crake's Paradice Project. The altruism of the project is exposed as a façade as the scientists reflect upon its corporate and commercial nature: 'It was big business, the BioCorps were backing it. People were paying through the ceiling for those gene-splices. They were customizing their kids, ordering up the DNA like pizza toppings' (Atwood 2013: 43). The scientists refer to the Crakers as 'a meat-computer set of problems to be solved' (Atwood 2013: 43), encapsulating a concrete, literal form of the posthuman 'material-informational' entity through the lexical compound 'meat-computer'. Such a reductive image continues to depict the type of posthumanism produced through biocapitalism as a dehumanising force. But as the novel progresses, the Crakers continue to exhibit some of the signs of human imagination that had started to manifest throughout *Oryx and Crake* (Evans 2010: 49),[2] particularly singing and storytelling. Atwood's views on the power of language and stories are certainly renowned,[3] so it is not surprising that the trope of storytelling becomes central to the development of the *MaddAddam* trilogy. Atwood states that humans are 'storytellers by nature', and so the Crakers are also drawn towards stories as 'they have that part of our human inheritance'.[4] Writing of the novels, the link between human biology and imagination is supplemented by Hannes Bergthaller (2010: 740), who posits that biological nature predisposes humankind to fiction and theology, whilst Deborah Bowen (2017: 697) also notes that 'it seems these things too are hard-wired in – too necessary'. Indeed, the Craker's deep-rooted tendency towards artistic expression becomes increasingly apparent over the course of the trilogy, despite these attributes

2   Also noted by Shari Evans, who argues that the Crakers grow beyond Crake's in-tended theme, proving that they can't be reduced to mere biological functions.
3   For instance, according to various interviews following the release of *MaddAddam*. In one interview, she states 'Storytelling is a very old human skill that gives us an evo-lutionary advantage' (Christie 2013). In another interview she positions language as a part of the genetic makeup of humans: 'the narrative programme that we come with' (Gallagher 2022).
4   Atwood, 'Margaret Atwood's Dystopian Future Interview', *BBC Radio 4 Online*, 16 September 2013, <http://www.bbc.co.uk/programmes/b039zg2c>, accessed 8 November 2013.

being purposefully omitted from Crake's original design remit in order to prevent 'any harmful symbolisms, such as kingdoms, icons, gods, or money' (Atwood 2004: 359).

Perhaps most significantly, Atwood's notion of storytelling as an intrinsic part of humanity gestures towards the existence of a biological, 'embodied imagination' (Gosetti-Ferencei 2018) – the understanding that imagination is not simply a function of the mind, but of the body as well. In *The Life of Imagination: Revealing and Making the World* (2018), Jennifer Anna Gosetti-Ferencei explains the evolution of human consciousness and cognition as intrinsically linked with the material world and embodied action (Gosetti-Ferencei 2018: 56–7). She further expounds upon 'the embodied nature of imagining' (Gosetti-Ferencei 2018: 160) and the way in which 'imagination is expressed through the body, just as the body extends imagination in action' (Gosetti-Ferencei 2018: 179). This premise of an embodied imagination refutes any Cartesian belief in the mind–body dualism, therefore allowing the singing and storytelling of the Crakers to be recognized as a function of both the body and the mind. In perceiving art as both reliant upon and an expression of biological features (Gosetti-Ferencei 2018: 160; Bergthaller 2010: 736), literature may also be considered a mode of expression of the biological imagination. Bergthaller explains how creative works of literature 'draw their meaning precisely from their relation to the life of the body' (Bergthaller 2010: 737), whilst Gosetti-Ferencei posits that 'literature is increasingly understood as arising from, and as engaging, embodied experience' (Gosetti-Ferencei 2018: 175). Additionally, Atwood considers language to be 'one of the oldest human technologies we have'[5] and so, as an 'anthropotechnology' (Bergthaller 2010: 734) that therefore straddles the natural/human and the technological/machinic, the written word may function to transcend the material–informational binary as well as that of the mind–body. If the shift from spoken to written language is crucial in the development of human imagination (Gosetti-Ferencei 2018: 58), then the arrival of literacy

5   Margaret Atwood, 'Seven life lessons from Margaret Atwood', *BBC Radio 4 online*, <https://www.bbc.co.uk/programmes/articles/5DQdfKq953Pq6DSkMkM1P5l/seven-life-lessons-from-margaret-atwood>, accessed 28 February 2021.

marks a pivotal point within the evolution of the Crakers as a medium of expression for their biological imagination, therefore facilitating an embodied posthumanism and negating any disregard for materiality.

Blackbeard is the first of the Craker children to be taught the art of writing by Toby, who is a central protagonist in the human survival story of both *The Year of the Flood* (2009) and *MaddAddam*. An inquisitive Craker child, Blackbeard harbours a keen interest in the community of human survivors, and he eventually elicits a relationship with Toby as his mentor and guide. Blackbeard's reflections upon his journey towards becoming literate mirror Gosetti-Ferencei's understanding of the imagination as grounded in embodied cognition (Gosetti-Ferencei 2018: 66), as he remarks on a connection between his internal consciousness and the external material world: 'I am Blackbeard, and this is my voice that I am writing down to help Toby. If you look at this writing I have made, you can hear me (I am Blackbord)[6] talking to you, inside your head. That is what writing is [...] This is my voice, the voice of Blackbeard that you are hearing in your head. That is called *reading*' (Atwood 2013: 376–8). The sensory nature of Blackbeard's experiences also demonstrate how the pen functions as a tool of extended cognition for the writer (Goretti-Ferencei 2018: 180), apparent through the manner by which the act of writing enables a manifestation of Toby's voice: 'And she showed me, Blackbeard, how to make such words, on a page, with a pen, when I was little. And she showed me how to turn the marks back into a voice, so that when I look at the page and read the words, it is Toby's voice that I hear. And when I speak these words out loud, you too are hearing Toby's voice' (Atwood 2013: 85). As well as mediating the mind–body/informational–material binaries through the expression of his own embodied imagination, Blackbeard's assimilation of Toby's narrative voice is a merging of human with posthuman imagination. The acts of reading and writing permit Blackbeard to successfully negotiate these binary categories with a fluidity similar to Braidotti's nomadic, rhizomatic approach (Braidotti 2013: 93, 188).

---

6   This is an intentional misspelling as written within the novel, symbolizing Blackbeard's developing state of language acquisition and his emergent literacy skills.

The developing relationships between the posthuman Crakers and some of the surviving human characters throughout the *MaddAddam* novel eventually culminate in the arrival of a new generation of interspecific hybrids – babies born to human women with Craker fathers. These children truly disrupt the categorization of human versus posthuman in crossing the physical boundaries between the two; they literalize the flexibility and interconnectedness of Braidotti's posthuman nomadic subject and provide a more hopeful vision for a post/human future. Crucially, this new generation is tasked with the continuation of literacy that will form the foundations of a new theology. By the end of *MaddAddam*, the responsibility for transcribing the ritualistic stories of the Crakers has passed from Toby to Blackbeard, who continues to impart the skills of reading and writing to the Craker–human children: 'And I have taught all of these things about the Book and the paper and the writing to Jimadam, and to Pilaren, and to Medulla and Oblongata [...] And they wanted to learn, although it is hard. But they learned these things, to help all of us together. And when I am no longer here among us. [...] then Jimadam and Pilaren and Medulla and Oblongata will teach these things to the younger ones' (Atwood 2013: 387). The continual passing down and transcribing of knowledge commences a process that Gosetti-Ferencei speculates as a 'potentially limitless variation' of recording imagined concepts, which in turn enables the further imaginings of others (Gosetti-Ferencei 2018: 57).

Throughout the *MaddAddam* trilogy, Atwood provides a stark warning as to the pitfalls of biotechnology and biocapitalism, which do indeed engender a perverse form of the posthuman. Whilst the Crakers exemplify ecological interdependency instead of the isolated individualism usually prevalent within posthuman culture, the fact that they are a direct result of a biocapitalist ethos that interprets biology as technology means that information technologies are prioritized, subsequently positioning the body as a commodity. However, the presence of an inherent biological imagination, most noticeable through the importance of stories within the Craker culture, moves towards an embodied posthumanism that overcomes the mind–body/material–informational binarism. Additionally, the arrival of the Craker–human hybrids effectively reworks and expands both human and posthuman subjectivity beyond definitive categorization and into a nomadic state, fluid and shifting and yet firmly located in its own embodied consciousness. The addition of blank pages at end of the new 'Book' that Blackbeard writes, which marks the end of the *MaddAddam* trilogy itself, allows for the continued imaginings of the new generation of cross-species subjects, demonstrating the possibility, and hope, for a limitless post/ human future.

Sarah Wagstaffe

Memory, Mourning and Nostalgia in *Oryx and Crake*

'He needed to forget the past – the distant past, the immediate past, the past in any form. He needed to exist only in the present, without guilt, without expectation' (Atwood 2003: 406). This is Jimmy/Snowman's desire as he leads the newly invented humanoids, the Crakers, out of their birthplace in the Paradice Dome and into the world, and towards the ruins of human civilization.[1] The story of Jimmy and his charges are central to Margaret Atwood's *Oryx and Crake* (2003), which chronicles one man's experience of the end of the world as we know it, and is the first instalment in the *MaddAddam* trilogy. Jimmy's shepherding of the Crakers takes place after a major catastrophe, engineered by Jimmy's best friend Crake, who distributed a wonder-pill throughout the population that promised sexual prowess and prolonged youth. When these pills became widespread, he began adding a deadly, incurable virus to the formula, wiping out most of humanity. Jimmy's nostalgic desire, expressed towards the end of the novel, is contradictory to the narrative preceding it, where the past is interwoven with Jimmy's life to such an extent as to be totally inseparable. Believing himself to be the only true human left alive, everything he does is influenced by his memories of—and nostalgia for—the past: from his own drive to survive to the new religion he imparts to the Crakers. Through Jimmy, Atwood uses ideas of memory and storytelling in a manner that defies traditional notions of nostalgia and turns them into a creative force that provides some semblance of purpose in an unfamiliar world.

Nostalgia, the longing for a lost past, has been studied as a psychological phenomenon and is often used as a means of exploitation, frequently

---

[1] Atwood's protagonist goes by both Jimmy and Snowman. For clarity I will refer to him as Jimmy throughout.

leading to negative consequences. In her key study *The Future of Nostalgia* (2001), Svetlana Boym identifies two main kinds of nostalgia, namely 'the restorative and the reflective': the former demanding a 'transhistorical reconstruction of the lost home' and the latter being 'the longing itself [...] wistfully, ironically, desperately' (Boym 2001: xviii). These ideas have become foundational to understandings of nostalgia. However, Atwood's protagonist is in a unique position and as such, neither reflective nor restorative nostalgia wholly fits his situation. He is the only human left (as far as he knows) and is therefore the last person able to preserve any memories of the time before the catastrophe which eliminated most of humanity. As such, the restoration of his past would be impossible and even pointless, while reflection would be unbearably painful. Despite this, he is unable to let his past go. Instead, he uses his past to provide meaning in his present. Through Jimmy, Atwood complicates Boym's nostalgia binary but creates space for a new and creative form of nostalgia that incorporates aspects of restoration, community, connection, and total fabrication.

Keightley and Pickering (2012) suggest that the nostalgic 'engages imaginatively with what is retained from the past and, moving across time, continuously rearranges the hotchpotch of experience into relatively coherent narrative structures', thereby giving their experiences 'meaning by becoming emplotted into a discernible sequential pattern' (Keightley and Pickering 2012: 43). This desire to generate a feeling of continuity and meaning through narrative is evident in Jimmy. His nostalgic desire and constant return to the past are the most convenient ways for him to hold on to his identity and sense of purpose when everything else has been lost, where the 'dissolution of meaning' is becoming more and more frequent (Atwood 2003: 43). The narrative is split into two: one which follows Jimmy's life leading up to the end of humanity, and one which is set in the relative present, where Jimmy is struggling to comprehend everything that has happened. This is a very explicit realization of Katherine V. Snyder's (2011) insistence that '[t]he future as imagined in dystopian speculative fiction must be simultaneously recognizable and unrecognizable, both like and not-like the present' (Snyder 2011: 470). One of Atwood's narratives within the novel introduces a familiar, if altered, world where life is at least reconcilable with our own present day, yet the parallel narrative is of a radically changed future. If the presence of genetically altered lifeforms and heavily controlled gated communities might initially seem jarring in the former, they become a relatively acceptable disfiguration of the norm when compared with the latter narrative's almost total annihilation of society. Through the use of two narratives, Atwood is already enforcing a 'dissolution of meaning': the explicit classism, perversion of nature and abuse of science present in the narrative of the novel's relative past become almost meaningless when faced with the narrative of the novel's present.

If Atwood's split narrative can support Snyder's requirement for readers to 'sustain a kind of double consciousness with respect to both the fictionality of the world portrayed and to its potential as our own world's future', it can also push beyond it (Snyder 2011: 470). Atwood's protagonist, Jimmy, is a vessel for a double consciousness himself. He is mourning the loss of everything he has ever known. In Freud's view, '[m]ourning is regularly the reaction to the loss of a loved person, or to the loss of some abstraction which has taken the place of one, such as one's country, liberty, an ideal, and so on', a feeling in which 'the world has become poor and empty' (Freud 2001: 243, 246). For Jimmy, who has lost everything Freud describes in one event, the only way to avoid the looming emptiness is to revisit the past. However, the past is becoming difficult to access; reflection on what was is becoming harder as meaning slowly slips away. The best he can do is fill in the blanks with his own creations, repopulating his existence by crafting stories based on the people he knew and events he experienced. This is aided by the two simultaneous narratives, which provide Jimmy's own 'double consciousness' as a means of surviving the present while trying to understand the past. 'Fictionality' comes in the form of Jimmy's storytelling to provide answers for the ever-curious Crakers, while also creating a more accessible past for himself, a means of navigating history to forge a clear connection between past and present. Without such storytelling, Snowman is stuck, as Snyder describes, 'marooned in time, cast away between a human past and a post-human future, cut off from the past and yet unable to move beyond it' (Snyder 2011: 472). Our very concept of Jimmy is caught between two narratives, one past and one present, mourning the former and fearing the latter. He can only escape by forming yet another narrative out of nostalgic constructions and fictitious designs.

Nostalgia, for the dually conscious Jimmy, is his only protection against the marching forward of time. To him, time feels like a form of currency that he is quickly losing. He feels as though

> he's been given a box of time belonging to him alone, stuffed to the brim with hours and minutes that he can spend like money. Trouble is, the box has holes in it and the time is running out, no matter what he does with it. (Atwood 2003: 44)

His fight against time is to use his memories to make the present more bearable, to give him more reason to live, even though he himself attempts to denounce 'pointless repinings' as wasteful (Atwood 2003: 51).[2] His past alone, though, is an imperfect solution, as it is too full of painful memories and purposeful avoidance of necessary truths. His answer is to create a mythology under his own control (at least in the beginning). This mythology eventually grows into a religion, which he passes on to the Crakers, who have themselves 'accumulated a stock of lore' about Jimmy and about their own creation (Atwood 2003: 9). While initially it seems that this stock of lore is self-made, it soon becomes clear that Jimmy has set it into motion himself. This creation cannot be considered in line with Boym's restorative mode of nostalgia, though, as Jimmy is not attempting to recreate the past. He is making something new. Called a 'storyteller-trickster' by J. Brooks Bouson (2004), Jimmy regains some semblance of control over the past by moulding it into his own narrative (Brooks Bouson 2004: 153). Bouson suggests that Jimmy finds a sort of challenge and joy in creating these stories for the Crakers, 'delighting' in his artistic attempts to 'thwart Crake' by denying his will for his creations to have no religion (Brooks Bouson 2004: 153). While this does appear to be true, there is also a distinct sense that these stories are required for Jimmy's own sake, for his sanity and his fragile sense of purpose. His creations may not be wholly restorative, but they still provide an ideal, one of few comforts in the ruined land Jimmy is forced to occupy.

A further foundational study on nostalgia, *Ethics and Nostalgia in the Contemporary Novel* (2005), contains John J. Su's claim that 'the vague, ambiguous, and shifting characteristics of nostalgic worlds enable

---

2   Emphasis in original.

individuals with diverse and often conflicting beliefs to identify with a common image', implying that nostalgia can be used to bridge certain societal gaps or misunderstandings, a way to find common ground between otherwise conflicting ideologies (Su 2005: 176). This study provides the necessary framework for understanding nostalgia in a social setting. Unfortunately, there is no shared history available for Jimmy and the Crakers. The Crakers have only an incredibly short history and no memory of the time before the catastrophe, and their history only overlaps with Jimmy's very recent experiences. However, Su's observations that 'nostalgia represents a necessary and often productive form of confronting loss and displacement' and 'nostalgic fantasies offer the hope of restoring a vital connection to the past despite cultural dislocation' are more easily applicable (Su 2005: 12, 118). Jimmy's creative use of nostalgic ideals enable him to re-establish links to his past which, while based in fiction, provide him with a method of processing his experiences of loss and displacement while keeping a relatively safe distance from the reality of his situation.

While nostalgia may provide comfort, it can also be an overtly negative force, one which Su explains as follows: 'The longing to return to a lost place frequently conceals feelings of fear and anxiety, and nostalgia has been repeatedly exploited for commercial and nationalistic purposes' (Su 2005: 3). Jimmy certainly shows fear and anxiety, but this cannot be exploited by any higher power; there are none left. However, Su's observation still applies in a non-conventional sense. Rather than a powerful figure exploiting the fear and anxiety of a particular group, Jimmy exploits others in order to reduce his *own* fears and anxiety. Jimmy has to creatively work his own nostalgic desire into constructions that the Crakers will understand and eventually come to take as truth. While Jimmy is certainly not exploiting the Crakers for political reasons (they have no concept of politics, race or culture), he is exploiting them in a more subtle fashion. He intertwines his memories and experiences with a new mythology which he passes onto the Crakers, deifying his old friend, his old lover and, to some extent, himself. His story of creation starts with '[i]n the beginning, there was chaos', and goes on to name Oryx (Jimmy's former lover and ongoing obsession) and Crake (his friend turned rival) as the creators of all life (Atwood 2003: 118–19). This is despite Crake's wishes that religion be avoided at all costs, as he was 'against the notion of God, or gods of any kind', and would 'surely be disgusted by the spectacle of his own gradual deification' (Atwood 2003: 119–120). Jimmy grants himself the position of 'Crake's prophet [...] whether he likes it or not' (Atwood 2003: 120). This is an odd concept, since surely Jimmy's position is by his own design. However, he is so caught up in his own fairy tale that it stretches beyond him, not entirely under his control. His nostalgia is guiding him, rather than the other way around, and gains a life of its own.

The exploitation, then, is not malicious or for any sort of physical or hierarchical gain. After all, despite authoring this mythology, Jimmy is not the most powerful figure in his own story. It is instead a sort of emotional exploitation. Jimmy's creations provide him with a way to 'interpret the present in relation to an inaccessible or lost past' (Su 2005: 4), as Su suggests, a method which is a psychological salve for Jimmy. It allows him to remain in contact with his memories and his lost home while giving him some (though not entire) control over how he processes his loss. In providing himself with this connection, he is also forcing it onto the Crakers. These people are too trusting and naïve, at least currently, to question the man who to them is guide and prophet. They willingly accept his stories and from them form a religion to which they strictly adhere. At first this is harmless. It gives the Crakers the answers they crave and is an emotional release for Jimmy. However, as the Crakers grow more curious, they begin to demand 'dogma: he would deviate from orthodoxy at his peril' (Atwood 2003: 120). If he lost the support of the Crakers, if they refused to acknowledge him as an authority, Jimmy would lose everything. His own fabricated connection to history would be severed and the Crakers would turn away from him, leaving him well and truly alone. As long as he can maintain his hold over them, he has an audience for his nostalgic constructions. If there is an audience, he can make it real. Jimmy's exploitation of the Crakers may not be malicious or even purposeful, to the point where exploitation seems too strong a word. However, he is using the Crakers, at least in part, to satisfy his own nostalgic desires, and this is already threatening to lead him into uncertain territory.

Andrew Tate (2017) highlights Jimmy's 'gift for narrative', which is 'ultimately revealed as a primary reason for his continued survival' (Tate

2017: 61). Before the disaster, when Crake is still alive, Jimmy claims that '[w]hen any civilization is dust and ashes [...] art is all that's left over. Images, words, music. Imaginative structures. Meaning – human meaning, that is – is defined by them' (Atwood 2003: 197). Crake, however, rebuffs this claim, stating that 'people can amuse themselves any way they like', but art simply serves a 'biological purpose' in making people more attractive to potential mates (Atwood 2003: 197). It seems contradictory, then, that Crake chose someone more artistically inclined to be the shepherd of the Crakers. As Tate says, the only reason Jimmy is still alive is because he has an aptitude for words, one which Crake used to get him a job at the Paradice Dome. There, Crake had the opportunity to handpick the person who would lead the Crakers to their new home. His choice was predominantly between the greatest scientific minds available, including himself. He rejected all of those options in favour of Jimmy, who was at best distinctly average at scientific and mathematical pursuits. When starting his new world, Crake chose a storyteller, not a scientist, as his guide.

Through Crake, Atwood is therefore suggesting that nostalgic desire runs deeper than it first appears, even in those who adamantly oppose it. Before the Crake-made catastrophe, when late capitalism is in full swing, Tate argues '[c]ulture is being disposed as a symptom of deeper vandalism and deliberate amnesia' (Tate 2017: 72). Throughout *Oryx and Crake*, we witness the continued devaluing and even removal of art and literature. Jimmy himself held a job 'going through old books and earmarking them for destruction' until he was fired for refusing to throw anything away (Atwood 2003: 283). Art in Atwood's dystopia has essentially become entirely disposable. Crake's actions, behaviours and words throughout the novel predominantly seem to be in favour of this practice. He even instils Jimmy with a warning about his Crakers: '*Watch out for art ... As soon as they start doing art, we're in trouble*. Symbolic thinking of any kind would signal downfall, in Crake's view' (Atwood 2003: 419–20)[3]. As Tate points out, Crake designed the Crakers so they would evolve 'without the need for symbolic thinking [...] free of the emotional lives that, in the geneticist's view, perpetuate territorial conflicts, desire and

3 Emphasis in original.

war' (Tate 2017: 76). In this quest, Crake failed. Whether it is because of Jimmy or some inherent need, or perhaps a mix of both, the Crakers begin producing symbolic images and practices. Perhaps this failure was also, in part, because of Crake. Though he was aloof, condescending and disdainful towards the arts, Atwood implies that Crake might have seen some intrinsic value in them, even if he never admitted it. If this is the case, it is possible he never acknowledged this himself. Contradicting his own warning about art and the symbolism that goes with it, Crake sent Jimmy, who specializes in symbolism, to teach the Crakers how to survive. Though his behaviour suggests that he is above such trivialities, in preserving Jimmy, Crake shows that he too has some inherent desire to exist beyond his natural lifespan and that he, too, was influenced by nostalgic desire. The only way to achieve his own preservation is through stories, and through art and culture, and so the very practices he claims to despise become his only continuing legacy through which he can survive. Some part of Crake, despite his best efforts, is still holding onto the past. In sparing Jimmy, he preserves that past (though in a massively altered form) and becomes a recognizable figure, a deity, in a world that was allegedly supposed to forget him.

It is interesting that the characters who could be considered nostalgic, both the obvious Jimmy and the much subtler Crake, are male. Both have idealized images of the world which they project onto their female companion, Oryx, who, on the other hand, appears entirely removed from nostalgia. When Jimmy enquires about her past and begins to piece evidence together, she tries to distract him or deny things, asking 'why do you dream up such things?' and continuing in a detached manner (Atwood 2003: 370). When she does share parts of her history, she seems to purposely call into question the truth of her tales. When Jimmy tells her he doesn't 'buy it', she simply asks 'what is it that you would like to buy instead?' (Atwood 2003: 167). Jimmy, often sentimental, always obsessed with the past, has fallen for a woman who seems to be his opposite. The simple solution is that Oryx has no reason to be nostalgic. From what we learn of her childhood, it was filled with trauma and abuse. She was trafficked, made to work for no pay and stay in poor conditions, and eventually was sold on to make child pornography. Even the traumas of Jimmy's childhood seem to pale into insignificance in comparison. However, her total lack of interest in providing a true, factual history for herself results in Jimmy weaving a fantasy about her even before she died. His constant idealisation of her (and, it is implied, Crake's as well) gives her a mythical quality. If, as Boym says, nostalgia is a 'romance with one's own fantasy', that certainly shows here because, through Jimmy, Atwood intertwines *romance with fantasy* and *romance with an individual* until the two become inseparable (Boym 2001: xiii).

This is a prime example of what Coral Ann Howells (2006) calls Atwood's insistence 'on the emotional and imaginative contexts within which human sexuality is embedded' (Howells 2006: 164). 'Emotional' and 'imaginative' contexts are critical as Jimmy's entire concept of Oryx is a combination of these things, notably lacking much of a solid reality. Jimmy's nostalgia is tied deeply to an emotional fantasy and emphasizes Su's observation that nostalgic reconstructions of an individual risk 'promoting static and homogenous identities that never existed historically' (Su 2005: 7). We know nothing for certain about Oryx and neither does Jimmy. We are never even provided with her real name, something Oryx herself claims to not remember. Jimmy is emotionally and sexually attracted to a woman who is simply an amalgamation of his own fabrications, a person who never existed yet is symbolized by a very real individual. Not only is she a semi-mythical creature to Jimmy even while she is alive, his deification of her after her death only furthers his own illusions. The emotional and imaginative contexts of his relationship with Oryx become central to his ongoing story of creation, related to the Crakers as fact rather than fantasy. In the instance of Jimmy and Oryx, the female is the passive subject of the male nostalgic desire. Jimmy's attempt to preserve Oryx through stories results in her becoming a mythical fabrication, bearing only superficial resemblances to the real woman.

The importance of Jimmy's position is emphasized by Howells in *The Cambridge Companion to Margaret Atwood*. She points out that Jimmy's private stories are different 'as he desperately tries to reclaim his identity as *Homo sapiens*, mourning his lost world' (Howells 2021: 175).[4] She gives Jimmy the title of 'the sole custodian of human history, culture, and

---

4   Emphasis in original.

language, living in a condition of radical isolation' (Howells 2021: 175). This position grants him the unique ability to mould history into whatever story he wants, which is what he does when building the Craker's religion and deifying Oryx and Crake. He is history's guardian but also its only orator, giving him the power to alter and embellish as he sees fit. However, while he can do this for the story he gives to the Crakers, he cannot completely change history for himself. No matter the embellishments, Jimmy is still aware of what really happened. To truly uncover the details of the past, and to come to terms with his complicity in the events leading up to the destruction of humanity, Jimmy retraces his steps to the Paradice Dome while simultaneously revisiting moments from his past, 'scattered like pieces of a giant jigsaw puzzle for Snowman to fit together into a narrative where the truth is finally revealed' (Howells 2021: 175). It is there that Jimmy's reliance on nostalgic fabrication truly comes to light.

Howells calls the Paradice Dome the 'traumatic centre' of the novel, the focal point that connects the 'before' and 'after' (Howells 2021: 175). Only upon arriving there, in its post-disaster state, is Jimmy able to truly reconnect with the darkest parts of his own past. Previously, Jimmy's memories were influenced by a certain level of untruth, or at least partial truths, allowing him to function as a passive hero. He remembers himself as the troubled child whose parents were indifferent towards him through no fault of his own. He saw himself as Crake's best and only friend, though he 'could feel it within himself to hate Crake, as well as liking him', and convinced himself he might even occasionally be Crake's idol (particularly when it came to relationships with the opposite sex) (Atwood 2003: 86). He was also Oryx's innocent lover: in Jimmy's eyes, her *true* love, hindered only by her admiration of Crake, who was 'her hero, in a way. An important way. As he, Jimmy, was not' (Atwood 2003: 377). He never admits that Oryx might have actually *loved* Crake in a romantic sense. In all of these cases, Jimmy was always (or almost always) doing the right thing, doing his best, and obstacles and bad things simply happened to him. He, in his own eyes, is a good man who might occasionally do bad things, but there is always an excuse to alleviate him of any serious blame. He is able to conveniently misremember, or to add extra details to the past which were not really there, or convince himself there was a reason where there was none. However, upon arriving at the Paradice Dome and encountering his literal 'skeletons in the closet, the bodies of Oryx and Crake', Jimmy is forced to contend with reality (Howells 2021: 175). His nostalgic reconstructions of the past falter and he must accept that he was, if not a main player in the end of the world, at least something of an accomplice. After all, he 'recoded the inner door, sealed it shut', and locked out everyone else, essentially condemning them to death, just as Crake planned (Atwood 2003: 394). For all of his creativity and deflection, Jimmy must come to terms with a harsh reality that threatens to collapse his nostalgia-driven fantasy.

When Jimmy finds Crake's and Oryx's bodies as he left them after the catastrophe, he reaches a critical moment. This is the point where everything could unravel; Oryx and Crake are dead, the Crakers are living in the fallout of a disaster and Jimmy is not altogether innocent. Jimmy's fictions are pushed into the light and examined for their inconsistencies and biases, not just for the reader but for Jimmy himself. He has to acknowledge his own failures, remember things he would rather forget and accept that his stories are just that: fiction. No amount of storytelling can erase the past, at least not for Jimmy. Here the narrative could have gone in many ways. Jimmy could have chosen the past, and let himself die there in the Dome alongside Crake and Oryx. He could have chosen an entirely new path and continued his journey into unknown territory (though his injuries may have prevented much success). However, Jimmy makes the decision to go back to the Crakers, to resume his imperfect, short-sighted present. He takes 'one last backward look at Paradice' and leaves his actual past where it belongs, behind him (Atwood 2003: 415). Despite everything, he will return to his land of make-believe and continue to live, 'existing and not existing', half man, half myth (Atwood 2003: 8).

Upon his return Jimmy is already planning new stories and ways to make his existence more bearable in the short term. He considers his need to 'invent some lies' about Crake and about himself (Atwood 2003: 417). Still, though, he cannot think too far ahead. Smith and Campbell (2017) develop a more positive approach to Boym's view of nostalgia, highlighting its potential to provide 'a sense of hope or longing for a better future', yet Jimmy seems to reject this (Smith and Campbell 2017: 612–27). When he tries to think about what to do next, he wonders '[w]hat to do next about what? That's too difficult' (Atwood 2003: 418). He has resolved to stay just where he is, thinking neither forward nor backward, except through his own fabrications. His memories will be recreated through stories, making them easier to bear and easier to forget. His future will remain untold. Jimmy has decided to live in a creative nostalgia, one that defies the past by forming it into something new, yet evades the present by remaining in the realms of fiction. Not only has Jimmy created a new form of nostalgia, separate from the restorative and the reflective, he has chosen it over reality.

This final decision seems monumental, yet it is thrown into question almost immediately. In the final pages, Jimmy realizes he is not quite as alone as he thought. There are more human survivors. Upon seeing them, he asks "What do you want me to do?", a query directed at empty space but one he nonetheless gets three answers for (Atwood 2003: 432). The first, '[i] t's hard to know', seems to come from Jimmy himself (Atwood 2003: 433). The second, '*Oh Jimmy, you were so funny*', mimics the tone and language of Oryx (Atwood 2003: 433).[5] The third, '*Don't let me down*', sounds more like Crake (Atwood 2003: 433).[6] In this revelatory moment, all of Jimmy's main influences hit him at once. He must again face the choice between past and present, only now, future has become a viable option. Howells asks, '[i]s it time to move forward, or time to exit the novel?', though there are far more questions at hand (Howells 2021: 176). Is Jimmy ready, or even able, to join human company again? Is Jimmy approaching salvation or death? Will he abandon the Crakers or will he turn his back on his own people? Will he somehow find a way to bring the two together? However, it *is* time to exit the novel and so these questions remain unanswered.[7] It is unknown whether Jimmy will embrace the future, both his own and the world's, or return to his present built on foundations of his own fiction.

Jimmy's journey is a journey through time. While he physically travels back to the Paradice Dome, he also travels psychologically through his past, from his childhood to the moments immediately preceding the end

5   Emphasis in original.
6   Emphasis in original.
7   That is, until the release of the rest of the trilogy: *The Year of the Flood* (2009) follows *Oryx and Crake*, and the third instalment, *MaddAddam*, was released in 2013.

of humanity as we know it. Every aspect of his journey is influenced by his past experiences, even if he tries to avoid it, and eventually becomes the foundation of the stories he passes on to the Crakers. Despite Crake's warnings, Jimmy imparts to the Crakers a new mythology that combines memory and fiction, creating a nostalgic vision that becomes religion, a phenomenon that will persist and grow long after Jimmy has died. After all, it has already preserved Oryx and Crake, so it will likely preserve Jimmy too. Jimmy comes to accept that he cannot entirely avoid the past, and so instead finds a way to mould it into a bearable fiction, at once preserving the aspects and individuals that are important to him while removing parts he finds painful. Through Jimmy, Atwood portrays a nostalgia that is neither restorative nor reflective, but entirely creative. The Crakers have no history, so Jimmy gifts them his own. While it may not be true to reality, it is a version that provides comfort and guidance not just for the Crakers, but for Jimmy himself.

Sarah Worgan

Surplus Life in Margaret Atwood's Oryx and Crake

Why is it he feels some line has been crossed, some boundary transgressed? How much is too much, how far is too far?

(Margaret Atwood, *Oryx and Crake*)

In *Oryx and Crake* 'life' is understood as the genomic, cellular-level life of biotech practices, and Atwood imagines that it is a commodity to be sold and marketed. Corporate control is manifested in the way biotechnology, as the 'new science', merges with consumer culture to reshape and reform society. Atwood envisages the development of what Gilles Deleuze calls 'control societies' (Deleuze 1992: 3–7), whereby there is no stable power core but rather a network of relations in which specific corporations gain global control of markets. In the process, biotechnology transforms into biotech company, as the field of genetics becomes inseparable from its corporate use. In Atwood's rendering, biotech companies are called Compounds and they organize society in place of centralized governments. With Compounds in control, life is cut or broken into commodifiable parts according to its marketing potential. For example, the 'body-oriented Compounds' (Atwood 2004: 339) of Helth Wyzer and ReejovenEssence have different transgenic aims: ReejovenEssence reaches for immortality, whereas Helth Wyzer develops organ-specific technologies. In the future of control societies that *Oryx and Crake* enacts, excess becomes integral to corporate power, and life becomes a material for human desires. How can life resist such limitless control in the new global order?

Life is not sacred in the new order. Concerns over biotech control are echoed in the sentiments of Jimmy's parents in *Oryx and Crake*. The pair argue over their diametric approaches to the genetic technologies of OrganInc, where engineers grow human transplant organs in a transgenic pig host. Jimmy's mother objects to the 'pig brain thing. You're interfering with the building blocks of life. It's immoral. It's [...] sacrilegious' (Atwood 2004: 64). His father's response: 'It's just proteins, you know that! There's nothing sacred about cells and tissue' (Atwood 2004: 65). Life as corporate material is desacralized, and *Oryx and Crake* is centred on the consequence of this shift: the removal of limits on what can be done to life. The hybrid bodies of the genetically spliced animals provoke a sense of sacrilege, despite the erasure of understandings of life through religious discourse, or nature 'with a capital N' (Atwood 2004: 242). Corporations can therefore gain control over life systems: if life no longer has value in terms of a moral or ethical respect, then experimentation is unrestricted. Jimmy questions unlimited exploitation of nonhuman life in terms of transgression, an inability of corporations to understand or ask 'how far is too far?' The boundary transgressed, however, is unclear until one considers the rampant commercialization and commodification of life.

Crake learns that his father had been 'executed' (Atwood 2004: 249) for discovering the extent of the Compounds' duplicitous manipulation of biomaterial. Indeed, Crake, from his father's findings, learns that Helth Wyzer has been manufacturing illnesses and cures for financial gain. In this future, the amalgamation of genetic technologies and marketing have led to what Donna Haraway calls 'gene fetishism', which 'is compounded of a political economic denial that holds commodities to be sources of their own value while obscuring the sociotechnical relations among humans and between humans and nonhumans that generate both objects and value' (Haraway 1997: 147). Genes become inextricable from their value, commodified beyond recognition of their form. Life as genomics is the object of this discourse; life is 'enterprised up' (Haraway 1997: 12) as the saleable and disposable product which, in Atwood's extreme of this version of life, becomes not about health maintenance but a business relationship which, to maintain itself, must also manufacture its object/reason: death. Crake describes the financialization of life and death:

> They put hostile bioforms in their vitamin pills [...] the way people slosh around out there it more or less runs itself [...] Ideally – that is, for maximum profit – the patient should get well or die just before all of his or her money runs out. (Atwood 2004: 248)

Biotechnology thus defines life as synonymous with the 'capital-accumulation strategy in the simultaneously marvellous and ordinary domains of the New World Order, Inc.' (Haraway 1997: 65). Life as capital denies human and nonhuman value – both are merely objects of the business discourse of the New World Order as it financializes both life and 'wholesale death' (Atwood 2004: 400). The 'sloshing around' of people in the Pleeblands, the non-Compound areas resembling contemporary society ('remember when everyone lived in the Pleeblands?', Atwood 2004: 72) propagates these manufactured viruses. No one in the Pleeblands can trace the source back to the corporations because of the random assignment of the hazardous biomaterial in the pills – it does not target all of its consumers so that it may continue its covert operations. For Atwood, as with Haraway, the genome has become 'a figure of the "already written" future, where bodies are displaced into proliferating databases for repackaging and marketing in the New World Order, Inc.' (Haraway 1997: 100). With life in commodifiable parts, so too the body has been abstracted; the human has a market value, and the limitless network of markets and corporations supplying product to these places assigns value to bodies (alive or dead) as objects of its discourse. *Oryx and Crake* therefore enacts the anxieties inherent to control societies; Atwood identifies that corporations hold unprecedented and unregulated power to exploit technologies of life for financial gain.

Melinda Cooper's *Life as Surplus* (2008) explores the relationship between economics and life sciences, using Foucault's theory of biopolitics to acknowledge the shift out of modern regulatory and disciplinary technologies which focused on 'an anatomo-politics of the human body' (Foucault 1978: 139) and 'a bio-politics of the population' (Foucault 1978: 139). Cooper's targets instead are 'the non-equilibrium models, post-Fordist flexibilization and financialization of life that lie at the heart of the neoliberal project' (Puig de la Bellacasa 2009: 321). Cooper uses this specific framework of financialization to analyse the development of the US bioeconomy, which she pinpoints to the 1970s, and how political and legal regimes within this led to the exploitation of life. Cooper remakes the link between capital and life. Indeed, she argues that 'the biotech revolution is the result of a whole series of legislative and regulatory measures designed to relocate economic production at the genetic, microbial, and cellular level, so that life becomes, literally, annexed within capitalist processes of accumulation' (Cooper 2008: 19). *Life as Surplus* delineates the specific forms of regulation which make this possible – for example, patenting and intellectual property laws. Cooper scrutinizes what the bioeconomy means in terms of limits and excess – the idea of growth linked to capital becomes limitless when it is fused with life. Life in the bioeconomy, she reveals, is considered as 'a *permanent source* of regeneration' (Puig de la Bellacasa 2009: 321). The bioeconomy promises to 'take us beyond all limits, transforming even industrial waste into surplus value' (Cooper 2008: 47). Cooper notes the inherent contradictions in this bioeconomic structure: 'the promise of a surplus of life will be predicated on a corresponding move to devaluate life' (Cooper 2008: 49). *Life As Surplus* is a rethinking of biopolitics which, in exposing these contradictions, invokes an 'administration of biological scarcity' (Cooper 2008: 50) and a re-establishment of limits. Excessive promises and biological scarcity are enacted for Cooper in the 'Pharmaceutical Empire' (Cooper 2008: 51) in which health is not for all. Rather, by restricting access to medication, it both creates and denies the life of the 'surplus population, of a life not worth the costs of its own reproduction' (Cooper 2008: 61). This notion of surplus or over-proliferation becomes the postmodern form of excess – it is both surplus value from manipulating life processes (the capital associated with the patenting and consequent proliferation of specific gene technologies for example) and is the excess of human life which is not provided for.

In Cooper's definition, the bioeconomy itself can be thought of as an excess, with its promise to push the limits of value. Atwood's interrogation of the desire to transcend limits is represented in the objective of the body Compounds to achieve immortality. Crake symbolically identifies 'the human condition' (Atwood 2004: 344) as the fuel and funding behind biotech research, as both grief and the desire to exceed the limitations of the human body drive research. Biotech corporations in *Oryx and Crake* thrive on the notion of perfectibility, of overcoming the limitations of the human body, and it is reflected in the consumer culture which has materialist and financial desires as its enterprise. A corporate conflation and exploitation of 'the human condition' drives this control of life. Desire is predicated on the marketed campaign for 'improvement' as people are told that they must overcome their limits, and so the companies thrive on the 'deformities' of the Pleebland inhabitants, who become the target for Jimmy's campaigns and other media slogans ('Herediseases

Removed. Why Be Short? Go Goliath!', Atwood 2004: 339). It is in the Pleeblands, as Crake observes, that their Compound 'stuff turns to gold' (Atwood 2004: 339). The pleeblanders enact the role of life as surplus, which has been produced by the bioeconomy. They also embody the inherent contradiction Cooper highlights in this bioeconomic structure, in which surplus life as capital is made only by removing the value of the life of these people. To Crake, and the corporations, the pleeblanders are merely the 'the ranks of the desperate' (Atwood 2004: 349), nameless consumers of compound products, a homogenous life form devoid of worth. Devaluing the pleeblanders thereby makes them the perfect target for the Compounds' acts of bioterror. Crake observes the financial ingenuity of Helth Wyzer's 'economics of scarcity' (Atwood 2004: 248) as they operate their vitamin bio-attack: holding back antidotes to the viruses they create 'so they're guaranteed high profits' (Atwood 2004: 248). The excessive promises and 'biological scarcity' (Cooper 2008: 50), which are played out in Cooper's pharmaceutical empire, are performed to their extreme by Atwood here. By restricting access to medication, corporations both create and deny the life of the surplus population. Atwood's pleeblanders are not only deemed unworthy of health, they are deliberately targeted for manufactured disease to produce more capital, and their deaths are part of this financial plan.

For Cooper, death as business discourse echoes the capitalist production of life, which was reliant on imposing limits that must then be transcended. The only difference today is '"merely" that the tensions of capitalism are being played out on a global, biospheric scale and thus implicate the future of life on earth' (Cooper 2008: 49). *Oryx and Crake* is a speculative imagining of how the system will develop, as it is concerned with reframing definitions of life in terms of the biotechnological impacts on the idea of 'the human'. In the near future, human life has proliferated beyond sustainable means, or so Crake believes:

> As a species we're in deep trouble, worse than anyone's saying [...] we're running out of space-time. Demand for resources has exceeded supply for decades in marginal geopolitical areas, hence the famines and droughts; but very soon, demand is going to exceed supply *for everyone*. With the BlyssPluss Pill the human race will have a better chance of surviving. (Atwood 2004: 347)

Crake obsesses over the solution to excessive human consumption and reproduction, which he articulates in the financialized terms of *supply and demand*. Human life, for Crake, is economically unsustainable. His answer is the BlyssPluss Pill: a pill marketed to combat sexually transmitted diseases – with the added bonuses of 'an unlimited supply of libido' (Atwood 2004: 346) and prolonged youth – while secretly, Crake reveals to Jimmy, acting as a sterilization tool to 'put a stop to hazardous reproduction' (Atwood 2004: 358). Crake's notion of secret sterilization mismarketed to the masses reinforces biological control. Compound control would be totalized, as corporations gain the power to decide an individual's reproductive fate with the pill. Crake notes that the effect could be altered 'if the populations of any one area got too low' (Atwood 2004: 347). Atwood's version of controlled life transitions 'from the comfortable old hierarchical dominations to the scary new networks of informatics of domination' (Haraway 1991: 161). Haraway's feminist framing of changing power relations is similar to Deleuze's societies of control in a sense, in that control is no longer in the hands of Western capitalist males but instead in networks. The informatics of domination reconfigures ideas of life in terms of code, as genomics provide the means through which to monitor and control life in unprecedented ways. Crake's pill initiates a discussion of the power of the corporation to act in a Big Brother fashion with life, establishing unlimited access to life as a raw material with control over the shape and future of the human.

Corporations strive for the exceeding of their own limits, envisaging global control over the future of life on earth. Crucially, however, Crake uses this system against itself. The unregulated forms of control allow Crake to insert his own hostile bioform in the BlyssPluss Pill to enact his vision of the future of humanity. The virus in the pill ensures a rapid and violent death. Oryx is responsible for distributing the death pill, limitlessly and indiscriminately, between the guarded borders of Compounds and Pleeblands. Marketing power grants her access to a global network and leads to the extensive dissemination of Crake's product. The virus breaks out simultaneously across the globe, represented on the monitor that Jimmy is forced to watch as 'dark pink [...] as for the British Empire once' (Atwood 2004: 397). Drawing attention to what Haraway (2004: 65) terms the 'imperializing essence' of genetic technologies (she cites the Human Genome Project as an example), Atwood interrogates the totalizing effects of aligning genes with life. Crake exploits the unlimited connectivity of marketing as the 'soul' of corporate culture, gaining this access to control.

With Crake's erasure of humanity through viral disease, Atwood plays out societies of control to their limit: the destruction of networks is enacted by their own means of control. Crake's influence within the system allows him unregulated access. In control of money, resources and people, Jimmy remarks that, 'whatever [Crake's] nominal title [...] he was obviously the biggest ant in the anthill' (Atwood 2004: 341). Crake recruits his own team, an entire group of biotech radicals from the anti-Compound website Jimmy and Crake used in their youth: 'what you're looking at is MaddAddam, the cream of the crop [...] they're splice geniuses [...] I just got to them ahead of the Corps, that's all' (Atwood 2004: 352). Crake ensures his team of bioterrorists is in control; their radical work with life makes them the perfect designers for both the undetected virus and the Crakers – his new race of genetically enhanced human beings. It also suggests a weakness in the Compound's power: while corporations drive for more power in the bioeconomy, and more control over its consumers, it is through this continual pushing for excess that Crake is able to exploit the system.

Atwood's rendering of life is reshaped by genetic technologies. The driving desire for excess engages with the 'human' as something dynamic and transformative, which is able to remake itself in terms of new versions of life. In *Oryx and Crake*, 'the human is always in flux, always becoming, always materializing, transducing, taking itself apart, putting itself back together, dis- and re- membering' (Cooke 2006: 80). Crake's new race of humans remakes and reinterprets their relationship with the world. Having destroyed life-as-commodity, what Crake enables is a reshaping of human forms. As Katherine Hayles recognizes, the posthuman 'offers resources for the construction of another kind of account' (Hayles 1999: 288). It offers opportunity and potential to transform the human beyond the creature created out of the Enlightenment, to replace 'the liberal human subject's manifest destiny to dominate and control' (Hayles

1999: 288). And the novel leaves us in this liminal space of potential, as Snowman is about to confront three human survivors of Crake's genocide. These two versions of human life seemingly cannot coexist: having already run away when the Crakers approached, Snowman imagines how easily these humans might have seen the Crakers as 'savage, or non-human and a threat' (Atwood 2004: 425) and respond with a violence precedented in human history. Knowing Crake trusted him to keep Crakers safe, he asks, 'what do you want me to do?' Atwood leaves the answer with the reader. Snowman's decision about what course is best to take with the survivors escapes the textual space – 'time to go' (Atwood 2004: 433) is his final remark. A final statement which is active and mobilizing, with a potential to transform and recreate. Snowman is not limited to his narrative; his actions are in excess of the text and indeterminate. The constructed life of the Crakers exceeds the narrative; they live on, and so the novel does not end with a return to 'human' life. The 'human' for Atwood is not the answer but rather a question in the future of understanding life.

Therefore, despite working with and for the Compound, Crake does not wipe out the human race in the name of corporations. It is not *homo sapiens* with which Crake is concerned, rather a way to remedy the negative corporate effects of human control: rampant and excessive consumerism. As Atwood claims, it is 'not biotech that's dangerous [...] It is people's fears and desires' (Atwood in Cooke 2006: 65). These desires are both generated and satiated by corporations, as they not only provide a service but also profit from their human consumers. Although Crake destroys this system, he does so by radically affirming corporate control to excess. What occurs is self-consumption as humanity gorges itself on Crake's pill. Snowman imagines the 'non-stop orgy' and the 'riotous behaviour of all sorts imaginable' (Atwood 2004: 124) which would have followed the over-consumption of the BlyssPluss pills 'until no one was left to keep it up' (Atwood 2004: 124). Snowman mythologizes this consumption in stories to the Crakers about 'the chaos' (Atwood 2004: 125) when humanity was 'eating up all the children of Oryx. They were killing them and killing them, and eating them and eating them. They ate them even when they weren't hungry' (Atwood 2004: 125). This repetitive and excessive consumption of animal life has nothing to do with need or hunger; there is no limit that would satiate desire. The imperative to consume became synonymous with the 'human condition' which fuels biotech. Crake's solution only succeeds because of the apparent limitlessness of human consumption in the bioeconomy. Demonstrating the destructiveness of understanding life as a commodifiable and consumable product, Atwood affirms this behaviour beyond its limit point, as humanity consumes itself in excess.

Part III

The Testaments

Coral Ann Howells

How Gilead Fell: An Ecocultural Reading of *The Testaments*

How did Gilead fall? *The Testaments* was written in response to this question.
(Atwood 2019: 417)

Atwood's return to Gilead thirty-five years after *The Handmaid's Tale* and its recent TV adaptation tells the story of the collapse of that totalitarian regime through three different female eye/I witness accounts. Like *The Handmaid's Tale*, it is about power politics and women's resistance to structures of oppression, and the collapse of Gilead needs to be understood as the struggle between two opposing narratives about human society and culture. State power politics is only one strand in this multidimensional novel, for Atwood, an astute political commentator, is also a passionate environmentalist, and my premise for this ecocultural reading is based on her longstanding feminist and ecological concerns which she beautifully encapsulated in her response to a question in 1978 about the traditional identification of women and nature: 'You aren't and can't be apart from nature. We're all part of the biological universe: men as well as women. So my answer would be that it's a potential source of power and vision' (Ingersoll 1992: 120). My central argument is that everything in this novel – its politics, plot, character relations, imagery – is underpinned by Atwood's ecological consciousness of the 'interactive relationships between biology, culture, and human agency' (Eisler and Fry 2019: 36). If survival was the key to *The Handmaid's Tale*, then restoration and renewal are the driving forces in *The Testaments*, symbolised by the colour green, 'spring green for fresh leaves' (Atwood 2019: 160). Though the emphasis here is on human and not nonhuman nature, the imagery and action insist on their interconnectedness as Atwood stages a dialogue between totalitarian and regeneration narratives.

In this context, an ecocultural reading which combines ecological and cultural elements would seem an appropriate method for untangling the intertwined forces of oppression, resistance, and reintegration which operate in this novel. My approach takes its direction from Hubert Zapf's *Literature as Cultural Ecology: Sustainable Texts*, though other critics like Jonathan Bate, Greg Garrard, and Simon Schama also use the concept of cultural framing for ecological discourse (Zapf 2016: 102).[1] Zapf argues that literature inscribes the ecological principle of universal interconnectedness: 'the ecological force of texts [...] gains its artistic potency through the *imaginative translation* of natural into cultural energies' in language and narrative (29). Moreover, he shares Atwood's awareness of the deep affinities between human and natural living systems: 'The unique rhythms of life [heartbeat, breathing] of every individual being in particular [...] have to be considered in any ecologically aware ethics and aesthetics of sustainable living' (144). At the same time, cultural ecology does not collapse the difference between human and nonhuman, but recognises the coexistence of culture and nature, without reducing one to the other. As Jonathan Bate summarises it, 'We are both a part of and apart from nature' (Bate 2000: 33).

The scandal of Gilead is that it perverts the concepts of 'human' and of 'nature' with its abuse of human bodies, especially women's bodies, and its denial of basic kinship relations of which the primary one is the biological connection between mother and child, together with its attempts to suppress socially constructed emotional attachments between human beings. Yet, flowing beneath these rigid structures are the primal life forces signalled in 'Bloodlines', for mothers, daughters, sisters, Handmaids (together with one ambiguous Aunt) are central to the plot, while Atwood interweaves biological determinism with wider female kinship structures when she introduces the affective dimension of the human need and capacity for love, embodied in culturally constructed social relationships. Together these women form an underground network of female resistance where 'sisterhood' provides the vital connecting link in a narrative of

---

1   I have adapted Zapf's triadic model of cultural ecological analysis, which combines 'a culture-critical metadiscourse, an imaginative counter-discourse, and a reintegrative interdiscourse' (2016: 102).

transformation and renewal. The power of sisterhood is confirmed when the two half-sisters escape from Gilead, emerging from the sea in Canada with one carrying Aunt Lydia's microdot document cache embedded in a tattoo on her arm, thus precipitating the fall of Gilead. This striking image conflates women's bodies, women's agency, and elemental forces, where culture and nature are blended together in the girls' symbolic rising from the dead. Bloodlines are restored when the two are reunited with their real mother, and this episode ends with a promise of new beginnings for individual lives and for the body politic. However, this is not the end of the story, for it continues to shift across space and time from the narrative present in Canada and in Gilead to a distant future (as Atwood's dystopias tend to do) when Gilead has become ancient history and women's stories of their lived experience have been transformed into archival documents. There is one last testament inscribed on a stone statue to a third sister, a figure on the margins whose claim rests not on biology but on a different kind of affinity based on love. Her memorial is testimony to the web of relationality which connects 'human' and 'nature' in a final gesture of resistance to Gilead's ideology.

Gilead is the paradigm of the totalitarian state, with its hierarchical structures of political and military power, its misogynistic divisions between the sexes, its systems of official secrecy and surveillance, and its ruthless policies of social control. All of this harks back to *The Handmaid's Tale*, that woman's record of a contemporary American society in profound transition where a new repressive ideology was being imposed on the population and the institutional abuses of child kidnapping and the Handmaid system were first put into practice. (There are many precedents and parallels with Gilead, e.g. the Nazi Lebensborn programme; the removal of children from mothers, as in the case of Australia's 'Stolen Generations' and Trump's policies at the US–Mexico border, a warning that 'History does not repeat itself, but it rhymes' (Atwood 2019: 407). In the Late Gileadean period, now rife with corruption, female bodies have become what Madeleine Davies describes as 'socio-cultural documents' where 'the body is the site on which political power is exercised and the site on which abuse is practised' (Davies 2006: 58). This is true of the Handmaids, who have been deprived of their human rights and reduced to 'two-legged wombs,' enslaved to a patriarchal elite and then robbed of their children who are reassigned to 'suitable families' in Gilead's grotesque deformation of natural kinship structures. All women are prisoners of the regime, from the younger generation of upper-class Gileadean girls (many of whom are Handmaids' daughters) who are groomed for early marriage and motherhood in conformity with a 'woman's destiny', to those educated older women now deprived of their former professional identities and forced to become collaborators in order to survive. In their role as Aunts, they have control over other women in the 'separate female sphere', for even within Gilead's rigidly gendered binary structure, there are still imbalances of power and privilege – and the woman with most power is Aunt Lydia, Director of Ardua Hall. She too carries traumatic memories of male violence at the time of the coup and has sworn vengeance against the regime:

> '*I will get you back for this. I don't care how long it takes or how much shit I have to eat in the meantime, but I will do it*'. (Atwood 2019: 149)

Aunt Lydia is a dangerous figure, one of Atwood's 'spotty-handed villainesses' who is not only Gilead's prime agent of women's oppression but also its unforgiving witness and implacable enemy, as her secretly written Ardua Hall Holograph reveals. That holograph is the 'master narrative', a term I use advisedly, for her counter-discourse erodes gender binaries, showing that bad behaviour is not the prerogative of men. As Atwood commented, 'Women [...] are fully human beings; they too have subterranean depths; why shouldn't their many-dimensional reality be given literary expression?' (Atwood 2005: 185). Old, disillusioned, and ruthless, Aunt Lydia has become both a collaborator and a double agent working for the outlawed Mayday resistance. Though her narrative is interspersed with the stories of the two younger women (who, incidentally, offer their versions of a woman-centred discourse which challenges her own), she is the arch-plotter. Ironically she is now the co-ordinator of female resistance, for she is the only woman in Gilead with political power, and 'knowledge is power, especially discreditable knowledge' (Atwood 2019: 35).

Aunt Lydia's is the first voice in the novel, where she introduces herself not as a human being but as a stone monument: 'Only dead people are allowed to have statues, but I have been given one while still alive. Already I am petrified' (3). With characteristic irony she exploits the double meaning of that verb, aligning herself from the start with death, both in her defiance and her fear of it. Atwood once suggested that writing is 'a reaction to the fear of death' (Atwood 2002: 157), and Aunt Lydia lives in constant fear in Gilead's world of treachery and intrigue. Her larger-than-life statue is a metaphor of power, and she speaks of herself as 'swollen with power' (32), though her memory of 'the cloth drape shrouding me' (3) at her statue's unveiling nine years ago carries strong associations of mortality. There is a complete mismatch between the woman's public image and her inner subjective life, as she reveals in a sudden disconcerting shift to present time when she moves into 'my private sanctum within the library of Ardua Hall' (4) to begin her dangerous written conversation with an unknown reader. This is the prelude to her last will and testament, where private memoir becomes ferocious social criticism in this 'definitive account of my life and times, suitably footnoted' (403).

Shifting back and forth across time, Aunt Lydia addresses her imagined future reader: 'Who are you, my reader? And when are you?' (61); she writes her narrative of self-examination and self-justification. This is the defence of her life, which she keeps hidden in a hollowed-out copy of Cardinal Newman's *Apologia Pro Vita Sua*: 'I am well aware of how you must be judging me, my reader; if [...] you have deciphered who I am, or was' (32), a metatextual reference to Ann Dowd's performance in the TV adaptation, which Atwood praised for making Aunt Lydia a much more well-rounded character than she was in the novel. Guilt-ridden and vengeful, Aunt Lydia is obsessed with death and blood – bloodstains and bloodlines – (but more of these in a moment) as she creates her memorial to Gilead's crimes and her own. She is a dark force, 'formless, shape-shifting', 'an unsettling shadow', and even nature withers under her gaze: 'the crocuses have melted, the daffodils have shrivelled to paper [...] What's next in the waltz of the flowers?' (111). Private and public bleed into each other, for besides her memoir, Aunt Lydia has assembled another set of files equally dangerous to herself and the state: the top secret crime files of Gilead which she has been photographing for years. This is the material that will feature on the incriminating document cache at the centre of her elaborate revenge plot. With that revenge accomplished, and shadowed by the moon's 'equivocal corpse-glow', she retires to the library to bid farewell to her unknown reader, whom she imagines as a mirror image of her own lost youthful self, 'a young woman, bright, ambitious [...] I will hover behind you, peering over your shoulder' (404). Everything is 'too late' as she sits in her sanctum waiting for death, ready with her stolen phial of morphine to exercise her final choice – of how to die: 'Isn't that freedom of a sort?' (32).

There is also another set of classified files under Aunt Lydia's charge, 'the Bloodlines Genealogical Archives,' which she describes as 'the beating heart of Ardua Hall' (35). That powerful organic image, so at variance with her usual dismissal of life-affirming rhythms, encodes the central narrative energies of the novel. These Archives kept by the Aunts are primarily tools of state, the official records on which the Handmaid system functions, spelling out the true biological connections between mothers, fathers, and children which Gilead has sought to conceal. But they are more than instrumental and administrative, for they are the living witness of primary kinship relations based on ties of blood, and as such they embody the means to what Zapf calls a reintegrative interdiscourse which 'turns the culturally excluded into a transformative force both for the cultural system and for human relationships' (2016: 116). How the forces of reintegration may be activated forms the dynamics of the plot, and the secret agent is Aunt Lydia, with her double-sided project of revenge and restoration.

That can only be accomplished through her recourse to Bloodlines, bringing together for the first time the now-adolescent daughters of the Handmaid Offred – Agnes and Nicole – who have grown up, one in Gilead and one in Toronto, ignorant of their true identities and of their real mother. Aunt Lydia's elaborate plot is presented as a fragmented narrative with her cool calculations embedded in the stories of the younger women, who are initially unwitting recruits in her serious spy game where, as they gradually discover, they have no choice but to play the roles already allocated to them. (There are strong similarities between Aunt Lydia and Jocelyn in *The Heart Goes Last* in their dealings with their unsuspecting accomplices.) Only when Nicole is returned to Gilead disguised as one of Aunt Lydia's Pearl Girl missionaries –'All things come to she who waits [...] Vengeance is mine', as she remarks (251) – does she reveal her strategy to her assembled group of young women – Nicole, Agnes, and her friend Becka; this is the first time they are all together, in the section significantly entitled 'Bloodlines'. As duplicitous as ever, she achieves their co-operation through a finely calculated series of appeals to their loyalty and their sense of justice and to the rhetoric of family coded into the concept of sisterhood. Only Nicole, the independent-minded Canadian teenager, protests against this as emotional blackmail, though her comments are sharply dismissed by Aunt Lydia as 'juvenile notions of fairness' which 'do not apply here' (337). Nicole is the key player in Aunt Lydia's revenge plot and her final stroke of irony, for Baby Nicole, the poster girl for Gilead now grown up, will become the poster girl for Gilead's collapse as a 'carrier pigeon', with the secret document already inserted in her arm ('So useful, Baby Nicole,' 33). Those documents are the catalyst for radical change, but their delivery depends not only on Nicole but on the cooperation of Agnes and Becka and a shadowy group of Mayday operatives, a collaborative effort with which Aunt Lydia has no empathy whatso ever.

For Aunt Lydia, Nicole and Agnes are merely instruments for revenge, her 'destroying angels' (392), and she is indifferent to them as individual human beings with their own affective lives. We note that Becka is excluded from the project for she does not fit into the Bloodlines pattern, the patriarchal model to which Aunt Lydia is committed. (Yet Becka is not so easily dismissed.) These young women's stories of trauma, loss, and longing for love and affection form a network of silenced feminine resistance to Gilead's life-denying social system and a radical alternative discourse to Aunt Lydia's singular narrative of opposition. Agnes, Becka, and Nicole, the second generation of Gilead girls, live in the fallout of Gilead's artificial construction of 'families' and all suffer its devastating consequences. For Agnes and Nicole, the revelation that their true mother was a Handmaid (Becka never discovers who her real mother was) brings on a crisis of identity for them both: 'I was a forgery, done on purpose' (Nicole, 39), and 'I was nobody's child' (Agnes, 85). Those painful feelings of abandonment and unbelonging are the direct result of Gilead's policies of social engineering which militate against the basic human desire for intimacy and love – as Offred had warned her Commander when he asked her what his new regime had overlooked:

Love, I said.
Love? Said the Commander. What kind of love? (Atwood 1996: 231)

Offed was talking about falling in love, but Gilead remains determined to overlook love of any kind in its deadly deformation of human nature. It is Becka who supplies the missing piece ignored in Gilead's calculations, for she embodies the social bonds of affection which redefine what is 'human' and extend the concept of 'sisterhood'. As feminist cultural historian Riane Eisler insists in her narrative about biological and cultural evolution, 'love is a dynamic that helps *explain* the emergence of humanity in both meanings of the word' (Eisler and Fry 2019: 49).

Brought up as privileged girls according to Gilead's patriarchal script, for Agnes and Becka there would seem to be no alternative to pious submission to their destiny as childbearers for the state – their fate is really no different from that of the Handmaids. That traditional identification of woman and nature is a 'legacy of oppression' in Gilead, as is perfectly illustrated in its rhetoric, where these girls are encouraged to see themselves as 'precious flowers' (10), though natural imagery is perverted to foster their sense of inferiority and vulnerability. These flowers are continually in danger of being ripped apart and their petals torn off by 'ravenous men' (10), and in Agnes's nightmare the message comes clear: 'with pink and white and plum fragments of myself scattered over the ground' (11), for this is a metaphor of bodily harm. Even seasonal imagery is corrupted, where the spring green colour of adolescent girls' costumes is the sign that a girl is ready for marriage. And always behind this floral façade lurks the brutal Old Testament story of the concubine cut into twelve pieces because of her rebellion. 'The adult female body was one big booby trap as far as I could tell' (83).

However, a few girls like Agnes and Becka manage to resist those imprisoning conventions, both violently refusing their arranged marriages and rescued unexpectedly by Aunt Lydia, who accepts them into Ardua Hall to train as Aunts. There they become close friends, finding an emotional kinship as 'sisters' in a loving relationship denied to them all their lives. The psychotherapist Juliet Mitchell observes the importance of siblings ('actual and metaphorical') and the construction of lateral bonding, especially in situations of trauma and loss: 'The presence and memory of the richness of lateral relationships are an underestimated part of the fabric of psychic and social life' (Mitchell 2003: 171). The concept of sisterhood is idealised by Becka, the lonely abused girl who longs fiercely for familial attachment, which she expresses in her love for Agnes: 'I wish I had a sister [...] And if I did, that person would be you' (301). Becka's devotion finds its tragic expression in her self-sacrifice for love when later she drowns herself in the college cistern in order to cover the flight from Gilead of her two adopted 'sisters'.

However, sisterhood becomes a problematic concept when Gilead's icon Baby Nicole suddenly comes to life as Agnes's newly discovered blood relation: 'This awkward girl shared a mother with me. I'd have to try my best' (336). And Nicole, who hates being Baby Nicole – 'I didn't ask to be' (187) – is just as uncomfortable with the idea. As a family psychologist has remarked, 'With so many ideals invested in sisterhood, rethinking it through the gap between the myth and embodied sistering presents a challenge' (Maunther 2005: 626). Radically different in upbringing and attitude, their only link is their shared fascination with their vanished mother, of whom we catch a glimpse when they look together at their mother's photograph, stolen by Agnes from the Bloodlines file. Placing their hands on it, they each search for genetic resemblance: 'Do you think she looks like me?' and 'I wondered the same thing' (338). In the end, realising that the image is only a symbol, they tear the picture up and flush it down the toilet for safety, in a place where natural feelings are excluded. Mother's love is only a concept for them, a deeply repressed memory, to be viewed with ambivalence by Nicole or with piety by Agnes:

'Just because people are related to you doesn't mean you love them,' she murmured.
'Love is a discipline, like prayer,' I said. (381)

That brief exchange is a damning indictment of the emotional damage inflicted by Gilead on all its mothers and daughters.

The deadly totalitarian order can only be destabilised by an outburst of violent energy where human agency and elemental forces combine in a creative effort towards deliverance. Atwood stages this scenario in 'Landfall', when the two half-sisters struggle out of the stormy sea, guided by the uncanny voice of Becka: 'Look up there. Follow the lights' (397, emphasis added) to deliver Aunt Lydia's document cache, a journey that is both toxic (Nicole nearly dies of sepsis) and transformative. The fall of Gilead is imminent, and Agnes and Nicole finally meet their mother, who hugs them and calls them her 'darling girls'. 'She smelled right. It was like an echo, of a voice you can't quite hear' (399) is Nicole's response. This open ending signals the potential for regeneration and renewal in the intertwined expression of individual and collective resistance to tyranny: 'Not yet [...] But it's the beginning' (398).

Those promises will be fulfilled, as we learn at a conference on Gileadean Studies long after Gilead has fallen, and affirmation comes with the evidence of another stone statue – not Aunt Lydia's but Becka's – decorated with flowers and birds, those traditional images of nature and freedom: 'IN LOVING MEMORY OF BECKA, AUNT IMMORTELLE, THIS MEMORIAL WAS ERECTED BY HER SISTERS AGNES AND NICOLE [...]' (415). Becka is finally enfolded into the mesh of family relations which she had always desired, and the inscription ends with her two favourite biblical verses:

> A BIRD OF THE AIR SHALL CARRY THE VOICE, AND THAT WHICH HATH WINGS SHALL TELL THE MATTER.
> LOVE IS AS STRONG AS DEATH. (415)[2]

With its celebration of the power of voice, the power of love, and the power of words which transcend time, Becka's statue is the final assertion of the value of these women's testaments of resistance. It bears mute witness to that 'reintegrative interdiscourse' which re-establishes the web of connections between 'human' and 'nature', which is vital for sustainability, change, and renewal in every society.

2   *Ecclesiastes* 10:20 and *Song of Songs* 8:6.

Blanka Grzegorczyk

Childhood Rites and Rights in *The Testaments*

The persistent strategy of infantilising female voices to keep them marginalised indicates that confines, not rights, define the status of childhood. American writer Joseph Epstein's mocking remarks in his *Wall Street Journal* op-ed (2020) about 'Madame First Lady – Mrs Biden – Jill – kiddo [sic]' Jill Biden's Doctor of Education degree, which he sees as failing to give her the right to use the honorific 'Dr,' might bring to mind Margaret Atwood's fictional Cambridge Professor James Darcy Pieixoto's repeated diminishment of female scholars in the 'Historical Notes' at the end of *The Handmaid's Tale* (1985) and *The Testaments* (2019). It is difficult, for example, not to identify Pieixoto's response to an enquiry from a female undergraduate in the new, expanded 'Historical Notes' Q&A in the 2017 audiobook special edition of *The Handmaid's Tale* as acutely condescending in its unsubtle mockery of young (and presumably female) academics' hopefulness, approached by Pieixoto more as willful naivete, for 'unhappy stories such as [Offred and her children's] to turn out well'. Patronising as it may be, however, Pieixoto's answer resonates with the suggestions in *The Testaments* that young people are on the other side of a historical threshold, looking towards a different future – a future that is not yet there but that, in the logic of Atwood's novel, it is their responsibility to pursue. And so, if Atwood's feminist dystopias have 'taken our times and made us wise to them' (Smith 2019), guiding us to a future that they cannot quite divine, 'with the hope that we will learn to act responsibly in ways which will make our [...] world a better place for ourselves' (Vevaina 2006: 97), *The Testaments* locates the burden of responsibility for bringing about this improved future largely with the young generation. This chapter explores the novel's ambiguous attitude toward the figure of the child, looking specifically at Atwood's constructions of the intertwining categories of the political and politicised, insider and outsider girl protagonist who is also at once constrained, self-thwarting, and rebellious. These girl protagonists' powerful and often playful rebellions force Atwood's audience to rethink the limits on young people's rights to protest, to play, and to know the past and put that knowledge to use, among others. Shown as uniquely capable of overcoming dominant interpretive habits and of engaging empathetically with those whose voices have been silenced or suppressed, the young female tellers, listeners – actual and implied – and discoverers of *The Testaments* allow us entry, dialogue, and mobilisation, while building a picture of childhood as an intricate network of vulnerabilities and resistances.

The young woman character in Gileadean dystopias is doubly oppressed. A continuation of Atwood's long-standing concerns with the question of 'who gets to do what to whom' (in Atwood with Brans 1982: 149; see also Howells 2006: 3), *The Testaments* takes the capacity of writing from and about 'herstories' to distil testimonies with those trapped by the systemic gendered imbalance as 'I-witnesses' to another level in its focus on the doubly marginalised positions of figures who are both young and female. In a world where one regime succeeds in subjecting its female citizens – considered by the male ruling elite to have 'smaller brains that [a]re incapable of thinking large thoughts' (15), brains that, as young girls in Gilead are taught, are 'soft and damp and warm and enveloping' and therefore make women particularly suitable to the 'duty of caring for other people' (87–8) – to the constraints of a number of inferior socio-political positions, the testimony of Gileadean young girls counts for even less than that of an adult woman witness (252). On the one hand, the erasure of girls' and young women' rights by Gilead systems is legitimised in the name of imposing protection on a group effectively seen as mothers – and carers – 'in waiting' (Wisker 2010: 63), seemingly shielding them from that whose force their minds are not strong enough to handle (Atwood 156). Access to reading and anything other than reductive versions of history would, under these principles, make young female minds 'fall apart under the contradictions' and destabilise the regime's own truth claims (303, 346); therefore, parts of pre-Gilead stories needed to be left out from the education of girls benefitting from an elevated rank (294–5), and even the old children's books that are used to teach reading to the most privileged group of Gilead women, the Aunts, had their pictures altered to reflect the changes that affected gender relationships in the society (292). An interesting parallel, indeed, opens up between Gilead's rules preventing young girls from witnessing a public execution and its neighbour Canada's omissions of what such executions entail from the school curriculum, which Nicole/Daisy/Jade (hereafter referred to as 'Daisy') – situated as a cultural insider in Canada and outsider in Gilead despite being born in the latter – herself attributes to a deeper structure of Canadian protectionism (16, 322).

On the other hand lies the Gilead regime's conviction that its young women need to be protected from themselves, whose underlying assumptions contrast sharply with the above tendency to sustain, and mythologise, their supposed innocence. Frequently described as impetuous and devious by those around them (373, 390), their not-quite-humanness and 'naughty core' appealing to the predatory instinct of men like Commander Judd and 'excus[ing these men's] treatment of them' (315–6), Atwood's Gilead-raised girl characters like Agnes Jemima are shown to internalise and invoke adult-established standards of judgement under which childhood is an undesirable state, marked by lack of restraint (89), melodrama (104), and make-believe (330). Yet readers of *The Testaments* are presented with a further paradox: with the adult female body tantamount to 'one big booby trap' both in its stubborn corporeality and socially recognized preparedness for marriage, Agnes Jemima 'dread[s] the thought of growing older' and 'consider[s] shrinking [her]self by not eating' (11, 83), implying not only a scoring out or self-erasure of the characters operating under erasure, but also the need to reverse the mechanisms that entail that silencing and subjection – the signifying practices of othering. It is important to recognize these and related contradictions that inhabit the novel's and its readers' conceptions of the child itself when considering the salience of childhood to processes of fictional- and real-world countercultural resistance as well as reading with resistance.

By writing the childhoods for which *The Handmaid's Tale* only sets the stage into being, Atwood reveals how boyhood and girlhood can be constructed around rights and freedoms or lack thereof. In an environment that is emphatically unsupportive or actively oppressive, she reminds her audience, children's capacity to exercise their various rights is imperiled. One of the ways in which the suspension of female protagonists' childhoods and the reclamation of youth agency make themselves felt in *The Testaments* is in opportunities for play. These occasions are drastically narrowed or discarded in the case of young girls in Gilead, whose very (regime-mandated) clothes, for example, constrict their freedom of movement, and therefore play: 'because of our skirts, which might be blown up by the wind and then looked into, we were not to think of taking such a liberty as a swing. Only boys could taste that freedom; only they could swoop and soar; only they could be airborne' (16). Indeed, the only games that are available to the Gileadean girl are the ones deemed useful for facilitating her social integration in their description and modelling of Gilead's societal codes and values, such as those revolving around dollhouses (the little pretend books on the shelves of a Commander's study are blank, we are told) with 'all the dolls [...] that you might need,' that is, Wives, Children, Marthas, Guardians, Angels, Commanders, Handmaids, and Aunts (14–5), and decks of cards (without any letters or numbers) where Handmaids are Hearts, Agnes Jemima thinks, to reflect the fact that these women have been chosen to become 'precious containers' (158–9). Once they are old enough to enroll in premarital preparatory schools, young women 'of good family' in this society learn to play-act as mistresses of high-ranking households. It is significant for our understanding of roleplay as both overdetermined by the state power here and a means of resistance to it that Agnes Jemima is aware of the performativity of the practices that are required of the girls on this path: 'we were to be actresses,' she explains to us, 'on the stages of our future houses' (161, 166). It is also poignant that close friendships are discouraged (24), presumably to undermine the liberatory potential of playmates in solidarity, community, or dialogue with each other, to diminish the resistant power of the collective.

Indeed, the focus of *The Testaments* on finding in play a transformative, or subversive, quality depends in part on the characters' resistant efforts in a shared play space, as reflected in Agnes Jemima and Shunamite's rewriting of 'proper' into 'pretend' prayers. Much as Agnes Jemima reads such behaviour as 'ineffectual [...] tiny rebellions,' they do lay important ground for her subsequent questioning of, and mobilisation against, this male-dominated nation in which 'when [husbands] were absent – as they would be often, since they would have to work late hours, nor should [the wives] ever criticize their lateness – it would be [a wife's] duty to say these prayers on behalf of what [their Aunt teachers] hoped would be [their] numerous children' (165). Stimulating a similar stance of attentiveness and questioning, or the work of, to borrow Marina Warner's term, the 'thinking imagination' (2018: n. pag.), is also another group play scenario, the 'Hanging' game, which Agnes Jemima supposes 'contained a beneficial amount of warning and threat' that ensured the Aunts' approval, but which for her raises questions about the terms by which punishment is conceived, narrated, and sanctioned (106–7). These resistances are repeated and reinforced within the novel across a wide spectrum of examples of individual play in which Agnes Jemima *gets her hands on* control – of actions, movements, and sensations – in situations where she attempts to reverse the exclusions imposed on her in violent ways by those around her, from locking the Aunt doll in the cellar of the dollhouse ('She would pound and pound on the cellar door and scream, "Let me out," but the little girl doll and the Martha doll who'd helped her would pay no attention, and sometimes they would laugh' (17)) to making men out of scraps of bread dough ('I never made dough women,' she tells us, 'because after they were baked I would eat them, and that made me feel I had a secret power over men. It was becoming clear to me that, despite the urges Aunt Vidala said I aroused in them, I had no power over them otherwise' (20)). That Atwood looks to play for resistance and to language and signs for play of meaning accords with her own valorisation of play that is evident, for example, in her obituary of Angela Carter (2005): 'Perhaps *play* is the operative word – not as in *trivial activity*, but as in word-play, play of thought, or play of light,' Atwood describes her friend and fellow writer's role in re-making history, in bringing it to life by throwing light on its underbellies. 'She was born subversive, in the sense of its original root, *to overturn*. She had an instinctive feeling for the other side, which included also the underside' (156). Not only would this description seem to apply to Atwood as well, but it could be applied to her – playful, rebellious, and genealogist – young female characters in *The Testaments*.

Seeing how Atwood deploys the figure of the genealogist child – understood in the Foucauldian (1980) sense as working to recover the 'subjugated knowledges' which are elided by dominant histories in Gilead – to argue about the urgency and difficulty of historical reconstruction makes the complexity of the relationship between official versions of the past and history as experienced by individuals all too plain. The prose in *The Testaments* is marked throughout by its preoccupation with the distortions and hidden truths that are either dug out from adults or purposefully divulged by them to young people like Agnes Jemima, Daisy, and Becka, whose journeys into growing awareness of the unreliability of accredited stories and records increasingly lock them into fighting for the right to the past, to 'have a story instead of a zero' (329). And while the gaps in knowledge between adults and children are also shown to characterise the exchanges between those from different generations outside of Gilead's borders (with Daisy thinking of herself, before learning of her true parentage, as being the 'age at which parents suddenly transform from people who know everything into people who know nothing' and of adults as 'in the habit of stating the obvious' (44, 130)), it is in connection with Gileadean buried histories that all three girls cannot resist the promise of records, traces, and conjurings of history that could create in them a sense of identity and belonging as well as help them to make meaning of the present and the future. In presenting them with example after example of how their (adult) others took ownership and control of the narratives that they have been feeding them (for Agnes Jemima, for instance, this includes her adoptive mother Tabitha's fairy-tale-like inventions (11–14), her Marthas' theories of motherhood (89), and the Aunts' cautionary tales (302–3)), Atwood has these young women realise not just the fictive character of all received interpretations but also the motives by which those offering such selective fictions act – as the three examples above demonstrate, all of Agnes Jemima's caregivers subordinate children's best interests to adult, and ultimately patriarchal, preferences. These revelations derive much of their significance from their liberating impact on the young characters – 'Once a story you've regarded as true has turned false,' Agnes Jemima acknowledges, 'you begin suspecting all stories' (307) – whose subsequent quests for truth and meaning work against Gilead's mass silences.

Inasmuch as *The Testaments* persistently questions both the uses of historical knowledge and the kinds of reading that direct the young imagination to conceive the past, their questing – and questioning – characters learn to see knowledge (and more specifically for Agnes Jemima and Becka, the knowledge-oriented model of education that training to be an Aunt opens up to them) as the means through which they can claim their power and enact, rather than playfully simulate, resistance, even though the reversals and disruptions that these girls manage are often almost invisibly complicit with adult power. 'It was how the Aunts got their power: by finding things out' (286), Agnes Jemima recognises during her stay in Ardua Hall as she comes to interpret secrets – or what Aunt Lydia earlier characterised as 'discreditable knowledge' (35) – as powerful weapons with the 'potential to judge the wicked in silence, and to punish them in ways they would not be able to anticipate' (309). But even in depicting the slow process of recovering their pasts that enables these oppressed young women to assert their resistant power, Atwood shows that whatever they discover about themselves and others – and when – falls under the control of adult plotters against Gilead, with much staying hidden. Appropriately for a novel that conveys the constructedness and difficulty in reconstructing history, then, the names of the girls' biological fathers, for example, have been redacted from the archival records that are slipped to them by Aunt Lydia (330, 338), and although Agnes Jemima is able to trace the identity of the Handmaid who died in childbirth in the young character's (adoptive) childhood home, her own mother remains an 'absence, a gap inside,' an unnamed figure from a torn-up picture to her for the majority of the novel's main timeframe (366). And if the Ardua Hall Library's innermost room can be accessed only by senior Aunts, limiting the secret files from which Agnes Jemima and Becka gain their confidential information to what Aunt Lydia considers to be useful in motivating them towards resistance against Gilead, the two girls also opt to hide their newfound knowledge about the inner workings of their society from each other – the primary reasons for these particular silences, Agnes Jemima posits, being the files' top secret classification and 'more importantly, [...]. wish[ing] to spare the other' (337) – in an interesting replication of adult perspectives on the tensions between child protection and participation.

Throughout the novel, however, persistence in the quest for knowledge and intense responsiveness to others appear to be innate traits of the youth, irrespective of adult direction being present or not: Agnes Jemima's description of her life as that of 'tiptoeing and eavesdropping,' of 'work[ing] hard at seeing without being seen and hearing without being heard' is one such instance, a decisive and desperate approach of striving for understanding in the face of incomplete knowledge and withholding of the truth (99; see also 159). The novel also emphasises how the critical thinking skills that reading and writing themselves demand of and stimulate in these young readers – 'Being able to read and write did not provide the answers to all questions,' we hear from Agnes Jemima. 'It led to other questions, and then to others' (299) – become one of the essential tools of genealogy. The trope of the young female genealogist whose efforts give a voice to the silenced women subjects reappears with other intellectually questing scholars in *The Testaments'* 'Historical Notes', but the graduate student Mia Smith, who is the first researcher to have realised the importance of the file containing the witness testimonies of Atwood's young Gileadean protagonists, becomes a mere (if not unnamed) footnote in presentations of senior scholars' (like Pieixoto) interpretations of the contents of her discovery.

As *The Testaments* makes clear, that young people are involved in socio-political action, that Atwood's young female characters are invested in – largely women-led and for the most part grass-roots – resistance to the regime in recording, actively opposing, and then moving on from the horrors of Gileadean life, does not mean that such activism was initiated by the young. For those, like Daisy, growing up outside of Gilead, it is a commonplace that 'defend[ing one's] principles' (48) and 'stand[ing] up against injustice' (52) are values inculcated in young people both at school and at home, with older children at Daisy's school in Canada encouraged to take part in anti-Gilead protests as part of World Social Awareness – and depicted as connecting the regime's brutality and oppressiveness with another cause that today is typically associated in popular imagination with real-life and fictional children through 'green' poster signs such as 'GILEAD, CLIMATE SCIENCE DE-LIAR! GILEAD WANTS US TO FRY!' – even if on condition of being accompanied by teachers and volunteer parents to 'make sure nothing violent happened to [them]' (48). It is this call to speak up against oppressive political powers and for the voiceless that stands behind Agnes Jemima's and Daisy's witness testimonies, which unlike Aunt Lydia's Ardua Hall Holograph manuscript (or Offred's cassette recording in *The Handmaid's Tale*) are not unprompted, although they are similarly self-reflexive. The two girls are asked to tell their unspecified initial audience about their experiences of growing up within and getting involved in these events from outside of Gilead in the first place, respectively (9, 39); their responses are shown to be guided by the concrete and often sociologically and anthropologically motivated questions (e.g. about the marriage process) from interested – and presumably adult – others (153).

Addressed directly a number of times in the novel, the young woman is also the implied reader of Aunt Lydia's manuscript: imagined as 'bright' and 'ambitious,' possibly a 'student of history,' and so another female genealogist, 'looking to make a niche for [her]self in whatever dim, echoing caverns of academia may still exist by [her] time' (403). Like *The Testaments*' young protagonists, this constructed (and hoped for (44–5)) reader is permitted an illusion of control over the presented material (169), an illusion that is punctured when the adult teller of the story presents herself as both a 'recording angel' and 'merely a dealer in sordid gossip' (277), both of which could be read as fuelling the reader's obsessive desire for knowledge, or when she reminds us that these wishes may then remain unfulfilled: if she were to destroy the manuscript, as Aunt Lydia leads us to realise, she would engage in a 'godlike' act of destruction of her readers, instead of a counter-historical act of reconstruction of narratives and histories so that vital lessons could be learnt for the future (317–8). At the same time, just as the passing on of news vital to women's survival in Gilead depends on acts of collective solidarity between those occupying very different social positions (232), the passing on of historical knowledge, or the means by which the past suffuses the future, cannot happen without some form of intergenerational solidarity and thus results in Aunt Lydia's obsession with whether she can trust her implied reader to give these lessons the weight that they deserve (172).

The politicisation of young people in Atwood's novel cannot exist independently of adults' narratives surrounding a set of features that they view as common to the quality of being young. It is not unreasonable, the adults around her young protagonists insist, to think that the female adolescent – that liminal being who stands in distinctive temporal disjunction from the people who control most of her existence, who is inherently empathetic and particularly alert to the difference between looking at and seeing others (103–4, 271), but entirely blind to the dangers of bravado (411), and who is idealistic and thirsty for justice (46, 411) – might be told to assume the ultimate responsibility for seeking a way forward into a different, more just future and consequently require instruction in the commitments that befit those future-carrying. Daisy notices that she 'somehow agreed to go to Gilead without ever definitely agreeing' to take part in a risky undercover operation, with 'everyone act[ing] as if [she]'d said yes', and saying 'how brave [she] was and what a difference [she] would make, and that she would bring hope to a lot of trapped people' (199); likewise, the younger Ardua Hall Supplicants like Agnes Jemima and Becka are continuously told that 'they had a crucial part to play, and that bravery was required of them,' which, Agnes Jemima observes, 'usually [...] meant giving up something' (334–5), and Becka's death can be interpreted as a willing sacrifice 'for the greater good of what she believes to be the purification and renewal (rather than the destruction) of Gilead' (Watkins 2019). Importantly, too, it is the iconic image of Baby Nicole, Daisy's previous identity, that, with all its connotations of fragility and abuse of children's rights, becomes a rallying point for the resistance movement against Gilead (45). And while the girls' mission to help set things right (and overturn the regime) is based entirely on adults' terms, Agnes Jemima and Daisy's survival is in the end aided by their sisterly solidarity as well as youthful strength, adaptability, and resilience, a resolution that captures the essence of girlhood in a manner that further belies the presence – and marks without quite yet thinking past the limits – of celebratory adult discourses around youth.

Received in part as a 'rallying cry for activism' (Clark 2019), *The Testaments*' tale of younger generations who are both empowered and circumscribed in their resistant perceptions of and responses to a repressive patriarchal regime is profoundly informed by discourses of rights. Against *The Testaments*' conception of the future as the responsibility of the young, there is a warning about a future marked by the ongoing, unassailable (if considerably less visible than in Gilead) disenfranchisement of young women, the prevision of a time to come that the novel's 'Historical Notes' – and additional materials – outline. This unequal future is one that readers are encouraged to strive towards changing but that requires a radical revision of adult rhetoric that can confuse young people's rights and responsibilities. Childhood in *The Testaments* provides a site where valuable intercultural and intergenerational solidarities for women may be claimed and recovered, one which does not, however, reject the adult story of youthful potentialities that are apt to release a society from the strictures of pain and crisis. That the novel is committed to so many tangled, contradictory conflations of rights-bearing and rights-suppressive discourses around youth is a sign of the difficulty in universally applying characteristics to a whole generation. It is only when adult-produced cultures recognise that children, like adults, are in quest of symbolic vocabularies with which to articulate, organise, and lay claim to the society's public and imaginary spaces that young people, fictional or real, may come into their own as both storytellers and listeners.

Sally McLuckie

Embracing the Witch: The Influence of Spiritual Feminism in Aunt Lydia's Transformation from Witch to Goddess

In *The Testaments* (2019), Margaret Atwood unveils Aunt Lydia as a spiritual feminist Goddess symbol, a reunion of the witch and goddess intended to provide an alternative post-Christian spiritual feminist mythology for suffering women (Atwood 2019). There are many complexities and complications with this statement, not least the complicity of Aunt Lydia in carrying out immoral actions, claims of political lethargy and reinforcing essentialism, but these are topics for future essays (Rountree 1999: 138). Herein, the focus is Atwood's renewed critique of the foundations of patriarchal and Western Judeo-Christian religion and the moral injury of women betrayed by its gender biases (Atwood 2022). This is not gratuitous; Atwood invokes the Goddess in Aunt Lydia's character as a symbol that 'legitimates and undergirds the moods and motivations inspired by feminism just as the symbol of God has legitimated patriarchal attitudes for several thousand years' (Rountree 1999: 156).

Aunt Lydia is symbolic of a spiritual feminist witch, a 'political revolutionary' and a 'symbol of woman as possessor of power and knowledge not sourced in nor requiring the legitimation of patriarchal institutions' (Rountree 1999: 141). In *The Testaments*, Aunt Lydia is a threat to the Divine Order, working as a Mayday double agent to expose the morally corrupt regime and its Commanders. On the surface Aunt Lydia conforms; covertly, she has rejected the regime's prescribed sex and gender role and created her own identity and feminist consciousness. In the process, Aunt Lydia invokes the Goddess, 'a political and psychological tool for women seeking liberation and empowerment' (Rountree 1999: 156). Aunt Lydia becomes a role model and a priestess through the process of reuniting the

witch and goddess aspects of her character (Rountree 1999: 141).[1] She is
not fooled by the Divine Order or the Commanders and as a Mayday
double agent, sets out to 'burn it all down' (*TT*: 379).[2] From the mouth
of a girl child comes a serious theological question, 'what if I were to pray
to Aunt Lydia at night, instead of to God?' (*TT*: 86). Atwood's critique of
the foundations of society includes the role of Western Judeo-Christian
religion in authorising and legitimising gender biases.[3]

By uniting the witch and the goddess in Aunt Lydia's character, Atwood
draws on mid- to late-twentieth-century spiritual feminism, a movement
'fundamentally concerned with women breaking free of the strictures of the
feminine as set forth by our culture' (Rountree 1999: 138). Spiritual feminists
make an 'ongoing challenge to and critique of patriarchal ideologies and
systems and working for the transformation of these systems in the real
world' (Rountree 1999: 138). One strand of the movement included
the employment of the 'witch as a symbol of frightening and deviant
womanhood' (Rountree 1999: 140). Spiritual feminists 'claim the witch
was once part of the Goddess, the crone aspect (seen in such goddesses as
Hecate)'. The crone was 'diabolised by Christianity and transformed into
the evil witch' and 'became separated from the Goddess and turned into
her moral opposite'. By 'embracing the witch', spiritual feminists 'feel they
are re-connecting the witch and the goddess and re-connecting with their
own female power (designated illegitimate under patriarchy)'. Rather than
mutely inhabiting the confines of patriarchal social constructs, embracing
the witch (and any number of other goddesses) enables women to self-
identify and liberate themselves from morally injurious and limiting
'patriarchal modes of definition' (Rountree 1999: 146). As pronounced by
Kathryn Rountree, this is 'a process at once sacred and political' (Rountree,
1999: 156). Atwood has previously commented on the strange occurrence
of 'a bumper crop of sinister Hecate-Crones' in Canadian literature, the
'notable absence of Venuses', and that 'Diana-Maidens often die young'
(Atwood 2012: 223). She concludes that perhaps the stories about these
older women are 'about the attempts of the buried Venuses and Dianas to

1   The witch is not purely a political revolutionary, but a priestess of a pre-Christian
    religion centred on a great Goddess. Rountree 1999: 141.
2   Atwood refers to this popular slogan in 'The Writing of the Testaments', 2022: xvii.
3   For further reading on tainted religious legacies see Guth (2018: 167–186).

get out, to free themselves' (Atwood 2012: 237). Atwood conjoins Aunt Lydia's witch-like character, made infamous in *The Handmaid's Tale* (1985), with her maternal, nurturing goddess character in *The Testaments* (2019).[4]

Figure 1. 'No one would think of looking inside GOD. Now you're a carrier pigeon, and all we have to do is transport you' (Aunt Lydia, *TT*: 333). Image reproduced with the permission of the artist.

The Testaments is both the sequel and prequel to the more popular *The Handmaid's Tale*. It contains withheld information about Aunt Lydia's capture and transportation across the border into Gilead. Once Aunt Lydia's timeline is reconfigured in chronological order, it is possible to view her, not as a 'parrot for patriarchal values' but as a symbol of the Goddess, a character who has invoked the Goddess by creating her own identity

---

4   For further reading about the witch, see Rabia (2017: 269–280).

and reuniting her witch and goddess aspects (Rine 2015: 57). We learn in
The Testaments that Aunt Lydia was a judge, she is an older woman (fifty-
three), she has had an abortion, been married once, briefly worked as a
schoolteacher, and was a volunteer at a rape crisis centre. Aunt Lydia has
similarities with Greco-Roman Hecate. She is an intermediary between
the women and Commander Judd, and between the world outside Gilead
and within (via the Pearl Girls). She is essential to the success or failure of
Gilead society in her position as head of the 'sphere for women' (*TT*: 175).
She has the power to choose whether to help Handmaids (Shunammite,
for example) or not. She has sovereignty over the 'sphere for women'. She
can use force (cattle prods, Particicutions, Testifying). Her role is to ensure
the fertility of the Handmaids is protected. She is a fostering, guiding
presence to Agnes Jemima and Nicole. She is a guardian or protectress of
exits and entrances for the Pearl Girls. She is independent in her oversight
of the 'sphere for women' but privileged by the support of Commander
Judd, 'carte blanche [...] within reason, and within budget. Subject, of
course, to my final approval' (*TT*: 176). Many of these roles and attributes
resonate with anthropological understandings of Greco-Roman Hecate
and are in keeping with Hesiod's 'Hymn to Hecate' in *Theogony*.[5] They
include being an intermediary, essential to the success or failure of society,
sovereignty, force, fertility, a fostering, guiding presence, having a mediating
function, a guardian or protectress of entrances, and being independent
but privileged.[6] In *The Testaments*, Aunt Lydia's power and influence goes
undetected by Commander Judd for most of the narrative. As a Mayday
double agent, she rebels against the establishment and encourages others
to do the same. Ironically, in his arrogance, Commander Judd unwittingly
gives Aunt Lydia all the power she needs to undermine the regime, because
she is a woman and not considered a threat: 'men have better things to do
than to concern themselves with the petty details of the female sphere'
(*TT*: 176). Like Hecate, Aunt Lydia is uniquely placed to secure either the
success or failure of society.

    Goddess Hecate has been adopted by men and women authors for a
variety of purposes that can equally be attributed to Atwood's portrayal

---

5   'Hymn to Hecate', Hesiod, *Theogony*, 8th–7th century BC.
6   For anthropological studies of Hecate see Boedeker (1983: 79-93), Clay (1982: 27–
    38), Marquardt (1981: 243–60) and Shamas (2007).

of Aunt Lydia as a Goddess symbol. Laura Shamas, for example, explores the underlying reasons for Shakespeare's portrayal of Hecate in *Macbeth*; a protest to patriarchy, a slight to patriarchal heritage, and an attempt to satirise and lampoon Anglo-Saxon mythology (Shamas 2007: 43). Viewing Aunt Lydia as a Goddess symbol incorporating the witch (Goddess Hecate) enables the reader to consider Atwood as engaging in spiritual feminist concerns regarding the gender inequality of women in patriarchal and Western Judeo-Christian societies. Aunt Lydia locates the divine within herself and, in the process, becomes an alternative or replacement Goddess symbol to traditional Western Judeo-Christian icons like the Virgin Mary. Astutely, Atwood gives Lydia the role of an aunt not a mother; she is not idealised as having conceived immaculately.[7] Aunt Lydia has witnessed suffering, but not of her own child, and this makes Aunt Lydia a neutral and arguably more widely acceptable Goddess symbol for a post-Christian/post-Divine Order society.[8] She is a guide and a mentor, rather than representing idealised femininity and motherhood (VanSpanckeren 2007: 153). Aunt Lydia is not aligned with Western Judeo-Christianity but rather in opposition and replacement.

Aunt Lydia is a witch, a 'political revolutionary', critiquing and attacking the authority of Commander Judd, the Divine Order, and the foundations of Gilead society. She rejects the authority of Commander Judd, who symbolises the patriarchy and religion (Divine Order) in the Gilead regime.[9] To an extent, Aunt Lydia succeeds in toppling Commander Judd when he admits, 'my stock is falling rapidly with the Council [...] I sense the cold shoulders, the abrupt greetings. I detect the symptoms of an imminent purge' (*TT*: 348). Commander Judd is a member of the Sons of Jacob group who conceptualised Gilead. With its resonance with the Old Testament, this would suggest that Atwood's attitude to religion and patriarchy is that they should be systematically removed as corrupt and dangerous pillars of society that have their roots in ancient Jewish

7   For further reading on Julia Kristeva's Stabat Mater philosophy, see Walton (2007: 110–113).
8   Lady Macbeth asks Hecate to 'unsex' her. Her meaning was to give her the strength of a man to carry out the regicide of King Duncan. In this reading, Hecate is viewed as 'unsex[ed]' because it frees the Goddess of gender roles.
9   For further reading see Atwood (2017), Allardice (2017) and Given (2019).

Christianity.[10] Her depiction of Commander Judd's character is not
flattering. He has misogynistic attitudes to women and humiliates Aunt
Lydia by subjecting her to an ordeal in the Thank Tank (Atwood 2019:
147–149). His attitude to abortion is pro-life: 'you are aware that this form
of person-murder is now punishable by death? The law is retroactive' (*TT*:
171). His attitude to marriage is Catholic: 'divorce is now a crime' (*TT*: 171).
His attitude to a woman's gender role is sexist: 'wasted your woman's body?
Denied its natural function?' (*TT*: 171). He also refers to the 'selfish choices
of women' as the cause of the decline in birth rate (*TT*: 174). Commander
Judd advocates that 'society is best served by separate spheres for men and
women' (*TT*: 174). He is resistant to the idea that the two spheres could
'meld' (*TT*: 174). He refers to a 'society congruent with the Divine Order'
that he builds 'out of charitable care and concern' (*TT*: 174). Women are
understood to be subordinate to the Commander and his power: 'it was
always a cruelty to promise them equality [...] since by their nature they
can never achieve it. We have already begun the merciful task of lowering
their expectations' (*TT*: 175). Atwood provides a powerful critique of the
ways women have historically been treated in patriarchal and Western
Judeo-Christian societies. As a Goddess symbol, Aunt Lydia represents
the rejection of and rebellion against the subjugation and oppression of
women in Gilead by the Divine Order.

Aunt Lydia's feminist consciousness develops after she suffers the loss
of her previous life and career in the world outside Gilead. She is captured
and transported to the stadium where she is re–gender-socialised in the
role of Aunt; her life as a judge ends, and a new life as Aunt Lydia, head of
the women's realm in Gilead is imposed (Christ and Plaskow 1992: 7).[11]

10   Commander Judd's file details many misdemeanours including the fates of his pre-
     vious Wives (he had disposed of them all, the first was pushed down the stairs, her
     neck was broken; two died in childbirth (their babies were Unbabies and he deliber-
     ately induced septicaemia or shock); he refused surgery when an Unbaby (with two
     heads) lodged in the birth canal and said nothing could be done because there had
     still been a foetal heartbeat; the fourth had cadmium poisoning that brought about
     stomach cancer (Atwood 2019: 308).
11   Carol P. Christ and Judith Plaskow refer to 'consciousness-raising [that] leads to a
     critique of culture and to the tasks of transforming or recreating it. Feminists have
     called their task a new naming of self and world' (Christ and Plaskow, 1992: 7).

After her ordeal in the stadium and the Thank Tank, Aunt Lydia resolves to overthrow the Gilead regime: 'I'll pull down the temple' (*TT*: 112).[12] She becomes a rebel with a cause. In becoming a Mayday double agent, Aunt Lydia is a witch, 'a political revolutionary', but in nurturing and guiding others to create their own self-identities, she takes on a spiritual priestess role. She is no longer acting solely for herself, but on behalf of others. As a Goddess symbol, she provides other suffering women with comfort, guidance, and hope. Aunt Lydia, for example, is instrumental in literally and metaphorically providing Agnes Jemima and Nicole (Offred's daughters) with a route to freedom outside the confines of Gilead and a reunion with their mother. Atwood has successfully created a Goddess symbol capable of undermining and destroying the Divine Order and Gilead regime, '*I will get you back for this. I don't care how long it takes or how much shit I have to eat in the meantime, but I will do it.*' (emphasis in original *TT*: 149).

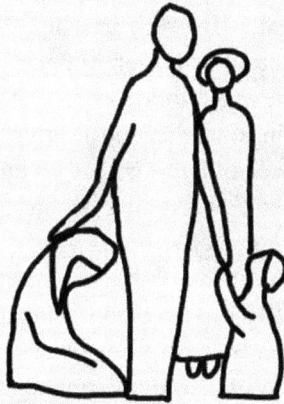

Figure 2. 'Votaries have taken to leaving offerings at my feet: eggs for fertility, oranges to suggest the fullness of pregnancy, croissants to reference the moon' (*TT*: 4). Image reproduced with the permission of the artist.

12   'Destroy this temple, and in three days I will raise it up', King James Bible 2:19.

Atwood unveils Aunt Lydia as a Goddess symbol on the first page of *The Testaments*. Her statue is revealed to us naked and vulnerable, 'I [...] pulled the rope that released the cloth drape shrouding me; it billowed to the ground, and there I stood' (*TT*: 3). There is something intensely private/personal/spiritual about the simple action of unveiling Aunt Lydia's statue. Though the cloth covers a physical object, the interaction between past and present tenses gives the illusion of covering her naked body at the same time. Her nakedness is exposed to us both as object and body. In *The Testaments* we 'see' (her statue/body) and 'hear' (the manuscript) her 'truth' (nightmares of living in purgatory/Gilead) for the first time. The present tense verb 'shrouding' has connotations of death (literal and metaphorical) and concealment (secret knowledge), both linking Aunt Lydia to the witch (Goddess Hecate). Aunt Lydia readily admits 'knowledge is power, especially discreditable knowledge' (*TT*: 35).

As the cloth 'billow[s]' to the ground, the statue of Aunt Lydia is disrobed/revealed. The verb 'billow' can be defined as a wave, especially a great wave or surge of water. The verb attaches spiritual meaning to the action of unveiling the statue; its import is heightened. This is as much the unveiling of her statue as Atwood's expose of Aunt Lydia's motives. Simultaneously, the opening of the text positions Aunt Lydia as a spiritual feminist Goddess symbol. Aunt Lydia is head of 'the separate sphere – the sphere for women' (*TT*: 175). Unveiling her statue becomes a political statement against gender equality.

At the unveiling of Aunt Lydia's statue, the audience respond with 'some discreet clapping' (*TT*: 3). The response signals Atwood's tongue-in-cheek anticipation of the reader's reception of her new novel, its attempt to conclude the unresolved fate of Gilead and its inhabitants from the prequel, and her version of a spiritual feminist mythology. From a position of spiritual authority, Aunt Lydia tells us that she 'forgive[s]' us in advance for being 'fatally hooked on life' (*TT*: 172). She knows there will be a personal price to be paid, 'for there was a bargain. Of course there was. Though I didn't make it with the Devil: I made it with Commander Judd' (*TT*: 173). The 'bargain' involved creating a 'sphere for women' with the dual goal of 'optimal [...] harmony, both civic and domestic' and 'optimal [...] offspring'

(*TT*: 175). This, of course, is ironic; Aunt Lydia has no intention of doing this. The author and Aunt Lydia are 'trickster[s]' (Wilson 2004: xiv). In the recent past, critics such as Sharon R. Wilson, Kathryn VanSpanckeren, and Karen Stein have commented on Atwood's expanding/transforming authorial intent: 'Atwood's tricksters are often iconic cultural heroes in tales that, together, are about saving, transforming, global human culture' (Wilson 2004: xiv); 'her attempt to move toward greater feeling while preserving important elements of myth' (Wilson 2004: xv), and 'recent texts not only continue genres and themes evident in her earliest work, but also intertextually advance innovative, genre-bending variations on these patterns' (Wilson 2004: xv). These critics generally agree that Atwood's oeuvre has developed/metamorphosed, and that the author has become 'more self-aware'; her texts 'move from victimisation' to 'talk[ing] back' (Wilson 2004: xv). Aunt Lydia, as Goddess symbol, is an extension of Atwood herself. The author writes with knowledge and understanding of spiritual feminism and post-structuralism. Aunt Lydia is a post-Christian Goddess symbol that implies a 'post' (after) Western Judeo-Christian religious perspective.

Aunt Lydia allows Commander Judd to believe he is in control. The power that he affords her, however, is not used for the purpose he intended. In similar vein to Zeus's gift to Hecate of a share of power in Olympus, Aunt Lydia provides a transfunctional role, 'to create laws' (sovereignty), to oversee offspring (fertility), and to use force when necessary (*TT*: 176) (Boedeker 1983: 84, 85). She is independent but privileged in the regime. This is mirrored by the deliberately obstructed outlook afforded to Aunt Lydia's statue, 'not that anything in the sky would be visible to my statue, placed as it is in a morose cluster of trees and shrubs' (*TT*: 3). Even in stone, dangerous women cannot be trusted and must be subdued. Like the Goddess Hecate, Aunt Lydia is independent within an overarching patriarchal structure.[13] We later understand that Aunt Lydia's statue is not simply a solo figure. It forms a female Holy Trinity – 'Clutching my left hand is a girl of seven or eight, gazing up at me with trusting eyes. My right hand rests on the head of a woman

---

13   For further reading on Hecate's independence see Marquardt (1981: 246).

crouched at my side, her hair veiled, her eyes upturned [...] and behind me
is one of my Pearl Girls, ready to set out on her missionary work' (*TT*: 3).
Atwood positions Aunt Lydia as the figurehead of her spiritual feminist
mythology, one that mimics but rejects Western Judeo-Christianity. Aunt
Lydia's 'fixed' gaze (representing 'idealism', 'unflinching commitment to
duty' and 'determination') is reminiscent of da Vinci's Madonna and
Mona Lisa paintings.

Atwood's portrayal of Aunt Lydia's statue invokes the Western Judeo-
Christian Holy Trinity (Father, Son, and Holy Ghost) and replaces it
with a pre-Christian matriarchal Goddess symbol that existed prior to
the Olympians and Western Judeo-Christianity. In Chapter thirty-four,
Atwood encourages/invites the reader to make an intertextual leap from
the Weird Sisters in *Macbeth* to the three sub-ordinates/'triumvirate'
of Aunt Lydia's 'sphere of women'; to conflate Aunt Lydia as a Goddess
symbol and Leader/Queen of Witches (Anglo-Saxon folklore) with
the Weird Sisters (Vidala, Elizabeth, and Helena).[14] She reinforces this
imagery in the reader's mind by referring to Aunt Lydia's 'turning point'
and the 'Wheel of Fortune' that 'rotates, fickle as the moon' (*TT*: 211).
Here, Atwood is not replacing Christianity, rather she is combining it, or
implying it can co-exist with spiritual feminist mythology headed by a
Goddess symbol.[15] Simultaneously, she implies this feminist mythology
exists *inside* the patriarchal structure, perhaps even implying that it stems
from or has been *overlaid/grafted* on to it. This is reinforced when Aunt
Lydia's manuscript is secreted/placed inside Cardinal Newman's text,
which implies her spiritual feminist mythology can be viewed as both
imprisoned *and* liberated by a patriarchal exo-skeleton.

14 'Triumvirate': in ancient Rome, a group of three men holding power (*Cambridge
Online Dictionary* n.d.).
15 In Chapter thirty-four, Atwood makes several implicit references to works cited to
Shakespeare plays, the handkerchief used to trick Othello by Iago in *Othello*; the 'triumvirate' formed to overthrow Julius Caesar in *Julius Caesar*. She is also deliberately
conflating Aunt Lydia with Hecate as Queen of Witches, which Shamas credits as
having been a Shakespearean invention.

Figure 3. 'What if I were to pray to Aunt Lydia at night, instead of to God?'
(Agnes Jemima, *TT*: 86). Image reproduced with the permission of the artist.

As part of the 'bargain' for creating the 'sphere for women', Aunt Lydia is provided with premises by Commander Judd. The setting for the administration of the 'sphere for women' is reminiscent of the Vatican, or convent (with Aunt Lydia as Abbess) – 'you will be given a budget, a base of operations, and a dormitory. We've set aside a student residential complex for you, within the walled compound of one of the former universities we have requisitioned' (*TT*: 176). Commander Judd gives Aunt Lydia 'Carte blanche' but 'Subject, of course' to his 'final approval' (*TT*: 176). He refers to her as Eve – If you fail, you will fail all women. As Eve did' (*TT*: 176). Aunt Lydia refers to her own 'recalcitrance' (*TT*: 113). This is a feature of Goddess Hecate, whose 'will' can be either beneficent or recalcitrant depending on her desire whether to fulfil the wishes of her votaries.[16] During the creation phase of her 'sphere for women', Aunt Lydia refers to herself as the 'alpha hen' in the 'henyard' (*TT*: 177). She acknowledges the need for a 'dark' side to her personality. As leader and 'spokeswoman' for the group, Aunt Lydia invents 'laws, uniforms, slogans, hymns, names' for the 'sphere' (*TT*: 177). Aunt Lydia sets out a 'new covenant' between herself and the women. The Hecate goddess has similar sovereignty over humans and is an intermediary between mortals (women) and immortals (Commander Judd) (Strauss 1984: 37).

Just as Aunt Lydia's character has transformed between *The Handmaid's Tale* and *The Testaments*, her statue has 'weathered' in the nine years that have elapsed since its unveiling (*TT*: 4). Ingloriously, it has been 'decorated' by pigeons, and 'moss' has grown in the 'damper crevices' (*TT*: 4). The adjective 'weathered' has connotations of being aged and matured by nature. Similarly, it implies that belief in the symbolism of the statue has matured and grown. This is evident by the leaving of 'offerings' at the foot of Aunt Lydia's statue: 'eggs for fertility, oranges to suggest the fullness of pregnancy, croissants to reference the moon' (*TT*: 4). Each of these 'offerings' has connotations of Triple Goddess mythology – Maiden (eggs), Mother (oranges), and Crone (croissants).[17] This implies Atwood intended the statue to represent an over-arching pre-Christian Goddess. The leaving of 'offerings' at the foot of the statue suggests prayer to a deity, along the

---

16 For further reading see Clay (1984: 34, 35).

17 For further reading see Helene Cixous's use of the orange, 'it is a vivid word linking fruit, flesh, her maternal home and writing. To write is to know the orange. To immerse oneself in its flesh. It is an overwhelming absorbing and sensuous experience, and a contrast is made between a hunger for this fruit and the need for disciplined action on behalf of suffering women' (Walton 2007: 152).

lines of a Virgin Mary paradigm – 'The black drawing ink I've been using is running out: soon I will switch to blue' (*TT*: 115). The use of colour imagery symbolises a union of the witch (black ink) and mother (blue ink) aspects of the goddess. The reference to 'blue' ink has connotations of the Virgin Mary. This may suggest faith generally, rather than the Virgin Mary specifically, 'faith in writing, in literature, as a divine force that transforms the political into the holy and discerns within human suffering the mysteries that beat at the heart of the world' (Walton 2007: 166). Atwood portrays Aunt Lydia as able to 'switch' or move seamlessly from one goddess (Hecate) to another (Venus) dependent on her need. For spiritual feminists, the authenticity and validity of an individual woman has to do with their ability to unite multiple goddesses rather than being flattened and constrained by patriarchal definitions of woman (Rountree 1999: 150). In creating the Goddess in themselves, women participate in a sacred and political act that liberates and empowers them from the gender biases of patriarchal and Western Judeo-Christian societies. Thus, Atwood presents Aunt Lydia as a Goddess symbol that embraces the witch and imbues her with the mystical and sacred qualities of the Goddess, providing hope, comfort, and guidance to other suffering women.

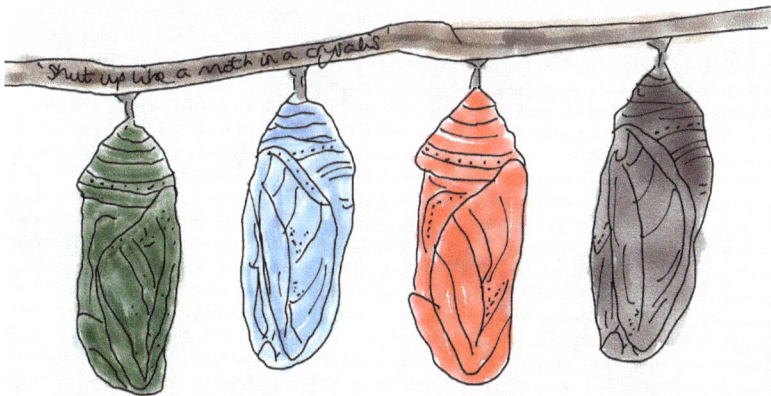

Figure 4. 'Society is best served by separate spheres for men and women' (Commander Judd, *TT*: 174) and 'shut up like a moth in a chrysalis' (Rine 2015). Image reproduced with the permission of the artist.

Jade Hinchliffe

Reading Atwood's Feminist Dystopian Fiction Alongside Feminist Surveillance Studies

Surveillance studies is a multidisciplinary field that is over two decades old. It originally developed largely from a social science base but now includes research from the arts and humanities. The value of literature, and of speculative fiction in particular, has been noted by many surveillance scholars, including Peter Marks, David Lyon and Mike Nellis (Hinchliffe (2021: 414–424). In fact, the leading journal in surveillance studies, *Surveillance & Society,* recently published a special issue on fiction, entitled 'Imagining Surveillance Futures', edited by Susan Cahill and Bryce Newell (2021). Scholarship on speculative fiction and surveillance has only recently emerged since the publication of Peter Marks' *Imagining Surveillance: Eutopian and Dystopian Literature and Film* (2017). The influence of George Orwell's *Nineteen Eighty-Four* (1949) on surveillance studies has been noted again and again by surveillance scholars but the influence of Margaret Atwood's *The Handmaid's Tale* (1985) has not been discussed in depth. Moreover, the genre of feminist dystopian fiction has not yet been explored in light of feminist surveillance studies. At the same time, whilst literary scholars have noted that surveillance is an important theme in *The Handmaid's Tale* (Wisker 2010), the portrayal of surveillance in the novel is often explored only in relation to Michel Foucault's scholarship on surveillance. This has meant that analysis of surveillance has focused mainly on the top-down monitoring of Handmaids by the state and has been less focused on other forms of surveillance, as well as surveillance and embodiment.

In this chapter, I will outline the importance of Atwood's *The Handmaid's Tale* and its Booker-Prize-winning sequel *The Testaments* (2019) to the field of surveillance studies and discuss what Atwood's feminist dystopias contribute to our understanding of surveillance and gender. In bringing together feminist theory, dystopian studies and surveillance studies, I will show why it is important that we re-examine Atwood's feminist dystopias in light of surveillance theory. By integrating surveillance theory with literary analysis, a more nuanced examination of the role of surveillance in Atwood's feminist dystopias can be revealed that discusses gender, surveillance and embodiment.

In 2009, *Surveillance & Society* published a special issue on gender and sexuality, wherein the editors stated that 'surveillance studies needs gender and sexuality' (Ball et al. 2009: 352). The editors acknowledged that the special issue on gender and sexuality was 'a long time coming' (Ball et al. 2009: 355), and they claimed that this issue was 'comparatively short' due to the fact that feminist surveillance studies had not yet been established. Since the publication of this special issue, there have been several major publications in feminist surveillance studies, including Shoshana Amielle Magnet's *When Biometrics Fail: Gender, Race and the Technology of Identity* (2011), Rachel E. Dubrofsky and Shoshana Amielle Magnet's (eds) *Feminist Surveillance Studies* (2015), Robert Heyen and Emily Van der Meulen's (eds) *Expanding the Gaze: Gender and the Politics of Surveillance* (2016) and Catherine D'Ignazio and Lauren F. Klein's *Data Feminism* (2020).

Feminist surveillance scholars argue that a feminist approach is important because it highlights how our experiences of surveillance are influenced by our bodies and how our bodies influence how we are surveilled. Heyen and Van der Meulen claim that 'gendering the field involves thinking about surveillance practices as socially located as embodied and as having differential impacts' (2016: 4). Dubrofsky and Magnet similarly state that surveillance practices 'remake the body, producing new ways of visualising bodily identities in ways that highlight othered forms of racialised, gendered, classed, abled, and disabled bodies, as well as sexualised identities' (2015: 9). Furthermore, feminist surveillance studies scholars highlight gendered surveillance practices, which are not usually examined by surveillance scholars or even viewed as surveillance practices. Nicola Shephard (2016: 7) argues that 'as relevant as conventional surveillance technologies, however, are public health screenings, birth certificates, social media postings, and other everyday practices'. The work of feminist surveillance scholars in the literature so far have analysed the surveillance practices Shephard mentions as well as ultrasound scans, transvaginal examinations, adoption, surrogacy and fertility treatments.

The Handmaid's Tale and *The Testaments* both highlight how women navigate spaces differently because of their gender, showing the relationship between surveillance, gender and embodiment. Moreover, the novels not only speculate on how women could be surveilled in a dystopian society, but also, they make us aware of the level of surveillance already involved in practices that are not usually considered as surveillance practices, such as ultrasound scans. These two concerns diagnosed in the novels are central to feminist surveillance studies.

The spatial layout and the division of space are important elements in speculative fiction. Marks (2017: 104) deconstructs the words 'utopia' and 'dystopia', noting that the common root word is 'topos', i.e. space, which is 'attached to prefixes with positive or negative connotations'. Dystopian novels usually portray a city space with boundaries and borders, where the characters are separated and segregated according to a hierarchy. The characters' identities – in particular, their class, gender and race – affect how they navigate these spaces and how they are monitored. Atwood's feminist dystopias explore how the characters' gender impacts how they are surveilled and how they navigate space.

Offred, the protagonist of *The Handmaid's Tale*, describes her navigation of public space in the time before Gilead, highlighting the fact that she has always considered her visibility in public spaces as a woman, even when there were no laws regarding gender and space. Offred states, 'I never ran at night; and in the daytime, only beside well-frequented roads. Women were not protected then. I remember the rules, rules that were never spelled out but that every woman knew [...]' (Atwood 2017: 34). Offred considered her visibility in the time before Gilead, choosing to exercise outdoors when it was light outside and where it was busy, in the hope that she would not be attacked and so that there would be witnesses, who could help if she was. Here Atwood shows how surveillance is embodied as Offred made decisions regarding her navigation of public space and considered her visibility based on her gender.

The official reason why Handmaids never walk alone is for their protection. Handmaids are viewed as walking wombs and as precious resources by the state, who need them in order to overcome the fertility crisis. The red robes that the Handmaids wear symbolise their important role. Offred says that 'now we walk along the same street, in red pairs, and no man shouts obscenities at us, speaks to us, touches us' (34). Aunt Lydia tells the Handmaids that there is 'freedom to' and 'freedom from' (34). Before Gilead, women had freedom to choose how to live their lives but knew that there were unofficial rules that governed space. In Gilead, women do not have the freedom to make choices but they can feel safer navigating public spaces. Offred even describes deliberately teasing the security guards in the knowledge that they could not touch her and considers the power that she feels from this interaction. Yet, the Handmaids are forced to walk in pairs for their protection, which suggests that they are only safe if there is another female witness. Presumably, if a Handmaid was attacked whilst she was by herself, her account would be viewed with suspicion because she should not have been unaccompanied. In the time before, Offred describes thinking that it was more dangerous to be alone in public spaces at night and making decisions based on this. In Gilead, Handmaids still cannot be alone, and this suggests that there are still the same risks for women navigating public spaces.

Through Offred's navigation of public space, Atwood shows that there are different types of surveillance practices that shape Offred's behaviour in public. As previously mentioned, analysis of surveillance in *The Handmaid's Tale* has focused on the top-down monitoring of Handmaids by the state, which includes Commanders, Eyes, Guardians of the Faith, Aunts and Wives. These groups all have more power over Handmaids. Less attention has been paid to what Mark Andrejevic (2005: 488) defines as 'lateral surveillance', which means 'peer-to-peer monitoring' by individuals rather than 'agents of institutions public or private'. When discussing her walking partner, Ofglen, Offred states 'the truth is that she is my spy, as I am hers. If either of us slips through the net because of something that happens on one of our daily walks, the other will be accountable' (29). Offred monitors Ofglen's behaviour to spot any clues that she is a rebel and notes that Ofglen 'walks demurely, head down, red-gloved hands clasped in front' (29). Offred notes that 'during these walks she has never said anything that was not strictly orthodox, but then, neither have I' (29). In order to prevent rebellions, the state makes Handmaids responsible not only for themselves but for their walking partners. This makes it difficult for Offred to ascertain whether Ofglen is a 'real believer' (29) or whether she is a rebel. Both Handmaids converse using the 'accepted' (29) greetings and responses and make themselves seem obedient to each other through their body language, just as they do with those who are superior to them. In this scenario, lateral surveillance is not separate from vertical, or top-down, surveillance. Offred also considered lateral surveillance when navigating space in the time before Gilead as she chose to run beside 'well-frequented roads' (34) so that she would be seen by other civilians. In these two examples, Atwood shows how people consider their visibility via top-down surveillance methods (e.g. CCTV) and via lateral surveillance methods (e.g. motorists) when making decisions about their use of public space. The decisions that Offred makes are based on her gender and this shows how surveillance is embodied and how our identity shapes our navigation of public space.

Self-surveillance is also an important aspect of *The Handmaid's Tale* as the vertical and lateral surveillance methods affect Offred's behaviour and her thoughts about her body, when she is in private. The more Offred thinks about her physical appearance and her visibility, the more detached she becomes from her body. When she is bathing, Offred says:

> My nakedness is strange to me already. My body seems outdated. Did I really wear bathing suits, at the beach? I did, without thought, amongst men, without caring that my legs, my arms, my thighs and back were on display, could be seen. *Shameful, immodest.* (72, emphasis in original)

Offred has internalised the idea that she should not be seen because of the vertical and lateral surveillance methods, which have changed her behaviour. As a Handmaid, Offred not only completely covers her body and her hair but she is also supposed to keep her head bowed and avoid making eye contact. She has not only internalised the idea that she should not be seen but she has also become accustomed to not seeing. Her naked body therefore seems strange to her because she has become detached from it. Offred says that she does not want to look at her naked body because it defines her (73) as she has a tattoo on her ankle: 'Four digits and an eye, a passport in reverse' (75). Offred's body, then, is a constant reminder to her of the surveillance systems.

Through the surveillance of Offred's body by the state, Atwood invites the reader to consider how some medical procedures that we do not normally consider surveillance practices could be viewed through this lens. Offred visits the doctor's every month for mandatory urine tests, blood tests, hormone tests and cancer smear (69). Offred describes how she feels being examined by the doctor:

> When I'm naked I lie down on the examining table, on the sheet of chilly crackling disposable paper. I pull the second sheet, the cloth one, up over my body. At neck level there's another sheet, suspended from the ceiling. It intersects me so that the doctor will never see my face. He deals with a torso only. (70)

Just as Offred detaches herself from her body during the ceremony as a coping mechanism, she detaches herself during the examination. The doctor, like the Commander, 'deals with a torso only'. As Atwood's novel shows, Offred feels dehumanised by this process and is also fearful because of the power relations between herself and the doctor, who propositions Offred. Offred worries that the doctor will 'fake the tests, report me for cancer, for infertility, have me shipped off to the Colonies, with the Unwomen. None of this has been said, but the knowledge of his power hangs nevertheless in the air as he pats my thigh' (71). It seems odd that Handmaids are not accompanied to the doctor's or that there is not another member of staff in the room, especially given the fact that Handmaids are not allowed to be alone in other situations. This incidence highlights the fact cervical cancer screenings and other procedures need to be seen as surveillance practices.

In their article on surveillance and cervical cancer screening, Anthony Corones and Susan Hardy (2009) discuss how this procedure is 'sexually sensitive for women in a way that other forms of health screening are not' (389). Corones and Hardy (391–392) suggest that there are many factors that may affect women's participation in cervical cancer screening, including risk perceptions, levels of support, shame and embarrassment and privacy, amongst other factors. They claim that one of the key strategies that the World Health Organization (WHO) invests in is health education, so that women comply with the screenings, and suggest that that the prevailing assumption on behalf of WHO is 'if *only* women understood the facts, they *would* comply' (392; emphasis in original). Whilst Corones and Hardy acknowledge that education is one of the factors that affects cervical cancer screening attendance, they show that there are many other factors involved. If this procedure was viewed by the WHO through a surveillance lens and if the other factors were considered, more support could be given to patients, which may increase attendance at cervical cancer screenings and make patients feel more comfortable with this procedure.

Reading Atwood's *The Handmaid's Tale* in light of feminist surveillance studies, then, shows how this novel highlights how surveillance methods are embodied and suggests why it is important for the term 'surveillance' to be applied to more practices. This novel was published almost four decades ago, however, and technology has evolved dramatically over this period. At the same time, feminist dystopian fiction has developed considerably. How then can *The Testaments* (2019) and Bruce Miller's Hulu/MGM Television adaptation of *The Handmaid's Tale* (2017–) further contribute to our understanding of feminist surveillance studies and feminist dystopian fiction?

In my research, I have noted several trends in twenty-first-century dystopian fiction, including feminist dystopian fiction, that differ from earlier works in this genre and which make this genre more hopeful (Hinchliffe 2021). These trends include more dystopias set in and written by authors from the Global South, more diverse authors, more diverse stories, settings and characters, multiple protagonists and perspectives and more specific contexts. These trends make the genre much more hopeful as often the multiple, diverse protagonists help each other. In twenty-first-century feminist dystopian fiction, there is often a sense of sisterhood in novels such as Bina Shah's *Before She Sleeps* (2018) and Leni Zumas' *Red Clocks* (2018). Whilst *The Handmaid's Tale* was told from the viewpoint of one female protagonist, *The Testaments* is told from the viewpoint of three female protagonists: Offred's daughters, Agnes and Nicole, and Aunt Lydia. Similarly, whilst the television adaptation centres on Offred, other characters are portrayed in significantly more depth. Both the sequel and the television adaptation explore the perspectives of those who are not Handmaids, and figures who were portrayed as antagonists in the original novel, such as Aunt Lydia and Serena Joy, have moments of redemption in the sequel and the television adaptation. Fiona Tolan (2021b: 162–164) argues that sisterhood is central to *The Testaments* in a way that it is not in the first novel and suggest that the sequel is much more hopeful as a result. One of the reasons why *The Testaments* and the television adaptation are more hopeful is because of the collaboration between the three protagonists and other characters, who are collectively engaging in activism and resistance.

The Testaments (2019), however, is not able to comment directly on current technologies, contemporary surveillance systems or current sociopolitical situations in the same way that other twenty-first-century dystopian fiction can because it has to remain faithful to *The Handmaid's Tale*. Susan Watkins (2020: 135–136) argues that 'the prominence of the sequel in contemporary women's writing within the post-apocalyptic genre allows the creative revision of many of the expectations created by the previous novels, as well as providing the opportunity to expose further some of the implications of the former text and the genre as a whole'. Atwood provides creative revision and explores the implications of *The Handmaid's Tale* further in the sequel, as Watkins suggests, but, even with the time jump, it was difficult for Atwood to draw parallels between dataveillance and current technologies and Gilead because technology and surveillance have evolved dramatically since 1985. Claire Wrobel (2021) notes that Atwood has briefly commented on dataveillance in *The Handmaid's Tale* as the Gileadean regime is able to take control through cancelling women's bank accounts, and Wrobel also points out that Atwood introduces CCTV cameras in *The Testaments* but these practices are not discussed in much depth.

In the television adaptation, connections have been made to current surveillance practices as well as to contemporary forms of activism and resistance, especially in the flashbacks to the time before Gilead and in the scenes in present-day Canada. Instead of a tattoo for identification, the Handmaids are tracked via a chip inserted in their ears. In various episodes where Handmaids attempt to escape, they have to remove their chips in order to not be detected by Gilead's security forces. In season two, episode nine, the physical letters written by women trapped in Gilead are leaked online in Canada, which leads to a wave of women's rights protests and results in negotiations between Canada and Gilead being terminated, to the detriment of Gilead. The television adaptation, then, showcases ways in which ordinary citizens can use current technologies to expose injustice in ways in which the novels do not. The television series is also able to connect with contemporary political situations, including, most notably, the 2016 presidential election and women's rights protests during the Trump administration. It remains to be seen whether the television series will draw any parallels with COVID-19 and the ways in which this has affected surveillance systems. There is, however, a reference to Zoom in the final episode of season four. For obvious reasons, the television adaptation can make connections between the contemporary world and Gilead in ways that the novels cannot.

Having said this, the insights that *The Handmaid's Tale*, *The Testaments* and the television adaptation provide surveillance studies scholars are immeasurable. Not only do Atwood's feminist dystopias comment on how women could be surveilled differently from men and how gender could impact our relationship with surveillance, she describes how surveillance is embodied. Atwood suggests why some practices that are not typically understood as surveillance should be seen through this lens and implies that these practices are not seen through this lens because they mostly affect women. Atwood's feminist dystopias have much to contribute to surveillance studies, as well as the subfield of feminist surveillance studies, and this is why her fiction should no longer be overlooked by surveillance scholars in favour of Orwell's dystopian classic.

Part IV

Later and Diverse Work: *Hag-Seed*, Music, Illustrated Texts and Poetry

Jessica Gildersleeve and Laurie Johnson

The Abuses of Shakespeare: *Hag-Seed*

The Illusion of Control

In *Negotiating with the Dead* (2002), Margaret Atwood observes the frequent assumption that literature's primary purpose is moral and social improvement. Literature is seen to be 'good for' us (108), she notes: it makes us better people simply through consumption. *Hag-Seed* (2016), Atwood's revision of William Shakespeare's *The Tempest* (1611), reflects on this supposition, as Felix, the former director of a high-profile theatre company, finds a new role as a teacher of theatre in a men's prison. Just as Prospero in *The Tempest* 'uses his arts [...] for the purposes of moral and social improvement [...] torturing people for their own good' (*Negotiating:* 115), so too Felix's work, his supervisor Estelle gushes, is 'a really wonderful example of discipline cross-fertilisation, showing the way the arts can be used as a therapeutic and educational tool, in a very creative and unexpected way!' (*Hag-Seed:* 71). In Felix's classroom, both he and his pupils shed their old identities and take on new roles, not only as performers, but also in the aliases they adopt and the labour they perform while in the theatre space. Atwood's consideration of the relationship between literature and responsibility has been the topic of some critical discussion (e.g. Bouson 2011): in particular, Yağmur Tatar (2020) addresses the metafictionality and metatheatricality of *Hag-Seed* as a means of providing contemporary social commentary, while Paul Joseph Zajac (2020) argues more particularly that *Hag-Seed* depicts the expression and working through of traumatic experience, mediated through the process of adaptation, and Merry Lynn Byrd argues that 'Felix seeks justice, not just punishment [...] making Atwood's revision very clearly about restitution and restoration rather than revenge' (2018: 77).

This chapter considers Atwood's critique of the simplification of literature as therapy, a substitute for a moral code or a vehicle for revenge. *Hag-Seed*, we argue, makes clear that literature (or theatrical performance) has effects and consequences, to be sure, but these cannot be predicted or controlled. Justice does not apply in this case; as Atwood asks in *Negotiating with the Dead*, 'if a man murders someone, then he is a murderer, and will be caught if possible, and put on trial, and so forth. But if a writer murders someone in a book [...] then what is he guilty of, and how are we to judge his crime?' (2002: 102–103). There has been no incitement to violence, and if the reader finds the events upsetting, that is a result of their own individual interaction with the text, rather than the responsibility of the text itself. To take this further, if Felix tortures someone within his performance of a play, 'what is he guilty of?' Although he can estimate the effects on this interactive audience, this is ultimately beyond his control. Indeed, even the effects on himself, in his simultaneous roles as director, actor and audience, are unpredictable. Felix's catharsis can thus be seen as an unplanned by-product of the chaos which results from his planned revenge on his enemies. Similarly, Prospero's power over Ariel is only limited, resulting in a great deal of collateral damage.

Felix also demands that his students use only Shakespeare's words as insult – as curse – just as the title of the novel does, in its reference to an insult hurled towards Caliban. In doing so, *Hag-Seed* calls up the performative power of language to make us feel, the way 'the words the writer writes do not exist in some walled garden called "literature," but actually get out there into the world, and have effects and consequences' (*Negotiating:* 97). But as with the insult, the affective consequence of the literary text ultimately cannot be controlled. The 'reader will judge the characters, because the reader will interpret', Atwood reminds us (111). *Hag-Seed*, then, observes the chaotic ethics of literature and its potential not only for improvement, but for destruction. To attempt to keep a tight rein on those consequences is a restriction, an imprisonment and an abuse of the literary text itself. Atwood's novel thus constitutes a significant shift from trends in earlier adaptations of Shakespeare's works, in which the tendency was 'to reduce possible misconstructions and minimise subversive interpretations', a strategy which, Jean I. Marsden argues, 'bespeaks a profound distrust of language, a fear that unless carefully controlled, words both printed and spoken can undermine social and political order' (1995: 20). This is perhaps best seen in the way Atwood reinterprets Prospero's final speech, and his imploration to the audience: 'As you from crimes would pardoned be / Let your indulgence set me free' (*Tempest* Epilogue: 19–20). Prospero, the artist-magician, personifies the chaotic ethics of the play, and of literature more generally. He 'uses his arts – magic arts, arts of illusion' for a range of purposes, Atwood identifies – not all of them virtuous: he 'plays God', 'the Grand Inquisitor, torturing people for their own good', he is at once a 'usurper', a 'sorcerer', a 'benevolent despot' (*Negotiating*: 115). But ultimately it is his art, his books, 'that give him his power' (115). To set him free is to recognise literature's free radical potential, to free it from the power craved by the artist-magician, and from the logic of redemption, revenge, and the assumption of a discourse of justice.

The Play within the Prison

Atwood's *Hag-Seed* is a contemporary and complex adaptation of Shakespeare's final play. Felix's own life is an echo of Prospero's: overthrown by his business partner for political gain, Felix now lives a solitary life with only the ghost of his dead daughter, Miranda, for company. In an attempt to '[b]reak out of [this] cell' of exile (*Hag-Seed*: 47), Felix takes a job at a nearby prison, running the Literacy Through Literature program, in which his students will learn through studying and performing the works of Shakespeare. After several years of success in teaching the inmates, he assigns *The Tempest*. The play and the adaptation (as well as 'its dark double', Howells 2017: 311) which Felix and his students create and perform are thus embedded within Atwood's novel, presenting a multilayered metanarrative about adaptation itself. *Hag-Seed* and its *Tempest*s show adaptation as 'inherently "palimpsestuous" works, haunted at all times by their adapted texts. If we know that prior text, we always feel its presence shadowing the one we are experiencing directly' (Hutcheon 2006: 6). For Dana Percec, the Hogarth adaptations are best understood not as '"reimaginings," but "reactions" to Shakespeare' (2018: 296). Indeed, the lives of Felix, his students, and those on whom he seeks revenge are all constructed in 'reaction' to Shakespeare's play and its multiple adaptations within Atwood's novel. Marta Dvořák's explanation of Atwood's adaptation is more specific:

> The novel belongs [...] to what Linda Hutcheon has identified as the double-voiced bitextual synthesis of parody, a transcontextualised repetition with a difference which mixes playful offhandedness with homage. By offering readers an adventure in intelligent vulgarisation which adheres to the classical functions of literature (to entertain and to teach), Atwood combats the current prejudices which have labeled Shakespeare's works irrelevant and boring, and installs in their place a new openness. (2021: 25)

What we must recognise, however, is the consequence of that 'openness': that freedom from the 'prejudice' of 'irrelevan[ce]' does not automatically constitute an acceptance of the play's wholesome or redemptive qualities. Like the inmates of the novel, who have the capacity to reoffend upon their early release, so too a literary text may not be wholly 'good'. Sociopathic in the sense that it cares not for its consequences or impacts, the literary text may be equally useful and abusive.

That Atwood's narrative and Felix's plot take place largely within a carceral setting also legitimates a certain latitude when it comes to the morality or rules which govern his plans for redemption and revenge. One is reminded of Oscar Wilde's sentiment in *The Picture of Dorian Gray* (1891): 'There is no such thing as a moral or an immoral book. Books are well written, or badly written. That is all' (Preface). Wilde's statement has ironically taken on a life of its own, floating free from its point of origin to be used by countless literary critics as a general principle to be restated, often without citation. Returning to Wilde's 'Preface' to *Dorian Gray* reminds us, however, that a particular work appears to have been on his mind as he penned this claim, since he writes shortly thereafter: 'The nineteenth century dislike of Realism is the rage of Caliban seeing his own face in a glass,' which he counters with the further claim that 'The nineteenth century dislike of Romanticism is the rage of Caliban not seeing his own face in a glass'. Caliban is here unmoored by Wilde to do service in making a point about the vagaries of literary tastes, but in so doing, Wilde also demonstrates that Caliban can be both one thing and another, depending on these tastes. More to the point, Wilde uses Caliban's duplicity as a mirror or glass to the figure he has created in Dorian Gray, a man who is at once both himself and his picture. By making such an allusion to *The Tempest*, Wilde is arguably also positioning himself as the equivalent of another figure in the same text, for whom the claim that a book is neither moral nor immoral but only well written can be ultimately seen as a cover for actions that do indeed have a moral or immoral dimension. As Atwood argues, morality and immorality, goodness and badness, are in fact a function of literary quality:

> If you're an *artist*, being a good man [...] is pretty much beside the point when it comes to your actual accomplishments [...]. However, whether you are a good man or a bad man is *not* beside the point if you happen to be a good *wizard* – good at doing your magic, making your 'marvellous clear jelly', creating illusions that can convince people of their truth – because if you are good at being a wizard in this sense, then power of various sorts may well come your way – power in relation to society – and then your goodness or badness as a human being will have a part in determining what you do with this power. (*Negotiating:* 113)

The prison, the carceral limit point of society, redefines morality and immorality: here, for instance, '[r]evenge is a known quantity [...] Boot in the kidneys, homemade blade in the neck, blood in the shower' (*Hag-Seed:* 76–77). The implicit rules of the theatre are upheld – respect for the director, for the language of the play, for the work of the 'team' (84) – but Felix must, by necessity, make free with the rules of learning and interpretation. The Fletcher Players must adopt a stage name, for instance, but all of these make reference in some way to the person's crimes; they may curse, but only in the terms of the play – and those who succeed in upholding this role win cigarettes (contraband property) at the course's conclusion. Felix's class thus create an exclusive group within the prison which abides by its own ethical code, one which does not necessarily align with either the rules of the prison or of the outside world.

Shakespeare, on the other hand, goes seemingly out of his way to make the setting a space for what Jonathan Goldberg calls a 'despecification', creating 'an island notoriously unmoored and variously located: a place between north Africa and Italy and yet an Atlantic locale' (ix). Attempts by generations of critics to specify the location by turning it into an allegory for this or that 'real' place invariably founder, if not within the surety of their own convictions about the location of the island, then at least with the appearance of the next reading that affixes the island to another location. As Goldberg points out, but only as an interesting point 'further worth mentioning', one of Shakespeare's sources may well have introduced this dislocation: 'in William Strachey's account of a shipwreck off Bermuda [...] he compares the New World hurricane to storms "upon the coast of *Barbary* and *Algeere*"' in Northern Africa (2004: 160, n. 25). The inability to pin the location down to an allegorically translated 'real' place was thus perhaps there all along in Shakespeare's source materials, but in taking Shakespeare's *Tempest* as a source, Atwood transforms the play into an allegory for a more modern reality and fixes the location as some place fictional and yet wholly familiar.

The Prison within the Play

Yet whether Shakespeare invented or inherited this sense of dislocation is neither here nor there; our point is that the play resists localising or limiting, even though this is what any reading will inevitably require of the text. In this way, the play casts its readers in the role of a Prospero attempting to limit the boundless power of the spirit he has bound. Having freed Ariel from the prison imposed by the witch Sycorax, Prospero enslaved the spirit, and so their first exchange in the play reveals that it is thus Prospero's magical control over Ariel that was the cause of the storm in which the King of Naples's ship is seemingly wrecked in the play's opening sequence. With his master's bidding having been carried out, Ariel begs for freedom once more but is threatened with a return to his former captive state:

> Prospero If thou more murmur'st, I will rend an oak
> And peg thee in his knotty entrails till
> Thou hast howled away twelve winters. (*The Tempest* 1.2: 294–96)

The irony is thus that Ariel's 'freedom' is to be enslaved, with only the deferred promise of being set free after the next charge to provide any hope. Even in the final moments of the play, which summaries of the play normally gloss as Prospero setting Ariel free, the spirit is in fact not set free; not yet. As Prospero says, 'My Ariel, chick,/That is thy charge. Then to the elements/Be free, and fare thou well' (5.1: 318–20), thereby deferring the long-awaited freedom until after yet another charge is undertaken. The play ends at this moment, with the appended 'Epilogue' only apparently delivered in some unspecified future by which time he nevertheless remains on 'this bare island' lacking 'spirits to enforce', begging the audience to set him free with their applause (Epilogue: 8–20).

If Prospero believes his books will enable him to control Ariel, the opening scene of the play already reveals that this power cannot be wielded without unintended consequences. 'No harm' (1.2: 14–15), he repeats to Miranda, insisting that the magic with which he caused the storm to swell also provides an assurance that the ship and all aboard will be transported safely from danger. There is in the previous scene, however, a palpable sense of mortal dread that overcomes the men on the stricken ship, the effects of which cannot be lost on audiences or readers. The mariners' cries, the prayers of the King and the Prince readying themselves for death and the talk of drowning from the characters on deck all speak to the undoubtedly psychological harm that the experience inflicts upon the ship's inhabitants. Moreover, in the dispute between Antonio and Sebastian on one side and Gonzalo on the other over whether to abandon ship or go down with the King – a conflict that could have been avoided had these men not been thrown together under such traumatic circumstances – the opening scene also sets in motion the play's assassination sub-plot as an unplanned consequence of Prospero's magic. 'No harm', then, to the persons on the ship, at least not in any immediate physical sense, but the damage done by Ariel's storm extends out through the play in ways that neither Prospero nor the book through which he maintains authority over Ariel had proscribed.

The subsequent demands made by Prospero on Ariel are in some sense necessitated by the spiraling consequences of the opening storm: first thwarting the attempt by Antonio and Stephano to kill the King in Act 2, then stopping Stephano's further coup in support of Caliban's uprising against Prospero across Acts 3 to 4, before bringing the various parties to Prospero's heel on the island in Act 5. Not all of the problems created in the opening act are resolved by play's end, with Caliban, for example, remaining in servitude, and the final fates of Antonio and Sebastien left unexplained, but Prospero has seemingly learned his lesson and vows, 'I'll break my staff' and 'I'll drown my book' (5.1: 53, 57). Again, though, as with the granting of freedom to Ariel, it is vowed by Prospero within the play but not yet acted upon by him at the play's end. It is only in Prospero's own words in the Epilogue that we gain any assurance that these things have eventually happened. What Prospero also reveals in giving us these reassurances is, however, that not all who populated the island and the play are free: Prospero is himself now a prisoner of the island and the play, and only the audience can now set him free by bringing the play to its conclusion. While invitations to applaud are normal in the epilogues to early modern plays, Prospero's appeal for freedom through this device might also be the play's final cruel irony – the reason this invitation is so expected in early modern plays is that, as Tiffany Stern has explained, a playwright would only receive payment for the play if it reached its third or 'benefit' performance, so the invitation to applause was included by playwrights to have audience's signal a desire to have the play performed again (2004: 172–73). In the case of Prospero's appeal for freedom, this repetition of the play would see him return in subsequent performances to the same circumstances under which we find him here, rather like Ariel appealing *ad infinitum* for and never quite achieving his freedom.

Prospero thus always already anticipates adaptation, repetition and infinite performance. Adaptation of *The Tempest*, then, does not conjure the 'pleasure' of 'repetition with variation' or 'the comfort of ritual', as Hutcheon (2006: 4) has it, but rather a fear of it. The fate of both Prospero and his play, it seems, are (literally) in the audience's hands. Felix offers his students an opportunity to imagine their way out of this prison of the text, to imagine an 'outside-text' via their final assignment. They are 'good readers' who have now 'become writers and claimed the text for themselves', Fiona Tolan observes (2021: 121). But most striking, perhaps, is Team Hag-Seed's (Caliban's) imagined futures for their character: a simultaneous vision of Caliban as at once a freak-show prisoner, subject to the insults and laughter of a mocking coloniser, and the wealthy son of a duke, later a celebrated rockstar. Their proposal refuses to resolve the after-life of the play, acknowledging it as a literary prison even as they work to set Caliban free via the 'freedom of interpretation' which Felix's assignment has offered to them (Jayendran 2020: 16). Nishevita Jayendran has thus argued that both Felix's reinterpretation of the play as well as the students' final assignment offer up the possibility of a creative retelling of Shakespeare's *Tempest* that can set Prospero and the characters free within and through new discursive spaces; a possibility that can be extended to *Hag-Seed* as a metacritical novelistic adaptation of the original play. With every new space come new discursive horizons and boundaries of freedom that necessitate constant negotiation of meaning (2020: 22).

Prospero and Caliban 'will be free', Jayendran adds, when they are 'not bound by a single crystalline interpretation' (2020: 24). The irony may yet be that, as Wilde noted, the freedom from a single interpretation may require that the characters assume a position that enables them to be at once seeing themselves and not seeing themselves in a glass.

The Control of Illusions

For their 2016 production of *The Tempest*, the Royal Shakespeare Company employed state-of-the-art technology to equip actor Mark Quartley with motion capture sensors to translate his movements into a digitally animated projection of Ariel onto smoke and mesh to create depth and contour. The technology was designed to give visual expression to the magical entity's other-worldly nature and shape-shifting abilities, while at the same time enabling Quartley to interact in real time with the other performers on stage through this avatar. The creative team planned for Quartley to provide the avatar's movements from backstage, but the decision was later made to bring Quartley onto the stage, showcasing both the actor's performance and the real-time wizardry of the technology (Aebischer 2020: 129–31). As might be expected with any such technology, the production was inevitably beset with glitches. The physicality of performance onstage meant Quartley occasionally skewed the calibration of the sensors, and the actor 'was even asked to restrict his *offstage* movements in order not to put the technology out of kilter' (Aebischer 2020: 131, emphasis in original). Instead of the anticipated freedom to express Ariel's differences in form and speed, the technology famously resulted in a production that was noted by many commentators for the relative constraints it placed on Quartley's body and therefore on the avatar's movements.

Lest we be seen here to be taking an easy route to the proof of our main point by using an example of an adaptation where things got glitchy, as technologies of adaptation inevitably do, it is also worth mentioning that when the imaging technology worked well, audiences were nevertheless struck by some specific limitations of the spectacle they beheld. Reviews of the production expressed fears 'that digital technology would upstage the actors' (Billington 2016) and while attempts to allay such fears were focused on the non-augmented performance of Simon Russell Beale's Prospero, a particular scene in which Quartley's body and avatar were merged on-stage strained such reassurances. As Pascale Aebischer notes, when in Act 1 Scene 2 Prospero reminds Ariel of how he had been trapped by Sycorax in 'cloven pine', the RSC production surrounded Quartley in the projection mesh to allow the magnified image of Ariel's contortions and pain to layer directly over the actor's smaller but identical gestures (2020: 137). The decision to directly depict Ariel's entrapment – an event that existed in the character's past – further heightened the feedback loops that the audience was already experiencing through the imagining technology, but ultimately also took the task of imagining the scene out of the hands of the audience: 'Instead of the magic illusionism of the masque as *texte de plaisir*, which left the audience reassured in their sense of separateness and control, the scene of Ariel's torture presented itself as an extratemporal, agonised, and queasiness-inducing *texte de jouissance* that sucked its viewers into its core to share in the spirit's anguish' (137).

Atwood's novel highlights a similar shift from the separateness and control offered to the audience of Shakespeare's play to something not unlike a scene of torture, albeit without the gimmickry of the RSC's augmented Ariel. Just as Beale's Prospero was, unquestionably, dwarfed on-stage by the scene of torture that Shakespeare's play only has him describe in just a few short lines, Atwood's Felix cannot help but be overshadowed by events he puts in motion within the walls of the prison that he otherwise enjoys the freedom to bypass. The riot may be the vehicle for his revenge, but its effects spill out beyond the measure of his imagination: Tony considers murdering one of his associates ('It's much better than I could have hoped for!', Felix declares, *Hag-Seed:* 222), the drugged grapes Felix has planted work with far greater effect than he had anticipated, while Anne-Marie and Freddie (playing Miranda and Ferdinand, respectively) really do fall in love. By representing the process of adaptation itself, Atwood allows us to bear witness to the glitchy messiness of adaptation even as it seeks to lock a specific interpretation or representation in place.

Ultimately, then, Atwood's adaptation of *The Tempest* exposes the paradoxical purposelessness of literature – or rather, the way in which its purpose, like Prospero's storm, is multiple, uncontrollable and wild. It untethers literature from rigid meaning and purpose, and the canon from unassailability. Just as Felix, in the novel's final moments, releases his obsessive memorialisation of his lost daughter, Miranda, offering her freedom, so too *Hag-Seed* releases *The Tempest*, Shakespeare, and literature more generally, from our restrictive ideas of how and why it works. 'To the elements be free', indeed (283).

Robin Elliott

Margaret Atwood and Music

While music has not been a major leitmotif in the creative work of Margaret Atwood, it does occasionally play an interesting role in her novels and poems. Composers have set her words to music frequently, including several libretti that she has written. Others have adapted her novels to create television shows with musical soundtracks, and also major musical stage works, often with Atwood's involvement in the creative process. Atwood's international celebrity status as an author has brought significant attention to all of her musical activities and has been an important part of the reception of the operas and ballets with which her name has been associated.

Atwood has been modest about her musical abilities and knowledge. Nevertheless, over the years, her musical interests have become notably diverse, and she has written with great insight and creativity about many kinds of music, from Laurie Anderson to contemporary opera (Atwood 2021; 2003). In the short story 'Wooden Box' from *Old Babes in the Wood* (2023), the favourite CDs of Tig (a character evidently based on Graeme Gibson, Atwood's life partner) include Elly Ameling (classical), Waylon Jennings (country) and Stan Rogers (folk). Atwood's musical tastes are similarly eclectic, ranging from folk and pop songs to classical music and opera. For the BBC radio show *Desert Island Discs* in 2003, and a similar selection of her favourite music for the BBC radio show *Paperback Writers* in 2016, Atwood's selections ranged from Bach and Beethoven to Tanya Tagaq and Neil Young.[1]

---

1   The *Desert Island Discs* selections are listed at <https://www.bbc.co.uk/pro-grammes/p00937l3> and those for *Paperback Writers* are at <https://www.bbc.co.uk/programmes/b0802npl>, both accessed 17 August 2025.

As a child, Atwood was subjected to the piano lessons that were then still a virtually mandatory part of a middle-class Canadian child's upbringing. The lessons evidently did not lead to mastery of keyboard skills but must have provided at least some knowledge of the rudiments of music. Atwood's first husband, Jim Polk, was a fine pianist and harpsichordist, and the couple attended Boston Symphony open rehearsals together. Perhaps inspired by his example, Atwood studied the recorder and attained a sufficiently proficient level to be able to play trio sonatas with Polk and a flautist friend. Choral singing was part of Atwood's early education; in secondary school she sang in a small choir and participated in school productions of the musical theatre standards *Oklahoma!* and *Brigadoon*. At the University of Toronto, Atwood contributed to theatrical revues and wrote occasional music reviews for the student newspaper, *The Varsity*.

Some Toronto-based musicians contemporary with Atwood include the classical pianist Glenn Gould (1932–1982), and the singer-songwriters Sylvia Tyson (b. 1940) and Gordon Lightfoot (1938–2023; he was born a year and a day before Atwood). Gould and Tyson both left their mark in fictional works by Atwood. The real name of Crake in *Oryx and Crake* (2003) is Glenn; he was named 'after a dead pianist, some boy genius with two n's' (70). In the story 'Isis in Darkness' from *Wilderness Tips* (1991), an unnamed folk singer who 'sang several mournful folk songs in a high, clear voice' (56) is clearly inspired by Tyson (Elliott 2006: 824). There are not many other musicians, fictional or otherwise, in Atwood's novels; the most substantial such character is West from *The Robber Bride* (1993). West is a musicologist at the University of Toronto; he plays the lute and spinet and is part of a cross-disciplinary research project with a team of neurophysiologists who are studying the effects of music on the brain. West's wife Tony is fearful that Xenia, the robber bride of the title, will steal West away from her, unaware that in fact Xenia long ago grew bored with West. West seems to be a conflation of two men in Atwood's life: her first husband Jim Polk, who like West was interested in early music, and her brother Harold Atwood, a neurophysiologist. Interestingly, West's cross-disciplinary research on music and the brain was prophetic, as the University of Toronto Faculty of Music in 2012 became home to the Music and Health Science Research Collaboratory, which is dedicated to fostering cross-disciplinary research in the fields of music and the health sciences.

Many Canadian composers have set Atwood's poems to music for voice(s) with instrumental accompaniment, including Aaron Davis (*Zombie Blizzard*, 2024), John Beckwith (*The Journals of Susanna Moodie*, 1972, rev. 1990), Stephen Chatman (*You Are Happy*, 1988), Timothy Corlis (*Notes Towards a Poem That Can Never be Written*, 2008), Thomas Kovacs (*Zodiac Driver*, 2004, rev. 2021); Patricia Morehead (*It Is Dangerous to Read Newspapers*, 1999), Bruce Pennycook (*Speeches for Dr. Frankenstein* for voice and electronics, 1981), Peter Skoggard (*Three Margaret Atwood Settings*, 2006 and *Half-Hanged Mary*, 2009) and E. Scott Wilkinson (*Memory*, 1997). The Toronto-based composer Dan Parr created an instrumental accompaniment in the style of Hollywood film-noir movie soundtracks to accompany a reading by Atwood of her poem 'Thriller Suite' for a concert by the Art of Time Ensemble in 2014.[2] The American singer-songwriter Orville Stoeber, with Atwood's blessing, provided varied settings of all fourteen hymns from *The Year of the Flood* (2009) for solo voice and instrumental accompaniment; the resulting CD was released at the same time as the novel, and Stoeber appeared with Atwood on a thirty-date book launch tour (Stoeber 2009).

Atwood has on occasion also been commissioned to write song lyrics. For the music group One Ring Zero's album *As Smart as We Are* (2004), which included lyrics by seventeen professional writers, Atwood contributed the words for 'Frankenstein Monster Song', which is sung on the album by Olivier Conan in a gravelly monotone somewhat in the manner of Leonard Cohen.[3] Atwood's most significant contribution to date as a writer of song lyrics is the cycle *Songs for Murdered Sisters*, written in 2018 and published in her poetry collection *Dearly* (2020). This set of eight songs (seven numbered poems plus a coda) was jointly commissioned by Houston Grand Opera

---

2   The performance can be seen at <https://youtu.be/Z_MBtkz_p8E>, accessed 17 August 2025.

3   Conan created a video for the song, which can be seen at <https://www.youtube.com/watch?v=7R4Ja2ko-Qg>, accessed 17 August 2025.

and Ottawa's National Arts Centre Orchestra for the Canadian baritone
Joshua Hopkins and was set to music by the American composer Jake
Heggie. In 2015, Hopkins's sister Nathalie Warmerdam and two other
women were all murdered within hours of one another by their ex-partner,
Basil Borutski. In response, Hopkins, Heggie and Atwood joined forces to
use their artistic talents to bring attention to the tragedy of gender-based
violence. 'I have known two women who were murdered, both by jealous
former romantic partners, so the killing of Joshua's sister resonated with
me,' Atwood noted. 'But I could not promise anything: with songs and
poems, they either arrive or they don't. I then wrote the sequence in one
session. I made the "sisters" plural because they are indeed – unhappily –
very plural. Sisters, daughters, mothers. So many.'[4] The song cycle, in a
first version for baritone and piano, was completed in February 2020 and
recorded later that year in both film and audio versions by Hopkins with
Heggie at the piano.[5] A second version with orchestral accompaniment,
completed in March 2020, was premiered by Hopkins with the National
Arts Centre Orchestra in Ottawa in 2023. Heggie notes that in the cycle,
the singer (Hopkins) is similar to the wanderer in Schubert's song cycle
Winterreise (Winter's Journey): 'He walks through the world wondering
how to make sense of this event and put the pieces together, filled with grief
and rage, on a quest for connection and transformation.'[6] The poignant,
profoundly moving and beautifully written cycle has received uniformly
high praise from reviewers.

Atwood's activities as a librettist date back to her high-school years.
In 1956, when she was in Grade 12, she wrote a short skit titled *Synthesia –
Operetta in One Act* for performance in her home economics class at Leaside
High School. The skit praises the qualities of synthetic fabrics and includes
six or seven songs set to pre-existing tunes (Elliott 2006: 826). Her first
professional libretto was commissioned by the CBC; Atwood was asked

---

4   From the website <https://songsformurderedsisters.com/>, accessed 17 August 2025.
5   The audio recording was released on Pentatone PTC 5186270 in 2021; the film,
    directed by James Niebuhr, was also released in 2021 and is available for viewing at
    <https://youtu.be/1vvjPKJi5So>, accessed 17 August 2025.
6   Liner notes for Pentatone PTC 5186270 (2021).

to create a text for a choral composition that was to be written by John Beckwith celebrating the 400th anniversary of Shakespeare's birth in 1564. The resulting work, *The Trumpets of Summer*, was first heard in a studio performance broadcast on CBC radio in November 1964. Atwood's text is about the place of Shakespeare in Canadian life and was inspired by the success of the recently established Stratford Festival in Ontario. The choral work, just over half an hour in duration, was subsequently heard several times in live performance and was recorded by Toronto's Festival Singers under the conductor Elmer Iseler in 1969.[7] A subsequent CBC commission for Atwood was for the radio series Anthology in 1970 and is titled *Oratorio for Sasquatch, Man and Two Androids*. Atwood requested that electronic music be used for the background music of the production and specified the types of voices to be used for the speaking roles. The work, published by the CBC in 1970, is a dark parable about the destruction of the natural world by mankind, whose destructive urges are voiced, ironically, by the two androids (Weaver 1970).[8]

Atwood's first libretto for a music theatre piece for professional performers was *Masque*, created in 1977 with the composer Raymond Pannell and the choreographer Ann Ditchburn. The work was workshopped by the National Ballet of Canada in April 1977 (retitled *Circe*), but after meeting with very negative reviews, it was scrapped and has never been revived, nor has Atwood's libretto been published.[9] Atwood's next effort was not much more successful. The Canadian Opera Company (COC) paired her with the composer Randolph Peters, who had recently scored a success for the COC with his opera *The Golden Asse* (1999), to a libretto by Robertson Davies (who had died before the music for the opera was completed). Peters and Atwood considered various subjects for their proposed opera, including John Gardner's 1971 novel *Grendel*, a story from

---

7   CBC SM 81 / RCI 340 / Capitol Records LP ST-6323 (1969), reissued on Centrediscs CMC CD 9103 (2003).

8   An erratum slip notes that the first 11 lines of *Oratorio for Sasquatch, Man and Two Androids* as printed are not by Atwood.

9   The manuscript of *Masque/Circe* is in the Margaret Atwood Papers in the Thomas Fisher Rare Book Library, University of Toronto, in MS Coll 200, box 41, files 9–11.

Ray Bradbury's *The Martian Chronicles*, and the life of Pauline Johnson (1861–1913), a Canadian writer and performance artist of mixed Mohawk and English parentage. Atwood completed a libretto on this last subject, but Peters was not happy with it and so a new one was created, titled *Inanna's Journey*, about Inanna, the ancient Sumerian goddess of love, fertility, and war. The music for *Inanna's Journey* that had been completed to date was given workshop performances in 2004 and 2005. A mainstage production was planned for the COC's 2006–07 season and again for the 2007–08 season, but ill-health prevented Peters from finishing the score in time (the composer later stated that he had completed and orchestrated 90% of it) (Terauds 2013). With the death in 2007 of Richard Bradshaw, the COC artistic director who had been championing the project, *Inanna's Journey* was dropped from the COC's plans and has never been performed.[10]

Meanwhile, Atwood's libretto for *Pauline*, which Peters had passed over, enjoyed a second life. In 2006, a new chamber opera company titled City Opera Vancouver (COV) was founded, and Charles Barber, the artistic director of COV, approached Atwood for a libretto. She suggested a revision of *Pauline* for chamber forces, and in 2008 Christos Hatzis was chosen as the composer for a scaled-down two-act version of *Pauline*. The plan was to premiere the opera as part of the arts programming for the 2010 Vancouver Winter Olympics. This proposal was not accepted by the Canadian Olympic Committee, and eventually, when a definite plan for the production of the opera did not materialise, Hatzis withdrew from the project.[11] The Vancouver-based composer Tobin Stokes replaced Hatzis in 2012. After a series of workshop performances in 2013, *Pauline* was premiered in Vancouver's York Theatre in May 2014. Set in Vancouver in 1913 during the final days in the life of the Canadian writer Pauline Johnson, the opera revolves around a struggle between Johnson and her strait-laced sister Eva over how Johnson's life story will be told and remembered.[12] The

---

10 A workshop performance of *City of Dust*, the prologue to the opera, can be heard on SoundCloud at <https://soundcloud.com/randolphpeters/city-of-dust>, accessed 17 August 2025.

11 Hatzis, Christos, Email communication, 16 August 2003.

12 Details about the opera are in the programme book for the premiere performance, available from the COV website at <http://cityoperavancouver.com/wordpress/

libretto unfolds in a series of vignettes and incorporates words by Johnson seamlessly into the narrative. Atwood's involvement brought international attention to the production, and the five shows in the small (371-seat) theatre were sold out. The original cast travelled to Quebec City for a subsequent concert performance of the opera in 2015.

The most frequently performed and by far most written about musical stage work to date based on a text by Atwood is the operatic version of her novel *The Handmaid's Tale*. This opera was commissioned by the Royal Theatre in Copenhagen from the composer Poul Ruders at the initiative of the British opera administrator Elaine Padmore, who was the company's Artistic Director from 1993 to 2000. It was Ruders's first full-length opera, and it was he who chose Atwood's novel as the subject matter for the commission. Ruders read the novel in 1992, and later told an interviewer that 'This book has it all: forbidden love, hope, desperation, violence, tenderness, public executions, grandiose processions. It is a vast drama all the way through, one that begs to be set to music' (Hvidt 2000).

The British actor, singer and writer Paul Bentley was tasked with turning Atwood's novel into a libretto (Bentley 2005).[13] Ruders and Bentley did not know each other prior to working on the opera together; it was Padmore who brought them together. Early on in the process, Atwood met with Ruders and gave her blessing to the project, but after the contract for the opera was completed (which took almost two years), she seems to have had little to no input into the adaptation. Bentley's libretto was written in English and the opera has been performed in English outside of Denmark; for the premiere in Copenhagen, it was performed in a Danish translation by the composer.[14] The opera is scored for a dozen vocal soloists, chorus and large orchestra, including digital keyboards, organ, a large percussion

wp-content/uploads/2014/06/City_Opera_Pauline_Programme.pdf>, accessed 22 August 2023.

13 Other useful sources about the opera include a dedicated issue of *University of Toronto Quarterly* 75/3 (July 2006), which contains half a dozen articles on both the novel and the opera; Canton (2007); Rasmussen (2007); and Reichenbächer (2021).

14 The premiere production in Danish from March 2000 was issued as a live recording: *Tjenerindens Fortælling / The Handmaid's Tale*, conducted by Michael Schønwandt, Dacapo CD 8.224465-66 (released in January 2021).

section and sound effects; Ruders later prepared a reduced orchestration of the opera for productions by smaller companies. Eric Domville notes that 'The frequent barrages of brass and percussion create a metallic edge to the sound, engendering a pervasive atmosphere of unease and terror' (2006: 878). Ruders's eclectic score draws upon diverse styles, ranging from freely tonal to stridently dissonant music, and includes occasional quotations, notably of the hymn 'Amazing Grace'. Ruders's music and Bentley's libretto were both widely praised by critics; indeed, the opera was so warmly received during its premiere performances that several other companies soon took it up. Productions ensued in London (2003), Minneapolis (2003) and Toronto (2004). After the huge success of the Hulu / MGM Television adaptation of *The Handmaid's Tale* in 2017, the opera was given a new lease on life with performances in Melbourne (2018) and Boston (2019). After a hiatus caused by COVID-19, new productions were also given in London (2022), Copenhagen (2022), Greenville, South Carolina (2023), Freiburg (2024), and San Francisco (2024). Reviewing the English National Opera's second production of *The Handmaid's Tale* in 2022, Matthew Rye noted that 'The opera makes for a tough, harrowing evening in the theatre [...] But it is also compelling, as both drama and music. Ruders's rather wide-ranging musical style, encompassing everything from dissonant clusters to gospel, is highly effective in conveying both the inhumanity and humanity on display' (Rye 2022). Atwood attended the Copenhagen premiere and also performances in London and Minneapolis, as well as the Toronto production by the Canadian Opera Company, where she received a rapturous reception from audiences when she appeared for a curtain call at the end of the performance.

The ballet world has also been drawn to Atwood's creative vision. In 2013, the Royal Winnipeg Ballet premiered a ballet version of *The Handmaid's Tale*, which was created at the initiative of the American choreographer Lila York. Atwood gave her blessing to the project, communicated with York about how to adapt the novel for ballet, and attended the premiere. Responding to criticisms that the original production was lacking in seriousness, York revised the work for a subsequent remounting in 2015 that was subsequently repeated in 2022. The revised version of the ballet is set to a pastiche score of pre-existing music by Leonard Bernstein, John Corigliano, James MacMillan, Andrzej Panufnik, Arvo Pärt and Alfred Schnittke. The Royal Winnipeg Ballet has performed *The Handmaid's Tale* for its home audience and also on tour in Alberta and Ottawa.

Equally as ambitious in scope as the Ruders/Bentley opera *The Handmaid's Tale* is the ballet *MADDADDAM*, which was commissioned by the National Ballet of Canada in association with Britain's Royal Ballet. Originally scheduled for November 2020, the premiere was delayed due to COVID-19 and took place in Toronto on 23 November 2022, five days after Atwood's 83rd birthday. Conceived by the British choreographer Wayne McGregor to an original score for orchestra and electronic sounds by the German-born British composer Max Richter, the ballet is inspired by Atwood's *MaddAddam* trilogy of novels. The 95-minute ballet unfolds in three acts of approximately equal duration titled Castaway, Extinctathon, and Dawn. Act 1 is scored mostly for orchestra, Act 2 is mostly for electronics (the orchestra leaves the pit after the first few minutes except for a few soloists) and Act 3 blends both orchestral and electronic sounds. In the programme book for the premiere, Atwood is listed as 'Creative Consultant'; she discussed the idea for the ballet with McGregor beginning in 2016 and worked with the British dramaturg Uzma Hameed to fashion the story arc for the ballet, but otherwise took a hands-off approach.[15] Speaking of her approach to adaptations in general, Atwood remarked, 'You can't control them. You have a choice to make: Do I give this person permission or not? I look at their work. I talk to them. And then I take a wild gamble' (Krashinsky Robertson 2022). Once again, Atwood received a wildly enthusiastic ovation from the Toronto audience when she appeared for a curtain call on opening night.

The most recent musical adaptation of the work of Atwood as of this writing is the opera *Oryx and Crake* with music by the German/Danish composer Søren Nils Eichberg to a libretto (in English) by the German novelist Hannah Dübgen based on Atwood's novel of the same title. The work was commissioned by the Hessisches Staatstheater Wiesbaden in

---

15 *MADDADDAM: Programme Book* (23–30 November 2022), National Ballet of Canada, 6.

Germany, which unveiled the first performance on 18 February 2023. A striking visual aspect of the production was the use of three-dimensional holographic projections created by the videographer Astrid Steiner. This is Eichberg's fifth opera, and it is scored for vocal soloists, choir, orchestra and electronic sounds. Like Ruders, Eichberg was drawn to the idea of setting Atwood's novel to music upon first reading it: 'I immediately fell in love with the novel Oryx and Crake (and its protagonist) [...] The characters and scenery immediately touched me and to me everything yearned for music' (Anonymous 2023). Atwood was predisposed to approve of an operatic treatment of this novel, and indeed had already envisaged such an adaptation as early as 2004, when she said 'I'm quite keen on doing Oryx and Crake as an opera. I think that would be quite bizarre. You'd have to have a number of uninhibited people willing to scamper around with parts of them painted blue, but that aside, I think it would make a really good opera' (Caldwell 2004). Initial reviews of the work are guardedly positive, and it remains to be seen if it will find a wider audience as the Ruders/Bentley opera has.

It is a mark of Atwood's prolific and multifaceted creativity that while music does not rank in the first tier of her interests, she has nevertheless left a profound mark on the musical world of her time, specifically through her work as a writer of texts for music, and more generally as an inspiration to a diverse and wide range of musicians. Recent activities as of this writing (August 2025) include a collaboration with the artist David Mack on a story based on Tori Amos's song 'Silent All These Years' for a graphic novel titled *Little Earthquakes: The Graphic Album* celebrating the 30th anniversary of the release of Amos's debut solo album,[16] and contributing recitations of seven of her poems from *Dearly*, paired with musical settings of those poems by Aaron Davis, for the recording of the song cycle *Zombie Blizzard* by the soprano Measha Brueggergosman-Lee with the Hannaford Street Silver Band.[17] Given the expansiveness of her output, it seems a safe bet that there will be many other future musical responses to the creative world of Margaret Atwood.

16   New York: Z2 Comics, 2022.
17   Leaf Music LM277 (2024).

Dunja M. Mohr

Refusing the Griselda Game: Fairy Tale Politics in Margaret Atwood's 'Impatient Griselda'

> The fairies gave up on humans years ago. We have been left to ourselves.
>
> (Jack Zipes 2023, xii)

We all grow up with stories. We tell and we listen to stories. We reconstruct and co-shape our world(s) through storytelling as a process of becoming aware of ourselves, our surroundings and our relations. Yet, although '[w]e live in a sea of stories, and like the fish who [...] will be the last to discover water, we have our own difficulty grasping what it is like to swim in stories' (Bruner 1996: 147). Over her long literary career, Margaret Atwood has repeatedly emphasized the importance of storytelling, something humans all over the world, in all cultures do[1]: 'Human beings are creative storytelling beings, they make art, because that is what human beings do' (2020). Storytelling is also a formidable power tool. Who shapes the narrative? Atwood's poem 'True Stories' (1981) rejects the notion of storytelling as a linear or exclusive truth bearer, demands contextualization and points to diffraction:

> Don't ask for the true story
> [....]
> The true story was lost
> on the way down to the beach;
> [....]

---

1   In her latest essay collection *Burning Questions* (2022), Atwood continues to explore, among many other topics, what function art has, what hope it might carry, the relationship between artist, text and reader, the power of words, politics and art, and storytelling's intricate relation to real world building, the imagination of (future) worlds and our realities being tied to '[w]hat kind of story [...] we think we're in, [...]? Because the answer will, in part, determine the outcome' (208).

The true story lies among the other stories;
a mess of colors, like jumbled clothing,
[....]
The true story is vicious
and multiple, and untrue
after all.

This unease with mono-perspectivism is symptomatic of Atwood's literary writings that delightfully bask in complex indeterminacies and multiple meanings, swimming in the 'notoriously slippery' (Atwood 2005: 173) pool of language and its poetic gaps. Critics have repeatedly analysed these recurring features of multiple versions and open endings, the ambiguity of metaphors, character and voice doubling, mirror imagery, duplicity, split selves and the chorus of perspectives, asking readers to negotiate between the narrative deceptions, the multiple truths and the story versions in her works. While 'Atwood's characteristic doubleness of vision' (Howells 1996: 4) certainly forms an integral part of Atwood's narrative style, her twenty-first-century texts often expand into multiplicity and multiple diffractions (e.g. the *MaddAddam* trilogy).[2] Unsurprisingly, Atwood is an unremitting expert at rewriting, palimpsesting and pilfering from the so-called literary canon and its themes, topics and myths, joyously 'signal[ling] a self-conscious engagement with the works of writers who have gone before her' (Tolan 2021: 109). These 'intertextual echoes' (Tolan 2021: 109) prominently include Shakespeare, Ovid, Homer, Mary Shelley, Swift, Orwell and The Brothers Grimm.

As an avid but critical reader of fairy tales, Atwood repeatedly draws on and refashions fairy tale lore in her work, typically from a feminist perspective, updating the older stories' 'archetypal motifs, characters, and narratives' (Appleton 2009: 7) for contemporary readers.[3] For Atwood,

2   See, for instance, Grace (1980; 1981); Lecker (1981); Relke (1983); Stovel (1986); Mycak (1996); Parkin-Gounelas (2004); Mohr (2005); Reed (2009); and Michael (2010).
3   Some of Atwood's works already openly employ fairy tales in their titles – *Bluebeard's Egg*, *The Robber Bride* – others include (inverse or satirized) often several overlapping fairy tale motifs or strategies, e.g. *The Edible Woman* (The Robber Bridegroom, Cinderella, The Gingerbread Man), *Lady Oracle* (Rapunzel, The Little Mermaid,

Refusing the Griselda Game   169

the Brothers Grimm's fairy tale compilation has been 'the most influential book I ever read' (Sandler 1977: 14). Exactly *because* 'many of these tales were originally told and retold by women [...] [who] left their mark' (Atwood 2005: 183), she argues, fairy tales comprise a whole cosmos of fictional characters and moral choices. Fairy tales have repeatedly been criticized for their often one-dimensional portrayal of female characters as submissive, passive and object prize status, in short for their misogynist and patriarchal content. Yet, as Atwood argues, we get a surprisingly 'wide range of heroines in these tales' (2005: 183), from 'passive good girls' to 'adventurous, resourceful women' as well as 'foolish ones' 'and a variety of evil witches', 'bad stepmothers', and 'wicked ugly sisters and false brides' (2005: 185).

While the exact evolution of the (Western European) literary fairy tale genre with its set phrases, highly symbolic language, recurring narrative patterns, stock characters and settings is a matter of scholarly debate, it is historically confirmed that the fairy tales' origin is orality.[4] It is 'a many-tongued genre, a cultural palimpsest' (Teverson 2013: 5) told and retold 'in a process of incremental adaptation generation by generation in the different cultures of the people who cross-fertilized the oral tales and disseminated them' (Zipes 2001: xi),[5] resulting in an overboarding 'plurisignification' (Teverson 2013: 6) that invites a variety of critical approaches (historical,

---

The Red Shoes), *The Heart Goes Last* (Hänsel and Gretel), *The Handmaid's Tale* and *The Blind Assassin* (Little Red Riding Hood) and Griselda in *Old Babes in the Wood*. There exists a considerable body of secondary literature on the use of fairy tale archetypes in Atwood's work. See, for instance, Fee (1993), Barzilai (2000), Wilson (2008; 1993/2010), and Appleton (2009).

4   For an overview of the genre and its origins, definitions, topics, themes and approaches, see Jack Zipes's *The Oxford Companion to Fairy Tales* (2015) and *The Irresistible Fairy Tale* (2012), Marina Warner's *Fairy Tale* (2018) and *Once Upon a Time* (2016) and Andrew Teverson's *Fairy Tale* (2013).

5   For the cross-cultural connections of the European and North American fairy tale, see Jack Zipes's essay 'Cross-Cultural Connections and the Contamination of the Classical Fairy Tale' (2001). For a more global perspective, see Mayako Murai and Luciana Cardi's *Re-Orienting the Fairy Tale: Contemporary Adaptations across Cultures* (2020).

folkloricist, literary, (post)structuralist, psychoanalytic, feminist and more). Many of the contemporary, seemingly timeless literary fairy tales that have come to dominate our collective memory – a 'global storytelling archive drawn upon by many cultures' (Tatar 2010: 57) – go back to a cross-cultural mesh of adapted anonymous oral folk tales and literary fairy tales by Giovanni Francesco Straparola (*Le piacevoli notti*, 1550–1553), Giambattista Basil (*Lo cunto de le cunti*, 1634–1636), Charles Perrault (*Histoires ou contes de temps passé*, 1697) and Jacob and Wilhelm Grimm (*Kinder- und Hausmärchen*, 1812–1815).

While '[m]etamorphosis', as Maria Tatar writes, is of course 'central to the fairy tale, which shows us figures shifting endlessly their shapes, crossing borders, and undergoing change', there is a didactic (and moral) intent, as these 'stories that traffic in transformation also seek to change listeners and readers in unconventional ways' (2010: 55). Unconventionality was a key element of many once popular literary fairy tales by bestselling female French *conteuses* – for instance, Marie-Catherine d'Aulnoy (*Les Contes des fées*, 1697) who also coined the very term 'fairy tale'; Marie-Jeanne L'Héritier (*Oeuvres meslées*, 1696), Henriette Julie Murat (*Histoires sublimes et allégoriques*, 1699) – writing against the increasingly stifling and repressive conservative seventeenth-century French society, where the clergy sought to ban art forms and railed at novels written by women for a largely female readership. However, their radical gender reversal fairy tales geared at an adult audience, critical of the patriarchy and its arranged marriages – but sometimes also running on an ambiguous morality – went out of fashion or were belittled as inauthentic.

It is this history of metamorphosis, ambiguities, regressive stereotypes and inequalities that Atwood's short story 'Impatient Griselda' toys with. Originally published online in May 2020 and then in *The Decameron Project: 29 New Stories from the Pandemic* (2020) – initiated by the editors of *The New York Times Magazine* in March 2020 as a contemporary writers' response to the COVID-19 pandemic modelled on Giovanni Boccaccio's *The Decameron* (1353) – and republished in Atwood's latest short story collection *Old Babes in the Wood* (2023), 'Impatient Griselda' is a witty combination of a pandemic narrative frame, a parodic feminist fairy tale rewriting of Boccaccio's Griselda and a tongue-in-cheek science fiction spoof.

Griselda has been a travelling text, circulating in various contexts and at different times for various purposes, predominantly constructed through male texts infused by patriarchal desires and morals to promote female submission or to undercut stereotypes about female sinfulness.[6] Griselda (*Decameron* X:10) is the last story in a long storytelling marathon in *The Decameron*, where ten aristocrats flee from Black-Death-ravaged Florence to the mountainous countryside and pass their time telling one hundred stories in ten days. This malicious and cynical tale of domestic and political domination and abuse is told by Dineo to sober up the aristocrats for the return to pandemic-ridden Florence and a life of endurance, pain and loss, adding a medieval-style trigger warning that the story about a vicious series of cruel tests and humiliations, relates 'a monstrous folly [...] I do not advise any to imitate' (Boccacio 1986: 781). In the story, the despotic Marquis of Saluzzo demands of his demure peasant bride to 'always seek to please him' (783). He sadistically pretends to murder their two children, sends placid Griselda back to her peasant father and, years later, stages a remarriage with a much younger bride (his own daughter in a covered incest allusion), ordering Griselda back as a servant to prepare the villa and the bride for the wedding. Stoically, Griselda submits to all ordeals, staying true to her promise of obedience, diligent service and patient endurance, proving that a truly noble character is precisely *not* tied to social status.[7] The story ends with the Marquis's confession that he sought 'to make trial of her patience' (784), testing her loyalty and Griselda's re-installment as his wife. Questionably, the zealous acceptance of absolute authority and the silent endurance of abuse are rewarded with a (contrived) happy ending.

---

6   Cf. for an overview Bronfman (2019).

7   Although Griselda never openly contradicts her husband, she does, however, voice a desire three times. Yet, each request is directly or indirectly linked to her children. She pleads not to expose her children's dead bodies to animals; she asks for a simple garment to cover her naked, now maternal body for the return to her father's house; and she protectively begs not to submit the child wife-to-be to the same ordeal she had to suffer.

Stressing morality and spirituality, Francesco Petrarch's Latin translation *Historia Griseldis* (1375) rather validates the inhuman testing with Griselda as a model of ideal feminine virtues and a Job-like figure. Geoffrey Chaucer's ironic response to Petrarch with 'The Clerk's Tale' in *The Canterbury Tales* (1387–1400) foregrounds materiality (clothes and gifts, etc.) and, undercutting the allegorical, seeks to entertain. Although shifting some elements and the tone and despite warnings not to imitate Griselda (Petrarch) or explicitly criticizing the Marquis/Walter (Chaucer), these two most immediate retellings largely stick to the misogynist tale of monstrous male brutality and female subordination and constancy *in extremis*. Only much later Perrault's ironical yet gallant dark fantasy version in the *Mother Goose Tales* (1697) casts Griselda rather as a deterrent example of how women should *not* be treated, clearly addressing her sufferings as senseless torture in an abusive marriage.

Atwood's 'Impatient Griselda' takes up Boccacio's pandemic frame story, but fuses it with a maximal defamiliarising but comic science fiction setting, assigning Dineo's role of the narrator to an unnamed alien of unspecified gender – obviously puzzled by human gender binaries, 'Thank you, Sir or Madam. I use both because quite frankly I can't tell the difference. We do not have such limited arrangements on our planet' (Atwood 2020: 69) – who looks like an octopus.[8] From this nonhuman, truly alien perspective on all matters human, the extraterrestrial 'mere entertainer' (70) retells, reinterprets, parodies and culturally adapts the 'ancient Earth story' (70) of Griselda 'as part of an intergalactical-crises aid package' of comfort narrations for locked-in, frightened humans endangered by a global pandemic (doubling us readers), 'No, you may not leave the quarantine room. The plague is out there. It would be too dangerous for you, though not for me. We do not have that type of microbe on our planet' (70), and trapped in a Lacanian state of anxiety because they

---

8   Possibly, this alludes to and satirizes the potentially threatening Kraken motif in English literature, e.g. the monstrous sea creature in Alfred Tennyson's 'The Kraken' sonnet (1830), or John Wyndham's alien invasion story *The Kraken* (1953), or China Miéville's more comical new weird portrayal of a venerable (occult) squid in *Kraken* (2010).

cannot clearly interpret the enigmatic other, the alien. With the help of a sometimes overwhelmed 'simultaneous translation device' (70) – which significantly adds to the story's comical tone, cultural mistranslations, misunderstandings and comical asides about puzzling human concepts such as nakedness,[9] and, metatextually, signposts as well as demonstrates the fairy tales' transgressive cultural translation history – the alien flippantly uses a rather casual vernacular.

The fairy tale is infused by the alien's ideological viewpoint, 'I was simply saying what I myself would have done in their place' (76), that jar with the fictional audience's (and our) expectations. Typically for Atwood, the female character is doubled. The twin sisters Patient and Impatient Griselda share the alien's inferior social status, and the alien's impatient replies to interruptions and advocacy of debatable courage underline a close affinity with Imp, potentially the alien's intratextual double. The twins are each other's opposites: Patient is submissive, docile, passive and obedient, whereas Impatient is outspoken, independent and actively refuses victimhood. Against emerging criticism of this retelling, the alien firmly requests narrative authority, 'Who is telling this story? I am. So there were two' (71), disclosing the storyteller's manipulative power on the metalevel.

The second significant change is the rather unusual end in which Impatient Griselda takes matters into her own hands and kills the Duke, a narrative development the abbreviations 'Pat' (for docility, easy to pat) and 'Imp' (for cunning intrepidity) foreshadow. This narrative twist holds up an uncomfortable mirror to the fictional audience, as it turns the usual contemporaneous readers' disgust at Griselda's infinite obedience into a disquiet at the alien's radical adaptation of the female submission story into a (violent) tale of liberation and retaliation, 'a militant feminist message of self-empowerment' (Däwes 2022: 12).

The alien entertainer's mission to reassure an obviously frightened audience with storytelling and snacks begins with a tongue-in-cheek cultural reference to Charles M. Schulz's ingenious Peanuts and sets the

---

9   That also includes the downright impossibility to immediately translate words that describe a cultural concept unknown to the other speaker, 'I regret that we do not have any snacks that are what you call vegan. We could not interpret this word' (69).

comical tone. The alien's questions and rebukes, 'Do you all have your comfort blankets?' and 'take your thumb out of your mouth, Sir-Madam' (69), unintentionally – and to the reader's amusement – recall a Linus-security-blanket, thumb-sucking moment. The alien chides the assumedly adult human audience for their childlike, inadequate behaviour – reminding "whimpering" members of the audience of their adult status 'No, you are not the children, Madam-Sir. You are 42' (69)[10] – and, at the same time, intimidates the audience, unsettled by the provision of blood-dripping raw meat snacks (a parody of the aristocrats' delicious food in *The Decameron*), by equating them with food, 'Those who are not snacks do not whimper' (76).

While the alien's orature comically mimics fairy tale dissemination, it also exposes the unreliability of the narrator. Much like the Craker Bluebeard at the end of Atwood's *MaddAddam* trilogy (2003–2013), who chooses which of the multiple possible endings he prefers, the alien takes liberties with the story, 'You didn't like this ending? It is not the usual one? Then which ending do you prefer?' (76). A story must resonate with the teller's personal and sociocultural perspective to be authentic, 'that ending is for a different story. Not one that interest me. I would tell that one badly. But I have told this one well, I believe—well enough to hold your attention, you must admit' (76), the alien explains, because what *really* matters is the audience's enchantment.

Atwood's intertextual game also palimpsests female rewritings of Griselda.[11] Christine de Pizan's adaptation of the Griselda theme in *The Book of the City of Ladies* (1404–1405) defends women against misogynist morals and negative characterizations and secularizes Griselda in Book 2 as a dignified, self-assertive woman of many virtues with her own agency, qualities the character Impatient Griselda displays, albeit in a much

---

10   For the initiated science fiction aficionados the number 42 is, of course, Deep Thought's answer to the 'Ultimate Question of Life, the Universe and Everything' in Douglas Adams's famous science fiction comedy *The Hitchhiker's Guide to the Galaxy* (1979–2009).

11   For a cross-cultural analysis of female Griselda story rewritings, see Smarr (2018: 205–229).

more deadly manner. Maria Edgeworth's novella *The Modern Griselda* (1804) foreshadows a doubling of Griselda characters when the (rather antithetical) 'modern' Griselda Bolingbroke – who first continuously tests her husband's devotion and uncompromising commitment to her until she *chooses* subordination much to his dismay – is confronted with her medieval alter ego at a reading, revealing how the unrelenting twisted ideals of womanhood ultimately (re)produce monsters.[12] Caryl Churchill's all-female feminist transhistorical drama about a rather brittle (universal) female solidarity in *Top Girl* (1982) presents a cacophony of historical and literary female characters and a feminist critique of Griselda's class-conscious self-objectification and martyrdom as a too often normalized female complicity with the patriarchy. It is this complicity Atwood's text denies and, instead, celebrates female solidarity. At the same time, the fictional audience's outspoken recoiling from Imp's unexpected violence – we get this audience reaction only through the alien's narrative filter, 'Excuse me? What is WTF?' (75) – and lack of reaction to Pat's fatalism, demasks the hypocritical moral doublespeak.

While Angela Carter's unpublished translation of Perrault's text, 'The Patience of Grizelda' (MS 88899/1/43), stresses the 'outstanding "patience" in the double sense of suffering and bearing pain or hardship without complaint' (De la Rochère 79–80), Atwood's story title instead marks the opposite, unruly impatience, an intentional deviation from the original story. Deeply critical of literature's 'recycled Patient Griseldas' (Carter 1979: 201), Carter's grim parody foregrounds Griselda, minus the litany about female obedience and passivity,[13] but uses Griselda as

---

12 In *The Modern Griselda*, another character, Emma Granby, partially takes on the role of the patient 'Griselda' wife, the 'pattern wife—a perfect Grizzle' (*Modern Griselda*), yet also displays rationality, a capacity that Griselda 'a petty, selfish, over-indulged child in place of a woman' (Langdon 2012: 9) lacks.

13 Carter has keenly clipped the story, cutting digressions and excessive descriptions, clearly characterising the prince as an abusive, misogynist psychopath. Her translation rather focuses on showing 'how a feudal system sustained by religious dogma and a misogynistic culture breeds oppression and misery in women, who go so far as to endorse their inhuman treatment and that of their daughter in the name of wifely submission, piety and virtue' (De la Rochére 2022: 79).

a 'hidden intertext' for 'The Bloody Chamber', her feminist rewriting of Bluebeard, 'pit[ting] religious myth against the fairy tale tradition to explore sadomasochism and the danger of internalizing patriarchal dictates exalting self-sacrifice and martyrdom' (De la Rochère 2022: 88). 'The Bloody Chamber' amplifies the nascent disobedience of the initially submissive child-like naïve wife by introducing a female double, here the wife's mother who, improbably, rides to her daughter's rescue at the very last minute and shoots the cruel Marquis. Refusing to play the Griselda game in Atwood's story and upending gendered expectations, Imp similarly comes to Pat's rescue, outsmarts the Duke, cuts his throat and then, in a narrative surprise move, the twins 'ate the Duke all up—bones, brocaded robes, and all' (75) in an act of anthropophagy, breaking a cultural taboo, as the fictional human audience immediately notes, that fairy tales, however, topicalize (e.g. in 'Hänsel and Gretel' the witch plans to fatten up Hänsel for later consummation).[14] Allegorically, the twins completely eradicate misogyny, patriarchy and sadism when they also eat the 'few suspicious relatives of the Duke [that] came sniffing around' (76).

Impatient Griselda, one could argue, represents position four, the creative non-victim, in the Canadian survival story (cf. Atwood *Survival* 1972). The refusal to play the Griselda game of female subjugation, rejecting victimization by tyrants and turning it into one of female resistance, serves as an inspiration for the physically and psychologically locked-in audience(s). The alien fairy tale mission contributes to human psychological survival, providing a form of escape from the pandemic through a moment of mental relief.[15] While storytelling fosters an emotional distancing from the pandemic, the fairy tales' content encourages the identification with Impatient Griselda and thus physical survival, fighting back against the physical threat the Duke represents, as an act of solidarity. Like Boccacio's Dineo, whose story prepares his audience for the return to plague-infested

---

14 Similar acts of consummation can be found in *The Robber Bride*, where the central character Zenia – another unreliable, manipulative narrator who offers various, conflicting stories or (un)truths about her past – metaphorically devours her friends' partners.

15 See Marcus (2020).

Florence, the alien's refashioned fairy tale leaves the audience with a sense of reinstated control and prepares the audience for a post-pandemic new normal that might demand changed attitudes. The alien's exit phrase, 'I hope the plague will be over soon, too. Then I can get back to *my* normal life' (76; my emphasis), reminds us that normalities too come in the plural and are very different, indicating that the human sense of normality will need to adapt to a post-pandemic future. The narratologically alienating setup of 'Impatient Griselda' and the fairy tale's retelling as a story of empowerment dare the human audience, including us, to imagine alternatives to traditional stories and to question a story's ending. It is from fairy tales and their potential to destabilise culturally learned behaviour and to expand our imagination that Atwood learned how powerful stories and words are, 'And where else could I have gotten the idea, so early in life, that words can change you?' (Atwood 1993: 292). New situations require changes and adaptations. We need to transform our stories if we want to find alternative solutions to messy and frightening situations and desire changed outcomes. Symbolically the alien leads the way, as they culturally and linguistically adjust to the new human cultural contact and physically modify in order to casually slide underneath the door at the end of the story, 'I'll just ooze out underneath the door. It is so useful not to have a skeleton' (76). If we read the alien as the symbol of storytelling, then freeing stories of narrow, traditional story skeletons give us all the liberties we need to explore new realms that may trigger surprising new story arcs. Because stories are multiple and arbitrary by nature, the truth of a story is essentially unattainable, obliterated by a layer of stories, as Atwood's 'True Stories' insinuates, 'The true story lies among the other stories', because stories inherently come in the plural.

Fiona Tolan

Feminist Killjoys: Happiness, Feminism and Troublemaking in Margaret Atwood's Fiction

As Margaret Atwood's 2010 novel *The Heart Goes Last* draws to its conclusion, the increasingly hectic narrative veers off into a kind of madcap zany comedy of mistaken identities, sexbots and Elvis impersonators. It begins, however, very persuasively, in post-economic-crash America, with Charmaine and Stan, having suffered redundancy and foreclosure on their dream home, surviving hand-to-mouth and living in their car. Atwood provides a vision of economic precarity in which a white, middle-class couple are suddenly plunged into the kind of subsistence living more commonly experienced by lower socioeconomic groups and 'subordinated ethnoracial others' (Engles 2018: 224). In desperation and seduced by marketing promises of 'maximum possible happiness' ('Who wouldn't tick that box?'), the couple sign up to a mysterious 'social experiment' that involves dividing their time between a picket-fence fantasy of 1950s suburbia and incarceration in a privately-run prison (Atwood 2010: 41).

Stan and Charmaine's pursuit of happiness via a highly securitised, gated, suburban community is rooted in fear, a retreat from trauma, and conservative nostalgia. Tim Engles contextualises the novel within the crisis of white masculinity, commonly diagnosed as a response to the feminist and civil rights movements of the mid-to-late twentieth century that prompted in white American men a 'desired return to previous eras of seemingly unchallenged eminence' (2018: 5). While Stan is certainly a study of anxious, left-behind middle-class masculinity – a software engineer whose employer 'packed up and moved west', leaving him overqualified and 'without a parachute' (8) – the novel also speaks loudly to female nostalgia for a fantasised, pre-feminist world of suburban housewifery.

In imagining Consilience, the gated-community/prison that Charmaine persuades Stan to join, Atwood literalises the second-wave feminist construction of the domestic sphere as a site of incarceration. Recalling seminal works such as Betty Friedan's *The Feminine Mystique* (1963), in which Friedan notoriously describes the white middle-class suburban homes of America as 'comfortable concentration camps' (336), and Germaine Greer's designation in *The Female Eunuch* (1970) of housewives as 'life contracted unpaid workers' or 'slaves' (329), second-wave feminism addressed itself to liberating women from the shackles of domesticity. In Atwood's novel, however, Charmaine dreams of such confinement. When Stan asks what she does during their weeks apart in the gender-segregated prison, her description ironically apes a vision of 1950s homemaking: 'We knit a lot [...] And there are the vegetable gardens, and the cooking [...] And the laundry of course. [...] I'm never bored! The days just fly by!' (Atwood 2010: 45). In her eagerness to subscribe to the Consilience project and its proffered protections from destitution, despite its evidently murky motivations, Charmaine represents the historical complicity of white middle-class women in accepting limitations on their freedom in exchange for domestic security and calling it happiness.

Such complicity is precisely what Simone de Beauvoir identifies and rails against in *The Second Sex*. In that pathbreaking 1949 study, Beauvoir tackles early on the thorny question of happiness, asking: 'are women in a harem not happier than a woman voter? Is a housewife not happier than a woman worker?' Rhetorical questions to which she then responds: 'We cannot really know what the word "happiness" means, and still less what authentic values it covers; there is no way to measure the happiness of others, and it is always easy to call a situation that one would like to impose on others *happy*' (16). For Beauvoir, committed to an existentialist philosophy of self-determination and the attainment of full subjectivity through the transcendence of brutish immanence, the pursuit of happiness is a false path, leading to 'stagnation' and 'immobility'. In focusing instead on 'the individual's possibilities' – what a person can and should strive to be – 'we will define these possibilities', she argues, 'not in terms of happiness but in terms of freedom' (16–17).

A similar suspicion of happiness will later pervade *The Feminine Mystique*. Indeed, happiness is Freidan's starting point in her exposition of what she calls 'the problem with no name' (1963 [2010]: 5). Examining the failure of the 'Happy Housewife Heroine' of post-war America to sustain pleasure and fulfilment through homemaking, Friedan documents a cohort of affluent, college-educated women exhibiting a host of psychosomatic symptoms and inconveniently confessing themselves to be unhappy (21). More recently, in *The Promise of Happiness* (2010), Sara Ahmed takes up this same feminist critical thread and builds on the work of late twentieth and twenty-first century feminist, black and queer criticism to argue that happiness is a tool 'used to justify oppression'. From the racist myth of 'the happy slave', to the heteronormative sentimentalising of 'the Angel in the house', feminist, black and queer political movements, suggests Ahmed, have commonly 'struggled *against* rather than *for* happiness' (2). Once happiness is better understood as acquiescence to the status quo and as a means to ameliorate the discomfort of others by suppressing any troublesome dissatisfactions of one's own, it is stripped of its veneer of contentment and exposed instead as an oppressive obligation. Crucially, for Ahmed, those who resist the conformity of the 'happiness script' – those who fail in 'passing as happy' – are typically vilified as troublemakers and their unhappiness located in their own internal failings rather than in any external systems of repression (59).

Atwood's fiction typically speaks to this feminist history of troublemaking. Repeatedly, from her earliest writings through to her most recent, Atwood's protagonists might be described as 'feminist killjoys' – women who, to borrow Ahmed's words, 'kill joy simply by not finding the objects that promise happiness quite so promising' (65). We can trace this function from Marian in *The Edible Woman* (1969), who confounds Peter by rejecting his marriage proposal, through Iris in *The Blind Assassin* (2000), who exposes her husband Richard as an abuser and eventually leaves him, to Agnes in *The Testaments* (2019), who resists an arranged marriage and becomes a defector from the authoritarian state of Gilead. Against this backdrop of feminist killjoys, Charmaine in *The Heart Goes Last* stands out in her determination to resist troublesome thoughts and remain cheerful. When the pressures of precarious living threaten to make Charmaine uncharacteristically 'irritable', 'she tries her best to stamp on that feeling and look on the bright side, because what's the use of complaining?' (4). Seemingly incongruent within Atwood's canon of troublesome women and feminist killjoys, Charmaine's habitual pep and cheer is soon revealed, however, as a defence against barely repressed trauma. As a victim of child abuse who dreams of security, she calls on our sympathies, but she is also a complicated and problematic figure. Later in this essay, I examine Charmaine alongside Agnes in *The Testaments* – both products of damaging childhoods, both coached in 'passing as happy' – and consider how their different choices and outcomes speak to Atwood's reflections on feminist troublemaking.

Troublesome Women

Atwood has long resisted the label 'feminist'. When Mervyn Rothstein, interviewing her for *The New York Times* in 1986 on the publication of *The Handmaid's Tale*, termed the book 'a feminist tract', she replied acerbically: 'Novels are not slogans. [...] If I wanted to say just one thing I would hire a billboard'. More than thirty years later, in one of the many interviews prompted by the 2017 Hulu television adaptation of the same novel, Atwood responds to being asked if she is a feminist writer by pressing the interviewer:

> Tell me what you mean. I don't sign blank cheques. Do you mean a 1972 feminist who felt that women were betraying their gender to have sex with men? I'm not that kind of feminist. And I'm not the kind that thinks trans women are not women. So you tell me what you mean and I'll tell you if I am one. (Conroy 2018)

The acuity with which Atwood parses the proposed label speaks to her keen awareness that the history of feminism is fractured and often fractious, with many different and occasionally contradictory incarnations gathered beneath the umbrella term 'feminism'. Nevertheless, and despite her best efforts to advise nuance and caution, she is seemingly irresistibly coded in popular consciousness as a feminist writer. This is largely due to the phenomenal and resurgent success of *The Handmaid's Tale*; as a now classic work of dystopian fiction, the novel has entered the popular lexicon as a feminist text. The Handmaids' red cloak and white bonnet have become in recent years a global symbol of protest, and women dressed as Handmaids have protested anti-abortion legislation in America, Ireland, Poland and Argentina. The success of the Handmaid's uniform as a symbol of political protest is intimately bound up with its aesthetics. The costume, as Atwood observes, speaks silently but eloquently to 'the requisitioning of women's bodies by the state'; as a visual symbol, the stark white cap contrasted against the bright-red, full-length cloak, like a patch of snow in a pool of blood, attracts attention while carefully evading potential arrest for noisy disturbance or censure for immodesty (Beaumont and Holpuch 2018). Protestors dressed as Handmaids, as Atwood observes, can sit in a courtroom or a legislature building and loudly and eloquently register their protest without saying a word.

These contemporary incarnations of protesting Handmaids join a long line of Atwood's troublesome women: female characters in her work that resist social pressures to be silent, submissive or simply happy with their lot. These characters are rarely self-identified feminists: indeed, very few such women exist in Atwood's work. Most notably, it is in two of her 1980s novels – *The Handmaid's Tale* (1985) and *Cat's Eye* (1988) – that Atwood specifically depicts feminist activists, in scenes that look back at certain points to the radical feminism of the 1970s. *The Handmaid's Tale* provides three separate vignettes of the early activism of Offred's mother: scenes in which she is depicted burning pornographic magazines in the park (48), returning bruised and bleeding from the 'abortion riots' (189) and marching at a feminist rally, where placards are waved that read:

TAKE BACK THE NIGHT [...] RECAPTURE OUR BODIES. DO YOU BELIEVE A WOMAN'S PLACE IS ON THE KITCHEN TABLE? Under the last sign there's a line drawing of a woman's body, lying on a table, blood dripping out of it. (130)

If Offred's mother is repeatedly figured in terms of public acts of feminist resistance and defiance, in *Cat's Eye*, instead, Elaine encounters feminism via consciousness-raising sessions in church halls, where 'Things are being said that I have never consciously thought about before. Things are being overthrown. Why, for instance, do we shave our legs? Wear lipstick? [...] Alter our shapes? What is wrong with us the way we are?' (343). In both of these novels, significantly, Atwood's protagonists feel excluded from the activism they encounter: Offred is too young and too disinterested in her mother's politics, while Elaine, as a young married mother, struggles to find a feminist praxis that speaks to her life. She feels implicitly excluded from the group: 'Women like me,' she reflects, 'with a husband, a child, have been referred to with some scorn as "nukes", for *nuclear family*. *Pronatalist* is suddenly a bad word' (344). *Cat's Eye* in particular here speaks to a historical moment when a mode of grassroots feminist activism was effecting social change but arguably leaving many women behind.

Atwood, like her near contemporary Doris Lessing – another woman writer with a famously prickly relationship with second-wave feminism – engages closely with feminist debates while resisting the overtures of the feminist movement. Famously stung by the almost exclusively feminist readings of *The Golden Notebook*, which she felt had ignored the novel's larger, more complex themes, Lessing later regretted that her necessary efforts to resist feminism's limitations left her in 'a false position' – 'for the last thing I have wanted to do', muses Lessing ten years later, 'was to refuse to support women' (Lessing 1973: 8). In her obituary of Lessing, written for *The Guardian* in 2013, Atwood likens her to the more readily feminist-affiliated Adrienne Rich, describing both as 'pivotal' in the landscape of twentieth-century writing: 'situated at the moment when the gates of the gender disparity castle were giving way' (Atwood 2013). If Atwood, like Lessing, resists a feminist affiliation that she deems too restrictive and too proprietorial of her work, I am interested in tracing the manner in which her novels, regardless of authorial reticence, espouse a persuasive politics that the writer herself is reluctant to name. We trace this politics, I suggest, by paying attention to Atwood's catalogue of female troublemakers.

Passing as Happy

Early on in *The Handmaid's Tale*, Offred recalls encountering a group of Japanese tourists who ask her and her fellow Handmaid Ofglen, via their interpreter, '*Are they happy?*' Ofglen says nothing, but understanding that silence can be dangerous, Offred replies: 'Yes, we are very happy', inwardly reflecting, 'I have to say something. What else can I say?' (39). Offred's public affirmation of happiness is demanded by the state: it signifies her submission and aids (but does not assure) her safety. Only in her private reflections can she articulate her sense of grief and loss. Returning to Gilead fifteen years after Offred's story ends, *The Testaments* radically expands the original novel's claustrophobic first-person account into three distinct narrative voices: Aunt Lydia's clandestine holograph, and the recorded testimonies of Agnes, a young woman raised in Gilead, and Nicole, a teenager raised in Canada. Of these three accounts, Agnes's is closest to Offred's. As the daughter of a Commander and his Wife, rather than a Handmaid, hers is a life of relative privilege, but it is similarly circumscribed by home and a limited sphere of state-sanctioned female activity, and she is similarly subject to the pressures of the regime, which demands of her, not just loyalty, but joyful obedience. Responding as a child to her mother's anxious questioning, Agnes recalls: 'What could I say but yes and yes? Yes, I was happy. Yes, I was lucky' (13). When she's offered as a teenage bride to a senior Commander, she's reassured by the Aunts: 'Your parents want you to be happy' (223). And when happiness fails, it must be mimicked; a school friend confides to Agnes: 'they put happy pills in the warm milk of the girls who were about to get married' (232). In Gilead, young women are taught that happiness is a duty, to their families and to the state, and that 'the good woman aligns her happiness with the happiness of others' (Ahmed 2010: 55). This is what Ahmed terms 'the sociality of happiness' (56): when ensuring the happiness of others becomes the object of one's own happiness, the imperative is that one must do whatever makes the *other* happy. For a good young Gileadean woman like Agnes, her happiness must always rest in submission and compliance. Happiness, in this manner, becomes a prison one must joyfully enter. And we might think here of Charmaine in *The Heart Goes Last*, happily signing up for her own incarceration.

   In that earlier novel, Charmaine readily adopts the role of a happy housewife heroine on the carefully constructed stage set of the Consilience project, finding requisite joy in the promise of 'a washer and dryer [...] a dining table [...] real china instead of plastic'. She recognises the artifice of the performance; the project, she intuits, represents a chance to peel

away her old self, 'to step out of that skin and be a different person'. It will
also, she hopes, shore up her marriage, sorely tested by homelessness and
unemployment; in the new home, she thinks, 'Stan will be happy too:
how could he not be happy?' (27). In an essay discussing *The Handmaid's
Tale*, Atwood identifies as one of the novel's key questions: 'How much
social instability would it take before people would renounce their hard-
won civil liberties in a trade-off for "safety"?' (Atwood 2011). As Coral
Howells observes, this same question underpins *The Heart Goes Last*.
Examining the novel's purposely excessive use of clashing, trashy genres –
horror, science fiction, romance, the gothic, erotica, fantasy and more –
Howells nevertheless identifies at its heart 'serious ethical questions about
institutional power versus individual freedom and free will' (2017: 305). The
alacrity with which Charmaine signs away her liberties is easily condemned
but Atwood makes clear that her sunniness – often irritating, seemingly
vacuous – is a learned trauma response. As a child eventually rescued by
her beloved Grandma Win from abuse and neglect, she is taught to bury
her nightmares and project positivity: '*you should forget those other things*',
advises her grandmother, '*a man's not accountable when he's had too much to
drink.* [...] *Let's make popcorn!*' (4, emphasis in original). For Charmaine, life
is 'thin ice with the cracks showing and disaster always waiting just beneath
her' (53), and although marriage to Stan promises 'solid ground' (53), the
banking crash leaves them living on the lawless streets, in constant threat
of being robbed, raped, or murdered. When offered safety and security,
therefore, Charmaine grasps it with both hands.

Towards the end of *The Testaments*, Aunt Lydia turns her shrewd eye to
her imagined reader, anticipating her objections: 'How can I have behaved
so badly, so cruelly, so stupidly? you will ask. You yourself would never have
done such things! But you yourself will never have had to' (403). In *The
Heart Goes Last*, Atwood similarly invites the reader to consider what she
would do in Charmaine's situation. As Ed, the Consilience spokesperson,
puts it, 'you can't eat your so-called liberties' (38). But while there is
sympathy for Charmaine's retreat to safety, Atwood is with Beauvoir in
calling for liberty over happiness. *The Heart Goes Last* is predicated on
the collapse of social order in northeast United States and the failure of
the implicit capitalist promise to protect the law-abiding middle classes.

As employers move west and the rich move offshore, the social contract is abandoned. Stepping into this void, the Consilience project offers no new solutions, but rather a dream of reviving the rotten, failing capitalist system. Speaking to a heady mix of nostalgia and fear, Ed warns that anarchy, chaos and 'the senseless destruction of property' might lead to calls 'for so-called revolution' and urgently asks: what can be done 'to keep the lid on?' (38–39). The obvious answer, of course, is that a revolution is needed. Capitalist, patriarchal, white-dominated society has repeatedly failed Charmaine, as it has failed whole swathes of American society, and yet she readily accepts its proffered solutions, designed only to reassert its dominion, and in doing so, becomes not just acquiescent, but entirely complicit.

As 'Chief Medications Administrator' (53), Charmaine's job in Positron – the prison element of the Consilience project – is to discreetly administer lethal injections to a succession of 'troublemakers' (65). Such people, rationalises Charmaine (who is rather proud of the skill with which she acquits her task), 'don't fit anywhere. They'll never be happy where they are' (69). Furthermore, the benefits of their absence are clear: 'safe streets, no homelessness, jobs for all!' (51). If she is at all uneasy, she has Grandma Win's twin strategies of repression and distraction to hand, as she reflects after killing a man: 'There are some things it's better not to think about. Tonight she'll join the knitting circle' (70). In an article that examines *The Heart Goes Last* as a response to America's 'post-recession nostalgia' (Kowal 2019: 146) in the wake of the financial crisis of 2008, Ewa Kowal reads Charmaine as largely 'naïve, kind and gentle' and suggests that her 'compliance and thoughtlessness' are used by Atwood as a 'telling illustration of the additional costs of a catastrophic economic crisis', when civic principles are overridden by base priorities (151). For Kowal, Atwood's novel is a cautionary tale about 'embracing responsibility' (153) rather than passively submitting to the cyclical crises of capitalism that can seem inevitable and unstoppable. This reading is certainly valid, but Charmaine's readiness to embrace the Consilience project, I suggest, has still further implications. In the novel's final scenes – when it is revealed that she never had an operation that supposedly made her uncontrollably in love with Stan – she instinctively regrets her autonomy, and the responsibility it confers: 'She wants the helplessness' (306). Charmaine does not just retreat into an inherently violent, repressive system due to economic necessity; she becomes fully invested in it.

In *Living a Feminist Life*, in which she extends her earlier writing on feminist killjoys into 'a killjoy manifesto', Ahmed offers, as a manifesto principle: 'We are not grateful when a system is extended to include us when that system is predicated on inequality and violence' (2017: 263). In *The Heart Goes Last*, Atwood imagines a female protagonist who retreats into safety and is willing to sustain a violent and repressive system in order to secure her own place within it. Crucially, the offences committed by 'the incorrigibles, the [...] troublemakers' (69) Charmaine dispatches are unknown and might include any number of activities or identities (political, racial, ethical, social) deemed unacceptable by the shadowy corporation running Consilience. Charmaine, however, works without qualms to 'reproduce the logics' of the project and 'to support a happiness fantasy' that requires the violent exclusion of troublesome others (Ahmed 2017: 263, 264). Atwood ends the novel with Charmaine, who has unwittingly helped bring down the project but who remains compliant and passive, being offered liberty and autonomy: 'Take it or leave it'. Her uninspiring response, on which the novel concludes – 'How do you mean?' (306) – leaves room for a possible future in which she finally rejects the happiness fantasy and considers becoming a troublemaker, but also little optimism that this revolution will ever occur.

In *The Testaments* instead, Agnes finds herself increasingly unable to pass as happy, and in her powerless state, she resorts to the only act of violence she can entertain and threatens suicide. From this abyss, however, she is offered a lifeline by Aunt Lydia, and the novel turns into a tale of espionage, female solidarity and daring escape. This most recent novel is, in many ways, one of Atwood's most optimistic. As I note elsewhere, while it commences on scenes of isolated young women, it concludes with acts of sisterly loyalty, cooperation and connection. 'You *are* a sister to me' (Atwood 2019: 357, emphasis in original), Agnes assures the self-sacrificing Becka, while Agnes's care leads Nicole to affirm: 'after that night she was really my sister' (397). In these sincere connections, Atwood 'provides a vision far more hopeful of female collaboration than was ever imagined in *The Handmaid's Tale*' (Tolan 2021b: 164). In addition to imagining a supportive sisterhood (while still providing a full Atwoodian cohort of spiteful schoolgirls and malicious mothers), many have noted a significant change of tone in the 'Historical Notes' that conclude both novels. While Professor Pieixoto notoriously questions and diminishes Offred's tale, yearning for a man's factual account rather than a woman's reflective memoir – 'What we wouldn't give, now, for even twenty pages or so of printout from Waterford's private computer! (Atwood 1985: 322) – he commences his address in *The Testaments*, in contrast, with an invitation to believe 'the authenticity of our two witness transcripts' (415). In a review essay focusing on the significance of testimony and bearing witness in *The Testaments*, Sophie Gilbert (2019) contextualises Atwood's novel against the backdrop of the #MeToo era, observing: 'A movement has swept her up, though she hadn't set out to write for one'. And for Susan Watkins, #MeToo and the corrosive spread of 'fake news' have motivated Atwood to replace 'incredulity with a much clearer sense of the validity of women's stories' (2019). Such readings commonly observe in *The Testaments* a more hopeful, positive trajectory for women than that offered by its more resolutely sceptical prequel.

With its tale of sisters and mothers reunited, and its promise that witness testimony will survive and will be believed, *The Testaments* comes much closer to a secure happy ending than most Atwood novels ever do. But having previously been made wary of happiness by feminist thinkers, and indeed by Atwood herself, we are left potentially troubled by the question of how to read this neat, happy resolution, this 'Shakespearean comedy of children lost and found' (Enright 2019). As one reviewer observes, 'there's a strong sense of goodness winning the day, even – whisper it – hints of something that might amount to a happy ending. Which actually feels a touch disappointing' (Myerson 2019). This sense of dissatisfaction – alluded to in a few reviews (Roupenian 2020; Williams 2019) – arguably resides in a suspicion of what Raffaella Baccolini terms the 'taming of dystopia' with comforting, reassuring endings, 'where hope is not maintained ambiguously but is substituted by a conformist happiness' (2020: 44). More complex, precarious endings, she argues, urge the reader to remain alert, which is the true purpose of dystopian fiction. While the conclusion of *The Testaments* rests on rebellion and the rejection of the 'conformist happiness' demanded by the Gilead state, it lacks perhaps the ambiguity and the precarity that Baccolini defines as necessary in order to 'invite readers to mobilize against the present and the risks of its possible outcomes' (44).

The Testaments is secure in the sincerity of Agnes's escape from happiness; she rejects social conformity and is prepared to risk everything for liberty in a way that Charmaine, certainly, is not. In this, the later novel more readily conceives of Agnes as another of Atwood's feminist killjoys. There is a danger, however, that the novel's comic resolution, while 'sad and happy, both at once' (399), as the unnamed Offred is described, undermines the power of the dystopian narrative. Instead, for a concluding and quite different vision of happiness from Atwood's work – we might even say one of feminist joy – we can turn once again to *The Handmaid's Tale*. Midway through the novel, Offred, imprisoned in Gilead and sentenced to silence and obedience, catches a glimpse of her mother in an old film, marching at a feminist protest, and describes her: 'Now my mother is moving forward, she's smiling, laughing, they all move forward, and now they're raising their fists in the air' (130). This resonant scene of female defiance is not complacent, conservative or static: it is provisional, dynamic, momentary, purposeful and – crucially – joyful. In such irrepressible glimpses, troubling the limits of the authoritarian regime, Atwood asserts the power and significance of the feminist killjoy in her work.

Helene Staveley

Empowering the Inner Nitwit: Margaret Atwood for Kids

Children feature prominently in most of Margaret Atwood's literary fiction. They are the interesting small people thrown into a difficult world who then grow up into the intriguingly fractured, traumatized, or dysfunctional writers and artists; dystopia endurers and sex industry survivors; convicted murderers; bartered heiresses; and the other damaged adult humans around whom Atwood narratives revolve. Some such childhoods are experienced by Elaine Risley, for example, in *Cat's Eye* (1988), Joan Foster in *Lady Oracle* (1976), Grace Marks in *Alias Grace* (1996), Iris and Laura Chase in *Blind Assassin* (2000), and in the *MaddAddam* trilogy (2003, 2009, 2013), Ren and Amanda, Jimmy/Snowman and Oryx, and Toby and Zeb. Examining Atwood's writing for children, though, enhances an understanding of her aesthetics and themes, especially regarding posthumanism. Atwood has written or co-written seven texts for young readers, of which the five she wrote on her own are considered here. The earliest, *Up in the Tree*, was published in 1978 in the pre–*Handmaid's Tale* era when Atwood was solidifying her central themes. *Princess Prunella and the Purple Peanut* was released in 1995 in a period Coral Ann Howells links with historical fiction (Howells 2020: 22). *Rude Ramsay and the Roaring Radishes* (2003), *Bashful Bob and Doleful Dorinda* (2004), and *Wandering Wenda* (2011) were all released within the years Atwood was writing the *MaddAddam* trilogy, often read as a posthuman dystopia. In refracting motifs from her books for adults onward into children's picture books, where children and animals coexist productively, Atwood playfully reconfigures core ideas about humanity and survival.

In their 2019 article 'Taking Age Out of Play: Children's Animistic Philosophizing Through a Picturebook,' Joanna Haynes and Katrin

Murriss identify picture-books for children as important sites of inquiry for posthumanist philosophies, representing relationships between child and animal in ways that replace taxonomy-based differentiation with cross-species friendships and kinships. Singly and collectively, Atwood's picture-books for young readers participate in such inquiries, as they 'philosophically reconfigure who and what counts as (fully) human and show why it matters' (Haynes and Murriss 2019: 290–309) by writing both child endurance and human survival as exceeding othered survivals; and Atwood, like most picture-book writers of such books, structures them comedically to achieve a happy ending. Given that many of Atwood's posthuman writings for adults ask directly and indirectly whether 'the survival of humanity "should be an ethical good to begin with"' (Tolan 2023: 137; quoting Bergthaller), they construct the adult human as unstable and unreliable. In *Cruel Optimism*, Lauren Berlant writes of 'the history of sentimentality around children' that children become 'the reason to have optimism,' because 'if nothing else, their lives are not already ruined' (Berlant 2011: 171). In this way child characters become icons of optimism for the future. Animals in children's books, on the other hand, make legible specific ideas about ethnicity, class, gender, the natural world, and similar sites of power and hierarchy (Jaeger 2018: 188–222), while also providing a 'sometimes ironic demonstration of a human frailty or moral lesson' (Coats 2018: 250). Thus it's the resonant figures of children and animals that embody much of the 'ethical good' of the human: what to carry forward despite arbitrary imposed constraints.

Interestingly, Atwood speaks of her writing for young people in terms of release, as a chance to free her 'inner nitwit' (Atwood 2003: 56). Generally construed as a 'term of abuse,' a *nitwit* denotes the irrational and absurd, 'a silly or foolish person' who is free in this case to say all those things Atwood refrains from saying in her interviews, poems, short stories, nonfiction, and novels. Reingard Nischik notes similar qualities in Atwood's comic strip art; she quotes a 1978 interview with Peter Gzowski where Atwood describes her 1970s *Kanadian Kultchur Komics* as "a medium in which I can do all those rude things that I don't usually do" (Nischik 2009: 204). Releasing the inner nitwit, then, involves getting away with something, or flouting that constantly surveilling social gaze under which Atwood's protagonists chafe in her fiction for adults. So we can read her writing for young people as providing licence for Atwood to think and write in ways that subvert, and exceed, many conventions that she herself has established.

In a 1983 interview Atwood identifies some affordances of writing for children as: the ability to privilege optimism and wish-fulfilment; the potential for the happy endings of comic and romance structures to fulfil expectations and close off anxieties; to permit silliness and play; and to empower nonsense and exuberance (Atwood with Ross and Davies 1986: 9–16). In *The Hidden Adult: Defining Children's Literature* (2008), influential theorist Perry Nodelman argues that, while definitions of children's literature are extremely diverse and still-evolving, it's useful to remember that such literature is made, edited, published, and sold by adults with their own often limiting ideas of what children can and should be, and that children's literature forcefully demonstrates what and how children are, teaching 'child readers subjectivity by offering them opportunities for identification with characters undergoing normative processes of coming into selfhood' (Nodelman 2008: 133–244). In *Up in the Tree, Prunella, Ramsay, Bob and Dorinda*, and *Wenda*, Atwood offers child readers options to see themselves in child characters whose evolving selves disrupt human-centering and adult-centering economies and, by being creatively abrasive, free themselves from normative scripts. Atwood writes her child protagonists as evolving toward what Rosi Braidotti might consider an in-between subject that can 'reject negativity and aim at the production of joyful or affirmative values and projects' (Braidotti 2019: 31–61). These characters and worlds enable Atwood to exceed the theories she outlined in *Survival* (1972). Atwood's picture books for young people empower her to write beyond both victimhood and creative non-victimhood and to pillory anthropocentrist and teleiocentrist thinking using posthuman pathways.

Up in the Tree

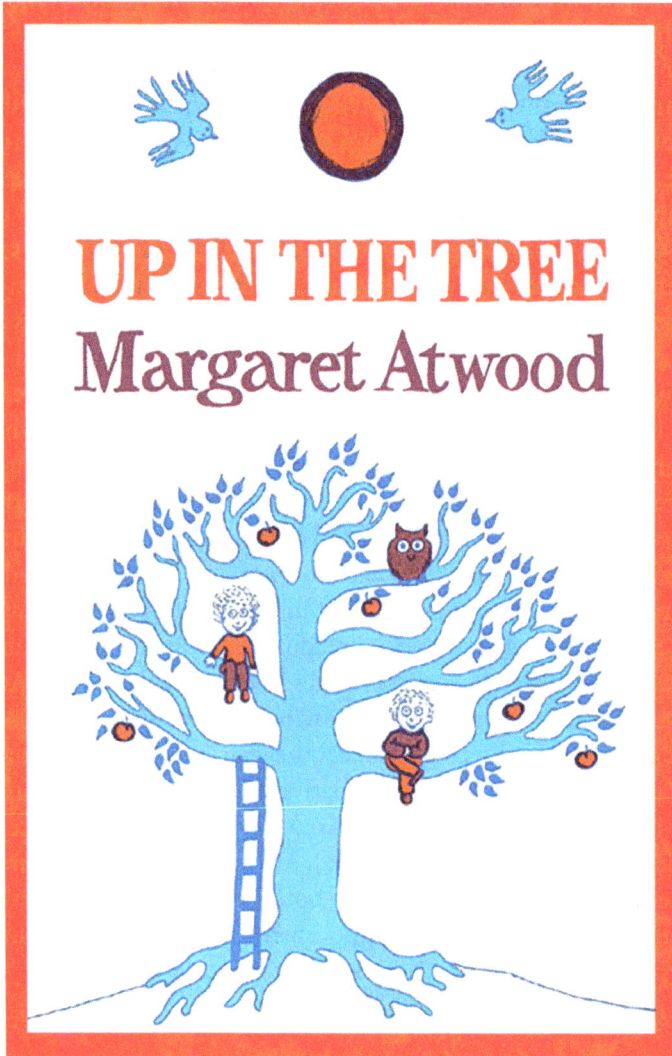

Figure 5. Margaret Atwood, *Up in the Tree* cover; words and image, c. 1978; reprinted 2006 by House of Anansi Press/Groundwood Books. Image reproduced by permission of House of Anansi Press and Groundwood Books.

The only one of her texts for young people to be written, illustrated, and hand-lettered by herself (Edwards and Saltman 2010: 69–98), *Up in the Tree* was published in 1978 as Atwood was becoming not just a successful writer but a famous one. Along with winning the Governor General's Award with her first book, she began publishing instalments of her self-parodic comic strip *Kanadian Kultchur Komiks* in *This Magazine* between 1975 and 1978; and she had published her screwball Künstlerroman *Lady Oracle* in 1976 and the pregnancy-invested *Life Before Man* in 1980. So it's easy to see Atwood's crafting of *Up in the Tree* as both producing joyful values while also remaining contiguous with her other literary and artistic practices.

The book is dedicated to Atwood's only child, aged two the year the book was published, and implies a pre-school-aged child 'reader' or user. The book's rhyming first-person-plural narrative is visually simple, with a designed airiness relating to generous whitespace and to the organic appearance of Atwood's hand-lettered text. The rhyming book totals fewer than three hundred words and tells of a pair of children who live in a tree and love it:

> We like our old tree,
> Our home in the tree;
> We swing in the Spring
> And we crawl in the Fall
> And we dance on the branches
> Way up in the tree. (Atwood 1978: np)

Life in the tree is delightful across seasons, perhaps because it's an experience of permeable space; three different species of birds, some apples, and the wind, in addition to the two children, all move within and around it, while familiar comforts like hot water and tea can be available there. Atwood draws the two child characters as nearly identical with pants and shirts, big eyes, friendly expressions, and short hair, and she illustrates the book in shades of blue and red and a brownish blend of the two, a minimal colour-scheme determined by publishing economics (Atwood with Ross and Davies 1986: 9–16; Nischik 2009: esp. 253–76). It's not clear which of the two children voices the text, perhaps both, and both usually meet the reader's gaze from within the book, as does the owl who keeps them company as though watching over them. It's relatively familiar for characters in picture books to 'break the fourth wall' by meeting the reader's eyes, and in Atwood's hands this move resembles a friendly indication that the characters can see the viewer/reader and are inviting play or interaction; it combines with the conversational direct-address narration to build reciprocal kinship and intimacy between speakers/characters and listener/readers. The children's gazes are friendly while the owl's nonthreatening gaze connotes startlement, concern, and wonder by turns.

The narrative's conflicts play out completely within the narrative, and so the book narrates an unfolding trauma of entrapment. The children's home is idyllic until two porcupines (Atwood with Ross and Davies 1986: 9–16) eat their ladder. Like the owl, the porcupines are not mentioned in the text; the illustrations alone show how the ladder vanishes. The shocked children do not cast blame but, despite their anxiety, look for a solution. While still airy, their home is now prison-like until their animal helper, the silent, unnarrated owl, leaves then returns with a larger bird who flies the children out of the tree to the ground. Since human structures like ladders aren't reliable, the children affix stairs to the trunk of the tree and on the last page are pictured snuggled up under blankets and sound asleep on their comfortable branches. The pair remain ungrounded, they actively prefer their aerial refuge and its unusual community; they have no predators and exhibit no malice but are equal to the dangers they face. They can live consequence-free in their Edenic tree, a playspace par excellence that will never expel them.

It's common for Atwood to polarize certain child character relationships such as those between *Lady Oracle*'s protagonist Joan and her bullying mother and husband, or the shifting 'frenmity' between Elaine and Cordelia in *Cat's Eye* (1988); but *Up in the Tree* seems the more unearthly because it does not narrate either child being bullied into acknowledging their own dependence and contingency on an adultist power structures. In short, *Up in the Tree* resists representing its child characters as subject to human-driven abjection. Instead they co-exist harmoniously with agents animal and environmental, managing problems and crises as they arise. The two birds are instrumental: necessary, silent, minimally acknowledged, agents of salvation. They live alongside the children, enabling their lives of whimsy.

Four Related Picture-Books

The next four picture-books are unified on several counts. First, Atwood's texts are accompanied by artwork from prominent children's illustrators. The earliest, *Princess Prunella and the Purple Peanut,* is illustrated by Maryann Kovalski, while the later three are all illustrated by Dušan Petričić, known in Serbia for his cartoons of political leaders. Second, the four narratives are fables in a couple of senses: they offer almost hyperbolically obvious morals, and they play with fairy tale structures and motifs in a recursive and self-conscious playfulness that Robert Scholes explicitly links with fable (*Fabulation and Metafiction* [1979]). The presence of talking animal helpers in all four contribute to an additional Aesopian sense of fable while also establishing a fairy-tale dimension to the four alliterative fables. Pauline Greenhill and Leah Claire Allen view fairy tales with animal helpers and animal–human transitivities 'as sites to launch critiques of alleged human nature, including kinship relationships and the cultural construction of normative human bodies,' noting also that 'Fairy tales are already species-queer, posthuman, and transbiological; their stories and characters destabilize and upend normative species relationships' (2018: 225–34). Atwood's alliterative fables link child protagonists with friendly animal helpers who, like the animal helpers described by Greenhill and Allen, speak human and animal languages with ease, transforming interspecies relationships that are conventionally dichotomized into dialogical and responsive ones. In fables, animals that speak, wear clothing, and walk upright – which describes these animal characters of Atwood's – 'simultaneously socialize [...] children and teach [...] them to put aside childish and thus animalistic behaviour' (Jaeger 2018: 188–222). The animal presences in Atwood's four fables underscore the child characters' experiences of vulnerability and of the poverty–wealth binary also common in fairy tales; together, child and animal characters co-perform kinships that exceed the biological. Thirdly, the four fables are comically horrific cautionary tales of young people in dire straits, participating in a tradition established by Heinrich Hoffmann, Hilaire Belloc, Edward Gorey, Lemony Snickett, and others. Such 'parodic cautionary tales,' in Katie Trumpener's terms, bifurcate 'content and form, using doggerel and comic rhymes to convey strict messages, juxtaposing stern narrative with playful or mocking pictures,' and they '[arm] children against didactic pieties and social conventions. Pedagogues expecting children to follow a strict moral and behavioural code, they suggest, have forgotten what it is like to inhabit a child's mind and body; meanwhile, they seem oddly blind to adult failings' (Trumpener 2009: 55–75). Fourthly and finally, all four rely on Atwood's outrageous alliteration. Ps, Rs, Bs and Ds, and Ws are all helplessly, obsessively prominent in their respective narratives, standing in for the doggerel and comic rhymes Trumpener discusses. The near maniacal alliteration of these four fables effectively joins them as an aesthetic unit and is outrageously consistent and inventive, exercising a broad register of vocabulary:

> Princess Prunella had a problem perceiving where she was going, because of the pocket mirror. At supper it was hard for her to place the spoon precisely between her lips, so she spilled parsley and potatoes on her pinafore, producing spots.
>
> She upset the pudgy palace lamps from their pedestals patterned with puffins and pelicans, bumped into the parlour piano draped with pewter-coloured polyester periwinkles, tripped over the powdered porcelain Pekingese perched near the fireplace, and tipped Princess Patty's powerful perfume all over the Persian carpet, making an unpleasant puddle. (Atwood 1995: np)

This text renders Prunella's spaces warty with animate and inanimate intruders, all denoted with popping 'p' percussives that delineate Atwood's 'inner nitwit' as a wordsmith egging on readers and listeners to get the linguistic joke.

As indicated by certain mainstream consumer reviews that invariably presume adults will read the book aloud (see in particular Ceep's 2015 consumer review of *Wenda* on *Amazon.ca*), Atwood's alliteration can register as abrasive, mocking, and problematically subversive of teleiocentrism and other restrictive practices. I like to think of it as Atwood playfully needling her loyal adult fanbase by bringing them to stutter and stumble while reading her books to their kids. That same fanbase has after all challenged and questioned her writing and her politics as much as appreciated them, and this is a chance for Atwood as writer to turn the tables and challenge readers with difficult and ludicrous but good-natured feats. Atwood's spectacular verbiage establishes that it's not just children, fictional or actual, who are fallible, incompetent, and subject to eternal authoritarian scrutiny: adults who craft and/or read the narratives can equally be derailed by such nonsense. Michael Heyman and Kevin Shortsleeve discuss nonsense as having 'an ancestral connection to medieval carnivalesque traditions' theorized as 'a genre of "absurd compositions" that revel in "linguistic freedom," illogical sequences, and the "inside out"' (Mikhail Bakhtin, qtd in Heyman and Shortsleeve 2011: 165–69). They continue, 'By its association with the word "grotesque," the term "nonsense" is understood to mean something unnatural, distorted, bizarre, ludicrous, or fantastically absurd; at the same time it is understood as amusing, quaint, immaterial—a place for simple, joyful fun.' Atwood's use of alliteration playfully renders grotesque, unnatural, distorted and fantastically absurd the top-down authority adults arrogate to themselves, not least through their power to prescribe the stories that model acceptable childness to actual kids (Nodelman 2008: 133–244.) Atwood's alliteration also carves out a space where the young can witness the stumbles of the mature, and from there perceive that the surveilling adult gaze is imperfectly competent, encouraging young readers/listeners to steal chances at joyful, subversive, nitwit nonsense.

Childhood as Fairy Tale Privilege

Princess Prunella is deeply attached to a silver mirror she carries everywhere, and this attachment codes her as narcissistic. Atwood's narrative shows others in Prunella's world as being concerned or harmed by her narcissism, since parents, servants, pets, and helpful visitors all bear the brunt of her self-absorption. Prunella achieves an apotheosis once her love affair with her own reflection is ruptured and she lifts her eyes to the larger world. But the mirror also suggests she possesses child knowledge that is neither understood nor valued by those around her; it helps Prunella keep her own beauty in constant view even while it interferes with her ability to recognize beauties outside the mirror's silver frame. She's not necessarily wrong about her own value. Children should have high intrinsic value irrespective of their socioeconomic status and identity; it's often adults who assess a child's value according to their compliance, cleverness, cuteness, and so forth, as happens when Prunella's parents devalue her for her vanity. But once she sees her beautiful world contextualizing and outshining her own beauty, Prunella witnesses how it exceeds her and is empowered to live harmoniously in the thickness of it.

Tellingly, it's animals that point the way for her. The adults around Prunella perennially fret about her self-centredness and vanity, but people are not around when the charm of her visage is ruptured by the curse of a purple peanut appearing on Prunella's nose. It's her pet pussycats who tell her to complete three good deeds: "'We pity you,' they whispered. "Your eyes are all pink and puffy, and that purple peanut is as big as a pumpkin. So we will remind you of what the white-haired wrinkly-wristed Wise Woman said: Perform three Good Deeds and your purple peanut will pop'" (Atwood 1995: n.p.). So she prevents parrots from destroying the laundry; rescues her pet pug from a poisonous puff-pig; and warns the prince not to swim in the pond where the pointy-toothed pike live. Kovalski's illustration identifies this as Prunella's happiest and least self-conscious moment; she's pictured crouched on the ground, face close to the pond, grinning besottedly at the pike, who is grinning besottedly back, ironically mirroring each other.

Each encounter with an animal takes the princess outside her head and relieves the painful epiphany that she has been 'a proud, presumptuous, and preoccupied princess' (Atwood 1995: n.p.) – which is just the kind of moral people under twelve are used to finding in books that adults encourage them to read. In other books this might be the pinnacle of the princess's arc: self-chastised and moderately humiliated, the flawed protagonist gains social approval by enduring abjection and thus submitting to acculturation. Prunella conforms to this somewhat, but as importantly, she's enthralled with and uplifted by the complex beauties of the world beyond her nose.

Figure 6. Maryann Kovalski, *Princess Prunella and the Purple Peanut*, text by Margaret Atwood, c. 1995, Key Porter Kids. Image reproduced by permission of Maryann Kovalski.

Kovalski's 'happily ever after' illustration presents Prunella at play in simple white clothes, pushing the petulant prince on a swing in an Edenic garden while her royal parents, her pets, and the wise stranger look on, beaming. This final image resembles the culminating major arcana tarot card, The World, wherein the World is anthropomorphized as a woman dancing and encircled by wreaths or laurels, as Prunella is posed encircled by greenery. The tarot card signifies fulfilment, achievement, success, and spiritual understanding, and Kovalski's illustration configures Prunella as empowered, unselfconscious, and freed, seeing the wonders around her with clear and adoring eyes, barely aware of the gaze of others. The obstacles that prevented her from living fully in her vibrant world are vanishing.

Prunella's fable was published in 1995 in the same decade in which Atwood was crafting her famed historical fictions, *The Robber Bride* (1993), *Alias Grace* (1996), and *The Blind Assassin* (2000), three historical fictions for adults interrogating the kinds of class and economic privilege that Princess Prunella enjoys. In fact, of the five human protagonists in the four alliterative fables, only Prunella is privileged and perverse, and only Prunella's story is situated in an exotic fairy tale past with fairy tale icons and archaisms such as palaces, royal parents, and suitor princes.

Childhood as Dystopia

The next three fables – *Rude Ramsay and the Roaring Radishes, Bashful Bob and Doleful Dorinda*, and *Wandering Wenda,* reprinted collectively in 2017 as *A Trio of Tolerable Tales* – are all set in grotesque versions of the twenty-first century world. These urban and urban-adjacent worlds linguistically and pictorially feature televisions, consumer capitalism, mass media, junk food, and sub/urban decay; further, Ramsay's world includes robot technology, Bob and Dorinda's includes feral communities, and Wenda's includes evil wizardry. Dušan Petričić's illustrations in all three books bring a zaniness that answers Atwood's own, caricaturing the antagonists in all their callous evil while the child protagonists are wily, resilient, and stalwart waifs whose main strength is their empathy for their animal companions.

All three were published while Atwood was composing the *MaddAddam* trilogy, and Ramsay and Rillah, Bob and Dorinda, and Wenda, Wilson, Wu, and Wahnapitae are all children who, like the

MaddAddam protagonists (see Bone 2016: 620–40), are literally or figuratively discarded by their parental figures, becoming vulnerable, impoverished, and radically disempowered within hostile human spaces. Ramsay's relatives prioritize convenience and rock and roll music over raising him well, while Rillah, the beautiful girl next door, was abandoned by her family as they ran away from their debt. Their instant friendship is their happily ever after. In *Bashful Bob and Doleful Dorinda*, Bob is raised from infancy by a trio of stray dogs in a park, and therefore he identifies and lives as a canine, not human; meanwhile, Dorinda's parents have vanished, so she must work for food and shelter.

Figure 7. Dušan Petričić, *Bashful Bob and Doleful Dorinda*, text by Margaret Atwood, c. 2004, Key Porter Kids. Reprinted in *A Trio of Tolerable Tales* (2017), Groundwood Books/House of Anansi Press. Image reproduced by permission of Groundwood Books/House of Anansi Press.

Her path crosses with Bob's, she becomes his caregiver, and the two save a buffalo together, for which they earn media attention, leading to their reunion with their four delinquent parents; they all fuse into a single household, including the dogs. Finally, Wandering Wenda is homeless and effectively orphaned when she befriends Wesley the Woodchuck; her parents were swept away by a wizardly whirlwind.

Figure 8. Dušan Petričić, *Wandering Wenda*, text by Margaret Atwood, c. 2011, McArthur & Co. Reprinted in *A Trio of Tolerable Tales* (2017), Groundwood Books/House of Anansi Press. Image reproduced by permission of Groundwood Books/House of Anansi Press.

The Widow Wallup enslaves Wenda and three other children at her washery, but Wesley enlists a neighbourhood wolfpack to help Wenda, Wilson, Wu, and Wahnapitae escape, forcing the Widow to confess that they are really the evil wizard in disguise. The Widow/ Wizard reluctantly destroys the whirlwind wand, returning all four sets of missing parents to the fold.

During the promotional tour for *Oryx and Crake*, Atwood described the book as 'a joke-filled romp through the end of the human race' (qtd in Bouson 2004: 139–56), a description that can also seem to apply collectively to *Ramsay, Bob and Dorinda*, and *Wenda*. The child characters in these books rarely take the adults in their worlds seriously, treating them as black jokes. Ramsay's family feeds him rancid, roach-infested food, and both the house they live in and the nearby rampart are virtually made of rubbish; he mocks and taunts them before abandoning them. Bob's, Dorinda's, and Wenda's parents are all hopelessly derelict in their duties; one is so careless she actually misplaces her baby, while the rest of the parents permit themselves to be waylaid by misfortune – a travel disaster for Dorinda's parents, the Wizard's magical whirlwind in *Wenda* – instead of returning home to help their suffering children. The books suggest through text and image that adults who leave their children behind are morally deficient and broken. Relationships with animals, contrastingly, are salvific, conversational, and expansive. Ramsay receives moral support from nearby birds and from Ralph the rat, who encourages Ramsay to 'Be rugged!' (Atwood 2017: 15) and overcome his reluctance to crawl through the rampart. Together boy and rat co-endure the rampart's filth, are co-delighted at the Edenic garden on the other side, co-feast on wholesome berries and vegetables, and eventually co-escape with Rillah to a sparkling-clean paradise under the rainbow. In *Bob and Dorinda*, the loving borzoi, boxer, and bulldog who raise Bob do so conscientiously and, at a crucial moment, help the children communicate with the bewildered bison to get him back home, generating the publicity that leads to them acquiring their own home. Wesley is half-starved until Wenda shares her scavenged wieners with him; they survive homelessness, deprivation, and enslavement together until Wesley digs an escape tunnel and enlists the wolves' help to defeat the Widow/Wizard. The verbal and pictorial hellscapes these children inhabit are as stark as *MaddAddam*'s Pleeblands and post-apocalyptic urban jungles. The animals' human/animal bilingualism facilitates a flow of vital information, empowering broader animal communities to disempower their tormentors by the same mechanism that frees the children of theirs.

Jane Bone's reading of Blackbeard and the Crakers from *MaddAddam* as child characters highlights the overlap of Bob the 'dogboy' with Blackbeard, and also the overlap of nurturers Dorinda and Wenda with Toby from *Year of the Flood* and *MaddAddam*. Toby is a gardener, beekeeper, and an intrepid explorer of the kudzu jungle, and likewise she is a storyteller and teacher to the semi-feral Crakers. Toby, Dorinda, and Wenda are nurturers and sharers: Dorinda helps Bob deal with the conflicts he faces in being semiferal in a barely civil world, even teaching him how to read as Toby teaches Blackbeard to read. Bob's near-feral qualities suggest the Rousseauvian concepts of the natural child and the noble savage, resembling Blackbeard who, for Bone, 'exemplifies the perfected child and yet his monstrousness contaminates the secured areas where the perfect child is always thought to exist' (Bone 2016: 627–40). For Bone, Blackbeard is also 'the chosen one [...], a child in the midst of chaos who can cross borders, is vulnerable, but who assumes new responsibilities mainly by being taught to read and write' (634). Dorinda helps her young friend become Brave rather than Bashful Bob; instead of hiding, he brings the dogs, who warn the baffled buffalo he is being pursued by zookeepers and so facilitate his return home. Gardens, parks, and wilderness spaces are as prominent across all four alliterative fables as they are in the *MaddAddam* books, and the home of Ramsay's repulsive relatives even has a rooftop garden like that of God's Gardeners, albeit a neglected one. The 'love at first sight' friendship between Ramsay and Rillah recalls the seemingly 'instant' love of Jimmy and Oryx, as though Atwood's nitwit narrator has seized a chance to differently resolve this doomed relationship.

Figure 9. Dušan Petričić, *Rude Ramsay and the Roaring Radishes*, text by Margaret Atwood, c. 2003, McArthur & Company. Reprinted in *A Trio of Tolerable Tales* (2017), Groundwood Books/House of Anansi Press. Image reproduced by permission of Groundwood Books/House of Anansi Press.

Conclusions

Donna Haraway derides the fantasy that 'technology will somehow come to the rescue of its naughty but very clever children or, what amounts to the same thing, God will come to the rescue of his disobedient but ever hopeful children' (Haraway 2016: 3). Animals, not technology, help

Atwood's child protagonists solve their problems, and their cross-species kinships configure a posthumanist ideal of a life of friendship beyond mere survival. Andrew Hoogheems reads in Atwood's *MaddAddam* trilogy the idea that 'stories and religion provide an evolutionary function: creating supportive communities, communicating knowledge, and teaching necessary social values' (qtd in Tolan 2023: 137) – an imperative in a thick posthumanist world binding together myriad levels of living organisms in a web of interdependence. In alliterative fables, Atwood's child protagonists are worlding with living beings that include humans and other living organisms, with animal helpers, familiar from fairy-tale narratives, actively enabling the child protagonists to best the conflicts they face. In her work for adults, Atwood writes children whose child knowledges and child truths are at best ignored and at worst punished. In her children's books, Atwood writes children whose experiences of radical precarity question teliocentric and anthropocentric knowledges and truths and are alleviated by animal friendships. Rosi Braidotti theorizes that producing knowledge in the posthuman era can show that 'there is no extinction/survival binary' and that what exists instead is 'complexity, embodied and embedded diversity and multiple becomings' (Braidotti 2019: 31–61). By releasing her inner nitwit and unleashing an aesthetics of delicious linguistic perversity and resilience, Atwood writes children who are betrayed and unhomed by adult human worlds that misread, mistreat, abandon, abuse, and neglect them. But with their animal helpers, they use this precarity as a transformative power that transcends the extinction/survival binary; joyfully resists the definitive limits adults and homes impose on them; and configures experiencing 'diverse and multiple becomings' as exuberantly creative processes.

Gina Wisker

'Poetry is the past /that breaks out in our hearts': Loss, Revision, Diversity and Survival in *Dearly* (2022) and *Morning in the Burned House* (1995)

Margaret Atwood has an extraordinary way of sensing future loss in presence. She imagines ahead from the rich ecology of lakes, land and the life of creatures, from the domestic, inhabited house, the breakfast table, the ageing parent, partner, the cat, into a future empty of all of these. Atwood's interest in diversity, survival and loss manifests in several ways, and the first thing some readers noted was most likely her energetic and acerbic undermining of the complacent controls of patriarchy, breaking out of its constraints, and contesting and opening up curtailed spaces for women to speak and be. Her work consistently exposes gender bias, and in her poetry, the revisionist feminist mythology she developed became a focus of early critical discussion. As an activist-writer across multiple forms, Atwood's concern with the misuse of power by both individuals and political regimes is of a piece with her work, alongside concern for ecological losses and imagined survivals in the microcosm of the individual, the family and the everyday.

Following an introduction to critical perspectives of her work – particularly the feminist revisionist approaches – and the use of free verse, we make links between Atwood's work on survival, or the lack of it, in nature, and loss, lack, and survival in her poetry of the domestic and personal, in her most recent collection *Dearly* (2020) and earlier poems in *Morning in the Burned House* (1995) (although, in various measures, these themes appear throughout her poetry). Poems considered in these collections focus mainly on spaces and those who inhabit them, or once did, and on presences and absences. In both *Dearly* (2020) and *Morning in the Burned House* (1995), whether fully embodied or disembodied, much of what is or was taken for granted in the world around us – particularly in the home, including loved ones, both humans and animals – is gone, stopped and evacuated, leaving only traces. Unease and sensed signs of impending loss are glimpsed in *Morning in the Burned House* (1995), while in *Dearly* (2020), lack, loss, and some lingering traces of survival infuse almost everything almost everywhere. Some losses are historic, some enacted in front of her and us, some predicted. Atwood's work returns, revisits and reviews issues, locations and characters, both between the texts and within them. The traces of past ways of existence ghost the sense of self, everyday certainties, atmosphere and being in individual poems, establishing continuities and links between past, present and future through action, image, language and sound. This is all serious and crucial. However, Atwood's wry, ironic and acerbic tone works actively against despair. Beyond the personal losses, in her most recent collection *Dearly*, there is a focus on the age of synthetics in the 'Plasticene' section, which contains the little poem 'Robot', a darkly Gothic yet upbeat, amusing and critical warning of loss of the human in the age of AI. This little figure is also ironic given the theft of Atwood's writing to feed and teach AI.

In both collections, *Morning in the Burned House* (1995) and *Dearly* (2020), representations of the lack of solidity and presence, and the emptiness hovering in the otherwise taken for granted everyday, reveal traces of continuing change and slippage. Some being is tentatively in flux, some fading away, soon to be gone or already only ghosting familiar spaces. While climate change, and the selfish acts of brash ignorant humans in the period of the Anthropocene are called out in these collections, as they are throughout her work, many of her poems are more personal here. Without being mawkish and sentimental, poems in both volumes mark the experiences of lived loss, both of the poet and the reader. Writing about departed loved ones conjures them back up, yet emphasises their absence. Slipping between the past, the present and the sensed future, she writes of the effects of her father's death, her mother's dementia and death, and the dementia and death of her husband, the writer Graeme Gibson. In telling of wanderers in liminal domestic spaces, Atwood imagines ahead to her own haunting presence as objects and places lose their immediate significance and solidity but still resonate with the memories of sounds, intentions and actions. This might seem mawkish or depressing, however, her tone is mostly aware, gentle, amused and wry, confirming both a caring sadness and a continuity in absence. It is not only humans who lose their full hold on everyday reality – Atwood's fluffy cat ('Ghost Cat' from *Dearly*) also wanders the house, confused both about the functions of places and what she should be doing.

While Atwood does not mention such influences directly, these ideas about continuities might remind us first of the Romantic poets' language, of images and words recollected in tranquillity (Wordsworth and Coleridge, *Lyrical Ballads*, 1798), and then of the oscillation between asserting the lasting qualities of artefacts, places and historical objects, and yearning for eternal existence in some form (Keats, 'Ode to a Nightingale', 1819). There is also a sense of circular time, (T. S. Eliot, 'Burnt Norton', 1936) since, when minds and bodies, homes and spaces, are ghosted, there is a continuing sense of all time being eternally present and of immanence alongside absence.

Impending potential loss is a significant warning in much of Atwood's writing, and in her ecological work, she urges that actions can and must be taken to preserve nature and diversity. Here, we largely concentrate on the human, the domestic and the personal poems; on the imagining of imminent fading and loss and the assertion of forms of continuity. In most of the poems discussed here from these two collections, ghosts and echoes of the past and future are the focus, and the domestic space is the location where loved ones and loss of them, memory and loss of it circulate.

Margaret Atwood's Poetry: Revisionist Feminist Perspectives

Atwood's poetry has been analysed from a variety of perspectives, and the revisionist feminist perspective was and is, unsurprisingly, very popular, whereas Liz Yorke (1991) and Charlotte Beyer (2000) also focus on spirituality, which can be seen as an ecological alert, a theme running consistently through her work at least since the novel *Survival* (1972).

Both these approaches insist on a revisiting of often limited understandings and views – a return to a familiar space to see and understand in a new light – and with this, Charlotte Beyer (2000) considers Atwood's revisionist feminist mythology, engaging with the earlier critical perspectives of both Alicia Ostriker (1986: 316) and Liz Yorke (1991) in her own exploration of Atwood's challenge to the poetry that precedes and surrounds her and what it is able to articulate. Ostriker exposes the negative nature of mythological representations of women, arguing 'mythology seems an inhospitable terrain for a woman writer' (Ostriker 1986: 316), and that 'It is thanks to myth we believe that women must be either "angel" or "monster"' (1986: 316). Beyer comments on Ostriker's views of revisionism that, 'Anywhere that experience, memory, fantasy or dream can be retrieved, whether in words or images, it may be revalued, and re-presented' (Beyer 2000: 278), noting that Ostriker argues that 'revisionism in contemporary women's writing is a significant strategy for redefining cultural discourses and constructions of femininity' (Beyer 2000: 278). Atwood's revisionist mythology drives her refusal to depict mythological women figures as always evil, always to blame, instead explaining their backstory, and either revealing the real villains as more likely to be men or showing that men constructing and retelling a classic mythic version of historical events lay the blame on women. Latterly, Atwood deliberately repurposes myths and representations of guilty, evil, problematic historical or mythical women in her fiction in *The Penelopiad* (2005) and *Hag-Seed* (2016) and in short stories and poems. These rewritings of historically deliberately constructed negative tales, lies and interpretations expose social bias turned myth or semi-religious doctrine. Atwood's idealised, mythical, painted, reified women of film, art, mystery and myth reflect on their own constructedness and, nobody's fools, undermine and taunt the men who constructed, invested in and paid for them. In *Morning in the Burned House*, women depicted in various kinds of art talk back and challenge stereotypical demeaning representations. Pin-up girl Miss July in 'Miss July Grows Older' (1995) reminisces and criticises her own earlier seductive allure, the pretences and the artifice. More assertive, Olympia in 'Manet's Olympia' (1995) calls out 'Monsieur Voyeur' in the painting, weaponising the stuffed sofa on which she reclines, seen as an object of desire, and refusing such objectification, telling him to 'get stuffed'.

Atwood often focuses on rewriting and on getting a story straight or presented from a different perspective. As Beyer notes, 'These representations are retrieved images of women, and what women have collectively and historically suffered. In some cases, they are 'instructions for survival' (Beyer 2000: 279). The women here from art, myth, film and the everyday have ageing and its accompanying insight in common when they reflect on being deified, reified, accepted or rejected in relation to their stereotypical or idealised body shapes and roles. They are aware of loss (of youth and allure) but, revisiting their body and role changes, emerge as insightful survivors.

Various critics have made similar comments on Atwood's re-readings and re-writing of negative, misogynistic myths and historical tales. Wagner-Martin noted of the 1988 poetry collection *Interlunar* (1988), in contrast to the feminist *The Handmaid's Tale* (1985), where its 'stark testimony to disaster' with the poet and humankind described as 'some doomed caravan' is voiced through a series of mythic personae, anthropomorphized in animal speakers (a series of snake poems), and generally different from the usual Atwoodian persona' (Wagner-Martin 1995: 81).[1] Indeed, a concern with disaster, both from a feminist perspective and one of ecology and survival, is present throughout Atwood's writing. Survival, the counterpart of loss, is the underpinning drive behind much of her sustainability work as well as her feminist rewritings and re-tellings. This focus appears early, not only in the novel *Survival* (1972) but also, as Beyer notes, through the recuperation, in poetry, of one of her women ancestors, Mary Webster, who was hanged but survived. 'Half-Hang'd Mary' (1995) is certainly a historically dissonant voice, a woman falsely accused of witchcraft as were so many women with dissonant voices. Atwood reminds us of Half-hang'd Mary when writing of the accused murderess, Grace Marks, in her novel *Alias Grace* (1996), troubling the received versions of Grace's guilt or innocence.

1   In turn, this refers to an interview with Kaminski (1992).

Feminist and Survivalist Poetics

Frank Davey (1984) also comments on Margaret Atwood's feminist poetics, noting her deliberate critique and undermining of a limiting, masculine, patriarchal perspective in her poetry. He sees her writing as a feminist act to disempower both gendered hierarchies and the deliberate differentiation, objectification and control of one story, one way, one set of relationships, one species. This refusal of hierarchies and divisions is, I argue, of a piece with her emptying out of the power of one view of life over another, the power of human over animal and nature. The disturbance of fixed hierarchy and assertion of changed forms, and new continuities, is shown in the way Atwood rejects dominance of language and worldview and avoids limitations and divisions, even between the living and the dead, and the present, the past and the future.

Returns, reminders and revisions echo through and between the novels and short stories and through poetry. Yorke talks of Atwood reimagining and revisioning painful stereotypes – the 'unfixing of stereotypic associations' (1991: 5–6) – while Beyer argues constructively for a reconciliation and merging of opposing feminist approaches and uses the work of Jacques Lacan and the French feminists – Luce Irigaray, Helene Cixous and Julia Kristeva – and an idea of 'self-in -process' (Beyer 2000: 281), which avoids replacing one fixity with another, as such fixities would variously curtail what woman can become. She argues that the 'significance and liberating potential of seeing identity in terms of a self-in-process, and the notion of this process as ongoing, rather than concluding in a static end result, that these theorists highlight', is relevant to 'an analysis of Atwood's poetic discourse' (Beyer 2000: 281).

Building on and extending beyond such a feminist perspective alone, we recognise that Atwood can envisage the possibilities of survivals, continuities and positive change in both public and personal spheres. In her ecologically focused work – such as in 'Frogless' (1995), which I have discussed earlier – this informs a call to positive social action, to listen to Indigenous wisdom and to stop polluting lakes and rivers (Wisker

2017). In the context of the personal, domestic and social losses which Atwood predicts or enacts in her work, particularly in her poetry, survival is expressed in the continued sensitivity to echoes, traces, memories and presences beyond the finality of loss.

Form and expression enable and enact both the losses and the continuities in her work. Of *Dearly*, Shelby Judge comments that the free verse enables 'a sense of intimacy and direct expression throughout the anthology' (Judge 2023, n.p.). But there is more than that. As a technical feature of Atwood's poetry in individual poems and between and within the collections, her preferred use of free verse creates an effect of returns and reminders. Seemingly not tied to strict stanza lengths, or patterns of rhyme, free verse is rather like memory, which enables the return of the familiar but different, reminding of newness, estrangement and loss. The rhyme or part rhyme recalls and echoes earlier sounds. Individual words and phrases recur and shift, adding slightly altered views like something half-remembered, still there but different. In both these collections, there also are some unusual, out of place, unique and strange images and presences in the familiar places, and slipping words which echo throughout a single poem, or between several of the poems, enacting unexpected absence and loss. Taken together, many of the poems in *Morning in the Burned House* (1995) and *Dearly* (2020) suggest and enact both the impending or actual absence of, and also the return of, the familiar, metamorphosed, changed and sometimes emptied out.

What Has Been Lost or Will Be Lost: Nature and the Personal

Early on in poems in *Morning in the Burned House* (1995), and more recently and specifically *Dearly* (2020), the mixed expression of what has been lost or will be lost and of what might be identified as surviving, is projected into both the emptying natural space and place and the emptying domestic space. Words and images enact absences as they also reach towards embodying signs of survival and continuities.

Davey looks at Atwood's poetry over time and points out that while she's using the same kind of language, latterly she uses it differently, deliberately refusing boundaries and hierarchies. He notes, 'this indeterminacy suggests habitual ongoing action and psychological estrangement from historical time' and that 'the result of such techniques is the removal of time as an operative dimension for much of the poetry'. The 'Speaker appears to be a spectator of her own life, standing outside both this life and its temporal context whereupon cause and effect disappear' (1984: 41). He is, of course, not writing about *Dearly* (2020) but his insights help us in our own reading of this collection. The personal and ethical continuities explored in *Dearly* are of a part with this deliberate refusal of (gendered and species) hierarchy. The language and image of indeterminacy and fluidity emphasises the links and continuities between human and other living things and nature, between the acts of the past and the continuities and consequences in the future, and between the living and the dead.

We briefly re-explore some earlier poems from *Morning in the Burned House* (1995) here to situate the most recent collection *Dearly* (2020) in a history of Margaret Atwood's writing. Also, importantly, Atwood is revisiting earlier territory in this later collection, and the sense of reimagining, of developing new understanding, is central to not only survival, but also much beyond bare survival – to becoming, continuing to evolve, and having one eye on the clock. In this act of revisiting and re-visioning, Atwood's poetry avoids being fixed, static and stagnant in perspective, rather it has the energy and imagination to return and see things differently. This is an energy that elsewhere informs her return to the context and much of the situation of *The Handmaid's Tale* (1985) in *The Testaments* (2019), where it is possible that there can be reconciliations, since not everything in the Gilead home of the three related girls is awful and to be discarded. Even Aunt Lydia, the main controller and colluder, can be appreciated differently in her role as recorder, keeper or revealer of secrets and as a re-interpreter. Returns enable continuities beyond seeming dead ends and revisions of both understandings and memories.

In Atwood's work more generally, she returns to places, characters, issues and problems to reimagine, sometimes to reinforce and sometimes to offer different perspectives. This energy and vitality characterises her work, as does the re-interpretation of older myths. In *Dearly*, a new appreciation of the potentialities of grief and loss – of both memories and a changing world – runs throughout the collection and prevents it from being merely memorialising or whimsical. Rather, it offers valuable new perspectives where histories, interpretations and lives could seem stuck, going or gone. Moreover, Atwood's wry humour generally accompanies even the most poignant moments of slipping away or loss.

Morning in the Burned House (1995)

It isn't just with the collection *Dearly* that Margaret Atwood deals with loss; her occasionally chirpy, a little bewildered, poignant tone runs throughout several of her collections, with peaks in *Morning in the Burned House* (1995). In free verse, the ways in which sounds and words repeat and echo usually confirm a pattern and provide continuities, but the first poem 'You Come Back' deliberately uses such techniques to disrupt the security of continuity. While clear echoes and patterns are asserted, they signal loss rather than confirmation of hold on the relationship between words, experiences, identity and meaning. Many of the concerns in this collection, as in *Dearly,* are about loss and lack of continuities, a slipping away of identity, of presence, of confirmation of the familiar, and of the links between self, identity, the shared world and language. 'You Come Back' takes us into a house, a room, no longer as familiar as some earlier time for the 'You' of the poem, which feels like a direct address (second person) to me/us as reader. The re-entry signals a disruption of continuities of recognition, of place, event and identity, and dislocates links between words, things, consciousness and identity.

> You come back into the room
> where you've been living
> all along. You say:
> What's been going on
> while I was away?

Like the three bears in the Goldilocks story, the house is disrupted; someone else, it seems, has been here, wearing the clothes but, unlike the three bears, the memory of the one addressed, returning, of 'You', repeated as if to confirm, is actually that which is disrupted. Although the repeated use of 'You' signals a return or 'setting foot', there is actually a problem, a separation between words and the embodiment they usually enable because there has been a dislocation in the mind of the one who returns, who comes back. They have actually been there all long. They never went away. They have, however, lost the connection between identity, actions and familiar place and things. They have also lost the connection between word ('say') and meaning, and any controlling sense of continuity of self ('I was away', which echoes 'say'). The entrance, 'setting foot' into the room, also signals a lack of connection between words, things, understanding and continuity of self and communication with others. It is like a dream, a half-remembered memory but also resembles the confusions of the onset of dementia.

They (poet, You, reader, someone) are

> Setting foot on the middle ground
> between body and word, which contains,
> or is supposed to, other
> people. ('You Come Back', Atwood:1995)

The poet, and the reader relate to the 'you' in the poem, but communication is undercut even as it is explained. Continuities of words, address, sounds, fix and assure a shared reality and create patterns, but here they are disrupted as Atwood uses free verse to enact lack of continuities.

'A Visit' (1995) picks up themes of discontinuity and insecurities of relationship between self, a shared reality, words and things and the familiar yet defamiliarised other person. The poem starts with a mix of a familiar phrases, an image of someone idealised, and then an immediate undercutting, a reduction, and a recognition of their losses, reflected in the speaker's loss of the once fuller (idealised) version of them>

> Gone are the days
> when you could walk on water.
> When you could walk. (Atwood 1995)

Both the speaker and the loved one now inhabit a world which slips away as they try to hold onto it – the loved one grasping at familiar reality, and failing; the speaker trying to understand the world as the other sees it, trying to recalibrate them, still near but somehow distanced by this fading away of their control over their own senses and movements and understanding. She writes of someone with memory loss reduced to the memory of just that day, to the working of one hand, which grips. The loved person inhabits a world of confusion over naming, while the one who watches suffers something palpable and painful and tries to make sense of it all. There is repetition, as with repeated words and behaviours, and lack – lack of the richness of the familiar past and its actions and objects. 'No' and 'not' repeat the denial of the familiar, while the suggestion they 'not panic' is part public warning and part an expression of unity and calm.

> That is not a train
> There is no cricket
> Let's not panic
> (Atwood 1995)

The person the speaker converses with – likely her unnamed father –once knew the detail and particularity of woodwork tools, but as these tools lose their functionality and reduce to just 'sullen metal', so the 'sullen' transfers to the loved one, now stuck in a reduced body, with reduced memory, and recognising of their old home only 'the bed'.

Against this memory loss of objects and anything familiar, the speaker becomes more gentle, acknowledging that it is, in a way, better to go with the flow and not push words towards clarification, recognising both the loss and confusion of the loved one, and their own loss. This is a way we learn to deal with dementia.

> Better to watch the stream
> that flows across the floor
> and is made of sunlight
> the forest made of shadows;
> better to watch the fireplace
> which is now a beach.
> (Atwood 1995)

Indoors and outdoors merge and transform. She responds very calmly, aware that for the loved one and so for her, things have changed into other things. This is a movement from loss to something imaginative and peaceful. She can go with the flow of his confused perception and expression.

In *Morning in the Burned House* (Atwood 1995), there are many traces of historical people, and the derailed memory of a family kitchen which seems to have been evacuated because of a nuclear attack but actually is (also?) a kitchen remembered from the past where the table is set, the food is laid out and memories linger but it is empty. We are reminded of 'Goldilocks' in both 'You Come Back', and this title poem which concludes the collection. The voice wanders, half recalls, like Virginia Woolf's bodiless voice in *To The Lighthouse* (1927), also a place filled with echoes of long dead lovers. The empty house is the speaker's family house of her childhood – a memory that is widespread beyond the individuals but focused on the individual detail. Here the mind, the loss, the remembering like a ghost in her own home, and in her own body, this family remembering is like the ghost in the body of the loved person, mother or partner as they drift away from sense making. Even lack of recognition and the confusion present in their eyes and movements are recalled by the speaker. The loss in the person is matched by the pained loss she feels. This is dementia as well as natural ageing. Atwood can be as wry in her novels and short stories but the poems are more pointed and poignant, emphasising confusion in familiar places.

Many of the poems in this collection concern traces, the difficulties of identification, differentiation between memory and the present and a lack of certainty about place, time, solidity and identity. The near identification of place, feeling and memory is of a piece with the way in which, reading her work, we are also reaching after a sense of Margaret Atwood the poet's influences, the echoes or traces in her work from the work of others and the echoes and traces between these two collections *Morning in the Burned House* and *Dearly* which evoke a sense of life although part of it almost completely slips away and refuses certainty.

Others have commented on her subjectivity (Nicholson 1996; Ward 1994), and perhaps philosophy, phenomenology (Husserl 1972 [1913]; Merleau-Ponty 1972 [1945]) and existentialism (Sartre 1972 [1943]) can also help us with an appreciation that we sense, interpret and construct meaning through words and images driven by memory and some kind of relationship between perception and words. We make links in reading these poems – as do Atwood's personae and the actors: family, pets, the house itself, the speaker – and are left with grasping after an ineffable understanding and fixity, a sense making which we are aware is a temporary, untrustworthy construction.

Ironically, ChatGPT (which I consulted, given the Robot poem in *Dearly*), has missed the point of *Morning in the Burned House*, seeing the collection as a single poem, beginning with the giveaway word 'delve' used at last twice with which it sums up the straightforward wording in the poem – places, people, time – and missing the underlying dissociation between word and things, the echoing, memory loss and the hanging on to continuities of self, family and loved ones – particularly Atwood's father, mother and her shared version of self – as the burned devastated remnants of a solid, safe home are contested and its certainties – ranging from toast to those who recognise where they are in the domestic space – drift and slip away. This AI summary focuses on themes alone and is not connected to past or present, to wordplay or to Atwood's other works. It is bland and informational:

> Margaret Atwood's poem 'Morning in the Burned House' delves into themes of memory, loss, and the passage of time. Through vivid imagery and poignant language, Atwood paints a picture of a house that has endured destruction, yet still holds remnants of the past. (ChatGPT).[2]

Yes of course. But everything else in the poem (and of course, that it is also part of a collection) is missed.

Dearly (2020)

It is probable that for Margaret Atwood, *Dearly* is first driven by sadness at the deterioration and loss of her ageing mother, the loss of memories and moments of childhood homes, the everyday, and then by the loss of her partner Graeme Gibson, who also had dementia. Throughout this

2   <https://essaygpt.hix.ai/essay/analysis-of-morning-in-the-burned-house-6c1356>

work, accompanying these personal losses, there is a running lament for the loss of nature and diversity in this period in which we all live, the Anthropocene, in which deterioration of natural habitats and climate change are mainly caused by human ignorance, thoughtless selfishness and a wilful taste for destruction.

In *Dearly* the word is used in several ways as 'dearly beloved' (we are gathered here today [...]; a term used for loss and celebration, at weddings and funerals) expressing a sense of personal loss, and also a sense of paying for something dearly, in the end. The confusion of the mind, the vague disconnectedness of her mother in the earlier collection reappears here as an imagined future for the speaker, as it was in the first collection, and also a current reality in the house in the life of the speaker. Wry, amused tones incur comparisons, drift off incomplete like the minds of those mentioned, are dreamlike as the past is, but first a curtain is momentarily lifted then the present also seems to be behind a curtain, intangible, fading, inchoate, sadly, dearly being lost. So, 'fading now, I miss you' references both vanishing words, and as Kate Kellaway (2020) notes, Atwood's partner, Graeme Gibson. Gibson died in 2019 and, slipping away, nearing the end of his life, he himself resembled a vanishing word (ie. a word such as 'dearly'). The book is dedicated to Graeme Gibson, who appears in several other poems, as a presence, or absence, or the figure to whom the work is dedicated. One of these is 'Invisible Man', which Kellaway calls 'a spare, withheld poem' in which 'his presence is bravely envisaged as absence, 'like hanging a hat/on a hook that's not there any longer'. Like children told to pencil in dotted lines to indicate an invisible man, there is, at the breakfast table, with remembered toast and eggs, or walking up a drive with rustling, fallen leaves, no body, only 'the shape of an absence'(Kellaway 2020).

Dearly (2020) is Margaret Atwood's twenty-first collection of poetry, and her first anthology in over ten years, preceded by *The Door* (2007), but she tells us in its opening pages that the individual pieces have, as ever, been written throughout that period, put away in drawers, perhaps for a future date. Knowing this gives the effect of premonition as well as haunting, looking forward to a gradually stepped loss and fading out. In people and the cat this can be understood as the seeping away of the complexities of those who are loved and whose presence also confirms our own. On a grander ecological scale, it keeps us concerned about the irrecoverable losses resulting from unbated free play of the greed of a few and the ignorance of many. Atwood's own work is varied and generous, neither divisive nor hierarchical. In a 2020 article for *The Guardian*, entitled 'Caught in Time's Current. Margaret Atwood on Grief, Poetry and the Past Four Years', Atwood offers a reflection on her own continuity and ageing, that of Graeme Gibson, and on the times post Trump in which she was working with *The Testaments*. She recognizes that the poetry collection is 'part of its own zeitgeist, while claiming not to be part of it. It's not exactly a memento mori; more like a memento vita' (Atwood 2020). She reflects that 'poems – like everything else – are created in a particular time'. They are 'embedded in their time and place' although 'they may transcend them' as readers reinscribe their meanings (Atwood 2020). She notes a number of personal and global contexts that influenced her writing of the poem 'Dearly' and the subsequent composition of the collection. In her personal life, experiences of ageing were an influence, as well as the death of her partner Graeme Gibson in September 2019, following a diagnosis of vascular dementia in 2012. The title poem was written in August 2017, before his death but, due to the degenerative and uncertain nature of dementia, 'Graeme was pre-mourned: all the poems about him in the book *Dearly* were written before he actually died' (Atwood, 2020). Professionally, at this time, she was enjoying great success. The MGM/Hulu series *The Handmaid's Tale* premiered in April 2017 and CBC/Netflix miniseries *Alias Grace* in September 2017. Atwood reflects that these series are 'inextricably caught in time's currents, since *The Handmaid's Tale* became newly relevant in light of Donald Trump's election and his misogynistic and anti-democratic demagoguery' (Atwood 2020). Chillingly, she talks of how the 2016 election stripped 'the precious elements of America's democracy'. And

> Both were also backlit by the lurid glow cast by the 2016 presidential election, which I'd experienced like those nightmare movies where you're expecting a girl to jump out of a cake and instead it's the Joker. Had Clinton won the election, *The Handmaid's Tale* TV series would have been framed as a bullet dodged. As things were, the viewership was not only very high but very horrified' (Atwood 2020).

The politically charged period up to the publication of *Dearly* (2020) was very disturbing, marking a loss of freedoms and values. Atwood comments, 'However, few expected at this point that the efforts to undermine the foundations of American democracy – an independent, functioning media, a judiciary separate from the executive branch, a respect for the constitution and a military that owes its loyalty to the country as embodied in the constitution, not to some king or junta or dictator – would go as far as they were to go by November 2020' (Atwood 2020).

The poems in *Dearly* (2020) speak of memory and loss and loss of memory, of passports and stones and birds, of imagining forward to being less clearly defined even to yourself.

In 'Passports', she tells of her own long forgotten trips to wherever, for reasons also forgotten. She, the persona, Atwood? ages through the lines, through sequences, from the kids 'cut curls' to alien versions of self, 'grey disks', 'wraiths photos'/claiming to prove that I was me'. She sees herself in particular passports and in the poem 'Passports' as aged, the memories both bright and seeping away. These are versions of self, whether like criminal poses (in photos of those arrested – one face forward, one sideways on) or something half-erased, and through them she is distanced from herself in 'sequenced', managed serial photographs, resembling 'a woman who's just been arrested', both herself and not herself 'fading', 'a little more than dead' but still lingeringly a little magical perhaps,

> like a mermaid doomed to appear onshore
> every five years and each time altered. ('Passports', 2020)

She is lamenting the loss of loved ones but this is accompanied by constant versions of presence through recording and reporting that loss. They are lost because they are no longer children or cat or partner, yet present because they are called forth in lines which present them gently and poignantly as they – lines and loved ones – slip and fade. Poetry does more than catch and record; it reimagines, reinterprets, reignites and revives. The act of capturing and putting into words reaches after the slipping particulars, creating new shapes and understandings, for coping and continuity. Through writing poetry, you turn the leaves of the passport, the photographs of the past, bringing those in the photographs back to a different kind of life. Beyond the enactment of loss, past, present and future, the emptying and grieving, the imagining forward to mourning, there is some hope for and expression of forms of continuity and transformation. This is what she's doing in this book. This is the action in 'Passports' in particular, which is written out in her own handwriting twice on the book's inside cover. The poem and collection were, it seems, set off by Atwood 'going through a drawer of old writing from my teenage and college years' 'I was a constant scribbler: fictions, essays, plays and poems: finished, unfinished, partly finished. Most were pretty bad, but there was a lot of them. These poems had many subjects covered, on peonies, the Hungarian Revolution of 1956, winter commerce, severed heads. The usual'(Atwood, *Dearly* 2020 prelims no page number.).. This mix of the political, personal and the Gothic recurs throughout Atwood's work. They are multiple poems written in ink or ballpoint, on all sorts of different kinds of paper. 'And some were sent out to magazines with return envelopes. And they were mostly returned'.

These handwritten poems, some of which form *Dearly*, accumulated and hidden in a drawer, were written and revised between 2008 and 2019, the period when, 'things got darker in the world. Also, I grew older. People very close to me died' (Atwood 2020). For Atwood, poetry deals with the core of human existence: 'life, death, renewal, change; as well as fairness and unfairness, injustice and sometimes justice. The world in all its variety. The weather. Time. Sadness. Joy. And birds.' At the end, she says 'I wish also for more birds in the world' (Atwood 2020 prelims). While her fiction has taken centre stage for engagement with critical gendered issues, politics, sustainability, equalities, Indigenous rights, rights of lakes and creatures, nonetheless, the poems have continued to flow, expressing the same concerns and continuities, even if popped in a drawer out of sight, for later. And now we have *Dearly*, in 2020.

In the opening poem, 'Late Poems', Atwood acknowledges:

These are the late poems.
Most poems are late.
Of course, too late,
like a letter sent by a sailor
that arrives after he has drowned.

Like many of the poems in this collection, the underlying question is whether, if, perhaps for the world it is too late to lament, too much has been lost already. Is it only whimsical to suggest that expressing and embodying the gradual, sudden or future losses might, in the act of expressing and sharing, somehow stimulate continuity? The poem ends with some such future, in the exhortation 'Sing on'.

Shelby Judge notes of the collection *Dearly* (2022), that it brings together many of Margaret Atwood's 'most recognisable and celebrated themes, but distilled – from minutely perfect descriptions of the natural world to startlingly witty encounters with aliens, from pressing political issues to myth' (Judge 2023). The themes here are 'grief, the passage of time and ageing, and environmentalism and conservation' (Judge 2023). Typically, the poems are in free-verse, avoiding any constraint of a set metre, rhythm or rhyme. As I noted earlier, in Atwood's careful use, free verse enables words, sounds to echo and remind of each other, without being forced into an imprisoning pattern. In the collection, this 'imparts a sense of intimacy and direct expression throughout' (Judge 2023). It also suggests learning to live with loss, the movement of memory returning, understanding patterns, progression or deterioration, making sense of the moments and events. Atwood's poems of loss reference the personal and the global, the world in the future bereft of creatures, the humblest, smallest creatures, particularly birds, and also flowers, building on the loss of frogs in the earlier 'Frogless' (1995), where each loss is usually the result of human selfishness and ignorance. In 'Oh Children', the lament is for a world without birds, insects, flowers and even clams:

> Oh children, will you grow up in a world without birds?
> Will there be crickets, where you are?
> Will there be asters?
> Clams, at a minimum.
> Maybe not clams.

Family and personal poetry is of a piece with care for the planet and for living things, lands, creatures, people. Everywhere there is loss, but also echoes, reminders and continuities. Making memories and retaining or losing them is a thread throughout; in 'Souvenirs', the mementos which we bring others are (paradoxically) only to remind the friends not of the holiday which only *we* experienced, but rather, of us.

A favourite for me is 'Ghost Cat'. The cat with dementia, wanting to be let in, her mind a dislocated scattering of memories not quite focused on her name, calls '*let me in/enclose me, tell me who I was*' and wonders what should she be eating? She is like loved ones who are there in body while the mind has wandered vaguely off. This could be reminiscent of the latter days of living with her mother, and her husband, author Graeme Gibson, as both suffered from dementia. When the cat appears, it's like it's there. But it is both presence and loss simultaneously.

She asks at the beginning of 'Ghost Cat' whether we know that cats also suffer from dementia.

> Ours did. Not the black one, smart enough
> to be neurotic and evade the vet.
> The other one, the furrier's muff, the piece of fluff.

The cat, unsure of what she should eat 'comes up the stairs moth footed' and wails to be let in the bedroom:

> So witless and erased. *O, who?*
> Clawing at the bedroom door
> shut tight against her. *Let me in*
> *enclose me, tell me who I was.*

As the house becomes a darkened cave, everything takes a Gothic turn. The cat's loss of identity and direction aligns with that of the speaker, losing her civilised presence and warning that no matter who the cat claims to be and how much it loves her, whoever she's speaking to must keep her out (like a vampire).This ghost cat, initially homely and loved, fluffy, probably a bit silly and trying to make friends, who never really had a complicated mind, turns at the end of the poem, as if predatory, beyond civilised behaviour, scratching to be let in. This could be a poem only of nostalgia, only of whimsy, but Atwood always manages to engage emotions and familiarity, bringing the scenario into the everyday then giving it a little dark twist at the end. No one wants a vampire/ zombie at their window, and they're probably also a bit worried about a vampire/ zombie cat. The humour prevents anguish but also reflects fears of otherness at this change of being.

While at the beginning of *Dearly*, she talks about words, hanging around or not being published, her ordering, and curation, of them here expresses an emerging design coming into view in new constructions. Its parts precious, its whole is a new kaleidoscope of re-formed fragments of light and difference. The act of writing experiences into poetry pulls it all together. Perhaps poetry can enable the mind to trawl and to travel and put the pieces – some sharply cut, some illusions only barely caught – into some new shape. This is a way of coping as well as crafting.

The Plasticene Suite

The notion of the plasticine in *Dearly* belies its common use for playful craft, rather suggesting an era in which the world is dominated by plastics that are ubiquitous, everywhere in our homes, and even in the stomachs of whales. This sequence of poems includes 'Robot', and is mainly focused on the substitution of the artificial for the human and animal, the flora and fauna – knowing this too will erode and decay in the end as human constructions and development do, but as part of *Dearly*, it is a survival /loss sequence, in the midst of the loss of memory, homeliness and familiarity. Merve Altin uses an ecopoetic lens 'to reveal Atwood's criticism of the anthropogenic factors contributing to the current ecological crisis, particularly the ever-increasing generation of plastic waste, and to comment on contemporary poetry's awareness of and power to address the pressing environmental issues' (Altin 2024). Atwood works with Fromm's work (1996) on the contemporary alienation of humans from nature which is 'artfully concealed by modern technology' (Fromm1996:33). Using the work of Fromm as a guide, work in the 'Plasticene Suite' can be read as alerting us to ways in which reliance on the convenience and comforts of technology has alienated us from nature, and also as Altin notes, our 'spirituality and morality'(Altin 2024). In particular, 'Whales' (Atwood 2020) as Altin notes, illustrates the audience's response when witnessing dead whales on television, in which a mother whale carries her dead baby, its stomach stuffed with plastic, while as Altin notes 'exposing their ignorance towards the detrimental effects of technology on the environment' (Altin 2024). The fundamental problem which the poem questions is whether we can actually sympathise and act against such destruction of the other living beings and 'begin to feel responsible, or whether our anthropogenic worldview and lifestyle prevent us from recognising our 'contribution' to environmental issues' (Altin 2024). Will we just keep watching, without either empathy or action to stop the destruction and loss? In this reading inspired by Altin, much of Atwood's ecologically oriented poetry from 'Frogless' (1995) to 'Plasticene Suite' (2020) acts like her activist writing in letters and newspaper articles collected in the archives (Collection Box/Brown Box) ie. to urge humans to wake up and act positively.

Margaret Atwood recently discovered that AI is being trained on pirated versions of 33 of her novels for their wordsmithing computer programs (Atwood 2023). Relating this theft and substitution of the artificial for the real to *The Stepford Wives* (1972), where wives are replaced by happy domestic replicas to please their husbands, she notes:

> The companies developing generative AI seem to have something like that in mind for me, at least in my capacity as an author. (The sex and the housekeeping can be done by other functionaries, I assume.) [...] Once fully trained, the bot may be given— 'Write a Margaret Atwood novel'—and the thing will glurp forth 50,000 words, like soft ice cream spiralling out of its dispenser, that will be indistinguishable from something I might grind out. (But minus the typos.) I myself can then be dispensed with—murdered by my replica, as it were—because, to quote a vulgar saying of my youth, who needs the cow when the milk's free? (Atwood 2023)

Her AI robot poem 'Worthy' presents a cute little robot, a lot more than a child's toy. AI, it seems, creeps up on you, offering to help and seeming unthreatening in its 'normal' human manner.

The newly invented little robot has a 'confiding' expression, cute, plastic doll face

> it's designed to learn like a child. ('Worthy' Atwood 2020)

The softness, childlike, malleable qualities are accompanied by reminders of pretence, artifice with 'invented' and 'designed'. Like a child, it is not going to be as innocent as it first appears. Humans give it objects which it absorbs, becomes bored with (and probably breaks). The poem turns into a question about the obsolescence of the robot destined for a 'cosmic trash heap' and that of the human:

> Or will you live forever?
> Will we become your ancestors,
> rapacious and tedious?
> or will you erase us?
> Will you drop us on the floor?
> Would that be better? (Atwood 'Worthy', 2020)

The human child's destructive tendencies are transferred to the robot. It will neither develop morality or conscience, nor bear the burden of its own decisions, as it does not have that capacity, thereby making it more terrifying. Although it might have been developed to support, help and entertain humans, and we thought we had the upper hand by teaching it, we will merely be ancestors, forgotten and smashed. The inherent danger of AI is that the humans who created it might be ultimately erased by their own creation,

The penultimate poem is 'Dearly', where Atwood depicts herself as quite frail but tough, with poor knees, balancing half a cup of coffee, walking carefully along the pavements while reflecting on the changing meaning of words and things. 'Dearly' – which is a common prayerbook expression for weddings and funerals: 'dearly beloved [...]' – brings together people who are not usually or regularly united. She addresses her own poems, stored in a drawer, details obsolete, alongside remembered objects, such as Polaroid photographs, which represent outdated technology. These serve as strings to link things together, like a string of pearls – however, she writes, 'I don't like stones around my neck'(Atwood,'Dearly', 2020) as they would weigh her down and chrysanthemums are 'flowers of the dead', each signifying dying and loss, for which she says 'I sorrow dearly'(Atwood,'Dearly', 2020), thereby creating a new combination, rather than signifying an ending. The next and final poem about picking blackberries, references new life, poetry, and berries 'the best ones grow in shadow'(Atwood,'Dearly', 2020) presumably like her own thoughts and the poems in the collection, saved in a drawer, not silent, growing, waiting for the right time.

Reading *Morning in the Burned House* and *Dearly* is like being part of a closely held secret – an alarming fear that is global yet domestic, and personal. They echo each other as each collection aligns the personal with the natural world, expressing and enacting losses and temporary tenuous holds on both. In *Dearly,* the lingering traces of family memories – members, people, pets and objects – re-animate the past, setting off questions about their future, and any kind of future, or survival, for the world. Atwood's concerns for the planet – for us, for creatures and the environment – and her awareness of and warnings about loss are imaginatively precise and both whimsical and threatening.

Bibliography

Aebischer, Pascale, *Shakespeare, Spectatorship and the Technologies of Performance* (Cambridge: Cambridge University Press, 2020).

Ahmed, Sara, *Living a Feminist Life* (Durham, NC: Duke University Press, 2017).

Ahmed, Sara, *The Promise of Happiness* (Durham, NC: Duke University Press, 2010).

Alder, Emily, and Jenny Bavidge, *Ecocriticism and the Genre*, in Clive Bloom, ed, *The Palgrave Handbook of Contemporary Gothic* (Cham: Springer, 2020), 225–242.

Alias Grace. Directed by Mary Harron. Episode 1. Netflix (25 September 2017).

Allardice, Lisa, 'Margaret Atwood: For a long time we were moving away from Gilead', *Guardian* (20 September 2017).

Altin, Merve, 'And now we're here: the Plasticene': Ecological Awareness in Margaret Atwood's Recent Poetry Collection, *Dearly*', *Litera Journal of Language Literature and Culture Studies*, 34/1, June 2024. <https://www.researchgate.net/publication/381609798_and_now_we%27re_here_the_Plasticene_Ecological_Awareness_in_Margaret_Atwood%27s_Recent_Poetry_Collection_Dearly>, accessed 27 August 2024.

Andrejevic, Mark., 'The Work of Watching One Another: Lateral Surveillance, Risk, and Governance', *Surveillance & Society*, 2(4) (2005), 479–497.

Ann, Judith, 'The Secretarial Proletariat', in Robin Morgan, ed., *Sisterhood is Powerful: An Anthology of Writings from the Women's Liberation Movement* (London: Vintage, 1970), 86–100.

Anonymous, 'World Premiere of Søren Nils Eichberg's Opera Based on Margaret Atwood's *Oryx and Crake*', *Wise Music Classical* (18 February 2023). <https://www.wisemusicclassical.com/news/4503/>, accessed 23 August 2023.

Appleton, Sarah A. ed., *Once Upon a Time: Myths, Fairytales, and Legends in Margaret Atwood's Writing* (Cambridge: Cambridge Scholars, 2009).

Atwood, Margaret. University of Toronto: Thomas Fisher Rare Book Library, Archive Manuscript. Collection Box /Brown Box (varied)

Atwood, Margaret, *Survival: A Thematic Guide to Canadian Literature* (Toronto: Anansi, [1972] 2012).

Atwood, Margaret, *Up in the Tree*, originally published 1978 (Toronto: Groundwood, 2006; *Kobo* e-book, February 2024).

Atwood, Margaret, *Life Before Man* (Toronto: McClelland and Stewart, 1979).

Atwood, Margaret, *Lady Oracle* (Toronto: McClelland and Stewart, 1981a).

Atwood, Margaret, *True Stories* (Toronto: Oxford University Press, 1981b).

Atwood, Margaret, 'An Interview with Margaret Atwood', interview by Catherine Sheldrick Ross and Cory Bieman Davies, *CCL* 42 (1986), 9–16.

Atwood, Margaret, *Cat's Eye* (London: Virago, 1988/1990).

Atwood, Margaret, *Interlunar* (London: Jonathan Cape, 1988).

Atwood, Margaret, 'For God and Gilead', *The Guardian* (22 March 2003).

Atwood, Margaret, *The Handmaid's Tale* (Toronto: Fawcett Crest: 1985/London: Vintage, 2005).

Atwood, Margaret, 'Articulating the Mute', interview by Karla Hammond, 1979, reprinted in Earl G. Ingersoll, ed., *Margaret Atwood: Conversations* (London: Virago, 1992).

Atwood, Margaret, 'Interview with Jo Brans', reprinted in Earl G. Ingersoll, ed., *Margaret Atwood: Conversations* (London: Virago, 1992).

Atwood, Margaret, 'Grimms Remembered', in Donald Haase, ed., *The Reception of Grimms' Fairytales: Responses, Reactions, Revisions* (Detroit: Wayne State University Press, 1993), 290–292.

Atwood, Margaret, *The Edible Woman*, originally published 1969 (London: Virago, 1994).

Atwood, Margaret, 'A Visit', *The Atlantic Monthly*, 275(5) (1995), 76.

Atwood, Margaret. 'Frogless', in *Morning in the Burned House* (Boston, MA: Houghton Mifflin, 1995).

Atwood, Margaret, *Morning in the Burned House* (Boston, MA: Houghton Mifflin, 1995).

Atwood, Margaret, *Princess Prunella and the Purple Peanut*, illus. Maryann Kovalski (Toronto: Key Porter Kids, 1995).

Atwood, Margaret, *Alias Grace* (New York: Anchor Books, 1996).

Atwood, Margaret, *The Blind Assassin* (Toronto: Seal Books, 2000).

Atwood, Margaret, *Negotiating with the Dead: A Writer on Writing* (Cambridge: Cambridge University Press, 2002).

Atwood, Margaret, *Oryx and Crake* (New York: Nan A. Talese, 2003).

Atwood, Margaret, *Rude Ramsay and the Roaring Radishes*, illus. Dušan Petričić (Toronto: McArthur & Co, 2003).

Atwood, Margaret, *Wandering Wenda and the Widow Wallup's Wunderground Washery*, illus. Dušan Petričić (Toronto: McArthur & Co., 2011).

Atwood, Margaret, 'Books Find Their Readers.' Interview. *Macleans* (20 October 2003), 56. Lexis Nexis, accessed 15 May 2012.

Atwood, Margaret, *Bashful Bob and Doleful Dorinda*. Illus. Dušan Petričić (Toronto: Key Porter Kids, 2004).

Atwood, Margaret, *Oryx and Crake* (Toronto: Seal Books, 2004).

Atwood, Margaret, 'Aliens Have Taken the Place of Angels', *Guardian* (17 June 2005).

Atwood, Margaret, 'Angela Carter: 1940–1992', in *Curious Pursuits: Occasional Writing 1970– 2005* (London: Virago, 2005), 155–156.

Atwood, Margaret, 'Spotty-Handed Villainesses: Problems of Female Bad Behaviour in the Creation of Literature', in *Curious Pursuits: Occasional Writing 1970-2005* (London: Virago, 2005), 171–187.

Atwood, Margaret, *The Penelopiad* (Toronto: Knopf, 2005).

Atwood, Margaret, 'A matter of life and debt', *New York Times*, 21 October 2008.

Atwood, Margaret, *The Year of the Flood* (London: Bloomsbury, 2009).

Atwood, Margaret, 'Margaret Atwood: The Road to Ustopia', *The Guardian*, 14 October 2011. <https://www.theguardian.com/books/2011/oct/14/margaret-atwood-road-to-ustopia>, accessed 20 May 2022.

Atwood, Margaret, 'Margaret Atwood on Fiction, the Future, and the Environment', interview at the Nexus Conference 2012, <http://opentranscripts.org/transcript/margaret-atwood-fiction-future-environment/>

Atwood, Margaret, 'Margaret Atwood's dystopian future interview', *BBC Radio 4 Online*, 16 September 2013, <http://www.bbc.co.uk/programmes/b039zg2c>, accessed 8 November 2013.

Atwood, Margaret, *MaddAddam* (London: Bloomsbury, 2013).

Atwood, Margaret, *The Heart Goes Last* (London: Bloomsbury, 2015).

Atwood, Margaret, *Hag-Seed* (London: Vintage, [2016] 2017).

Atwood, Margaret, 'Margaret Atwood on What *The Handmaid's Tale* Means in the Age of Trump', *New York Times* (10 March 2017).

Atwood, Margaret, 'The Handmaid's Tale' Author Margaret Atwood: 'I Have Never Believed It Can't Happen Here', *CBS News* (8 September 2019).

Atwood, Margaret, *The Testaments* (London: Chatto & Windus, 2019).

Atwood, Margaret, 'Caught in Time's Current: Margaret Atwood on Grief, Poetry and the Past Four Years', *The Guardian* (7 November 2020), <https://www.theguardian.com/books/ng-interactive/2020/nov/07/caught-in-times-current-margaret-atwood-on-grief-poetry-and-the-past-four-years>, accessed 19 July 2024.

Atwood, Margaret, *Dearly* (New York: Ecco Press, 2020).

Atwood, Margaret, 'Impatient Griselda' in The New York Times Magazine, ed., *The Decameron Project: 29 New Stories from the Pandemic* (London: Simon & Schuster, 2020), 67–76.

Atwood, Margaret, 'Margaret Atwood Teaches Creative Writing', Masterclass.com (5 October 2020), <https://www.youtube.com/watch?v=U_dotIugpSA>, accessed 10 September 2023.

Atwood, Margaret, '"It Has Never Been More Pertinent": Margaret Atwood on the Chilling Genius of Laurie Anderson's *Big Science*', *The Guardian* (8 April 2021).

Atwood, Margaret, 'Seven Life Lessons from Margaret Atwood', *BBC Radio 4 online*, <https://www.bbc.co.uk/programmes/articles/5DQdfKq953Pq6DS kMkM1P5l/seven-life-lessons-from-margaret-atwood>, accessed 28 February 2021.

Atwood, Margaret, 'The Writing of *The Testaments*', in *Burning Questions: Essays and Occasional Pieces, 2004–2021* (London: Chatto & Windus, 2022).

Atwood, Margaret, *Burning Questions: Essays and Occasional Pieces, 2004–2021* (London: Chatto & Windus, 2022).

Atwood, Margaret, *Old Babes in the Wood: Stories* (Toronto: McClelland & Stewart, 2023).

Atwood, Margaret, 'Murdered by My Replica?', *The Atlantic* (26 August 2023), <https://www.theatlantic.com/books/archive/2023/08/ai-chatbot-training-books-margaret-atwood/675151/?utm_source=email&utm_medium=social&utm_campaign=share)>

Atwood, Margaret, *Trio of Tolerable Tales*, illus. Dušan Petričić (Toronto: Groundwood, 2017. *Kobo*, February 2024).

Baccolini, Raffaella, '"Hope isn't Stupid": The Appropriation of Dystopia', *MediAzioni*, 27 (2020), 39–49.

Baker, Daniella Irene, 'From Enduring to Living: An Ecofeminist Reading of Margaret Atwood's *The Edible Woman* and Han Kang's *The Vegetarian*', *Margaret Atwood Studies*, 18 (2025), 8.

Ball, K. et al., 'Editorial: Surveillance Studies Needs Gender and Sexuality', *Surveillance & Society*, 6(4) (2009), 352–355.

Barthes, Roland, 'Toward a Psychology of Contemporary Food Consumption', in Carole Counihan and Penny Van Esterik, eds., *Food and Culture: A Reader* (London: Routledge, 1997), 20–27.

Barzilai, Shuli, '"Say That I had a Lovely Face": The Grimms' 'Rapunzel', Tennyson's 'Lady of Shalott', and Atwood's *Lady Oracle*', *Tulsa Studies in Women's Literature*, 19(2) (2000), 231–254.

Bate, Jonathan, *The Song of the Earth* (London: Picador, 2000).

Baudrillard, Jean, 'The Pseudo-event and Neo-reality', in *Revenge of the Crystal: Selected Writings on the Modern Object and its Destiny, 1968-1983* (Sydney: Pluto Press/Power Institute of Fine Arts, 1990).

Beaumont, Peter, and Amanda Holpuch, 'How *The Handmaid's Tale* Dressed Protests Across the World.' *The Guardian* (3 August 2018), <https://www.theguardian.com/world/2018/aug/03/how-the-handmaids-tale-dressed-protests-across-the-world>, accessed 8 December 2020.

Bentley, Paul, *A Handmaid's Diary* (Copenhagen: Edition Wilhelm Hansen, 2005).

Benyus, Janine, *Biomimicry: Innovation Inspired by Nature* (New York: HarperCollins, 1997).

Berlant, Lauren, *Cruel Optimism* (Duke, NC: Duke University Press, 2011).

Bergthaller, Hannes, 'Housebreaking the Human Animal: Humanism and the Problem of Sustainability in Margaret Atwood's *Oryx and Crake* and *The Year of the Flood*, *English Studies*, 91(7) (2010), 728–743.

Beyer, Charlotte, 'Feminist Revisionist Mythology and Female Identity in Margaret Atwood's Recent Poetry', *Literature and Theology*, 14(3) (2000), 276–298, <https://www.jstor.org/stable/23925612>.

Billington, Michale, '*The Tempest* Review: Beale's Superb Prospero Haunts Hi-Tech Spectacle,' *The Guardian* (18 November 2016).

Blos, Peter, *The Adolescent Personality: A Study of Individual Behaviour* (New York: Appleton-Century, 1941).

Boccacio, Giovanni, *The Decameron*. Trans. John Payne. Rev. and Annotat. Charles S. Singleton (Berkeley: University of California Press, 1986).

Boedeker, Deborah, 'Hecate: A Transfunctional Goddess in Theogony?', *Transactions of the American Philological Association*, 113 (1983), 79–93.

Bone, Jane, 'Environmental Dystopias: Margaret Atwood and the Monstrous Child', *Discourse*, 37(5) (2016), 627–640.

Bottingheimer, Ruth, *An New History of Fairytales* (New York: State University of New York Press, 2009), <https://doi.org/10.1017/9781108626651.013>, accessed 12 September 2023.

Bowen, Deborah, 'Ecological Endings and Eschatology: Margaret Atwood's Post-Apocalyptic Fiction', *Christianity & Literature*, 66(4) (2017), 691–705.

Braidotti, Rosi, *The Posthuman* (Cambridge: Polity Press, [2013] 2017).

Braidotti, Rosi, 'A Theoretical Framework for the Critical Posthumanities', *Theory, Culture and Society*, 36(6) (2019), 31–61.

Bronfman, Judith, *Chaucer's Clerk's Tale: The Griselda Story Received, Rewritten, Illustrated*, originally published 1994 (New York: Routledge, 2019).

Bouson, Brooks, Jane, "It's Game Over Forever': Atwood's Satiric Vision of a Bioengineered Posthuman Future in *Oryx and Crake*', *Journal of Commonwealth Literature*, 39(3), (September 2004), 139–156.

Brooks Bouson, Jane, "'We're Using Up the Earth. It's Almost Gone": A Return to the Post-Apocalyptic Future in Margaret Atwood's *The Year of the Flood*, *Journal of Commonwealth Literature*, 46(1) (2011), 9–26.

Bruner, Jerome, *The Culture of Education* (Cambridge, MA: Harvard University Press, 1996).

Boym, Svetlana, *The Future of Nostalgia* (New York: Basic Books, 2001).

Bruch, Hilde. 2000. *The Golden Cage: The Enigma of Anorexia Nervosa*. London: Open Books.

Bruhm, Steven, 'The Contemporary Gothic: Why We Need It', in Jerrold E. Hogle, ed., *The Cambridge Companion to Gothic Fiction* (Cambridge: Cambridge University Press, 2006), 259–276.

Byrd, Merry Lynn, 'Maybe the Answer was Miranda All Along', *Femspec*, 18(1) (2018), 75–80.

Cahill, Susan., and Newell, Bryce Clayton., 'Surveillance Stories: Imagining Surveillance Futures', *Surveillance & Society*, 19(4) (2021), 412–413.

Caldwell, Rebecca, 'Atwood Finds Opera "Powerful"', *Toronto Globe and Mail* (18 September 2004).

Canton, Kimberly Fairbrother, '"I'm Sorry My Story is in Fragments": Offred's Operatic Counter-Memory', *ESC: English Studies in Canada*, 33(3) (2007), 125–144.

Carr, Emily, 'The Riddle Was the Angel in the House: Towards an American Ecofeminist Gothic', in Andrew Smith and William Hughes, eds., *EcoGothic* (Manchester: Manchester University Press, 2013),160–176.

Carter, Angela, *The Sadeian Woman: An Exercise in Cultural History* (London: Virago, 1979).

Carter, Angela, [Created 1987–2002], *Angela Carter Papers*, British Library Manuscript Collections, GB 58 Add. MS 88899/1/43: Unpublished Short Stories, 1962–77.

Ceep, 'Review: *Wandering Wenda and Widow Wallup's Wunderground Washery*', Amazon (21 December 2015), https://www.amazon.com/Wandering-Wenda-Wallops-Wunderground-Washery/dp/1770870008, accessed 16 August 2025.

Christ, Carol P., and Judith Plaskow, eds., *Womanspirit Rising: A Feminist Reader in Religion* (New York: HarperCollins, 1992).

Christie, Janet, 'Interview: Margaret Atwood on Her Novel MaddAddam', *The Scotsman Online* (1 September 2013), <https://www.scotsman.com/arts-and-culture/interview-margaret-atwood-her-novel-maddaddam-1562906>, accessed 28 March 2021.

Clark, Alex, '*The Testaments* by Margaret Atwood – First Look Review', *The Guardian* (4 September 2019), <https://www.theguardian.com/books/2019/sep/04/the-testaments-by-margaret-atwood-first-look-review>

Clay, Jenny Strauss, 'The Hecate of *Theogony*', *Greek, Roman and Byzantine Studies*, 25(1) (1984), 27–28. <https://grbs.library.duke.edu/index.php/grbs/article/view/5671>

Coats, Karen, 'Tales We Live By', in Karen Coats ed., *The Bloomsbury Introduction to Children's and Young Adult Literature* (London and New York: Bloomsbury Academic, 2018), 243–274.

Conley, Carolyn, *Certain Other Countries: Homicide, Gender, and National Identity in Late Nineteenth-Century England, Ireland, Scotland, and Wales* (Columbus, OH: Ohio State University Press, 2020).

Conroy, Catherine, 'Margaret Atwood: "When Did It Become the Norm to Expect a Porn Star on the First Date?"' Interview. *The Irish Times* (1 March 2018),

<https://www.irishtimes.com/culture/books/margaret-atwood-when-did-it-become-the-norm-to-expect-a-porn-star-on-the-first-date-1.3408922>, accessed 16 May 2022.

Cooke, Grayson, 'Technics and the Human At Zero-Hour: Margaret Atwood's Oryx and Crake', *Studies in Canadian Literature* 31(2) (2006), 63–83.

Cooper, Melinda, *Life as Surplus: Biotechnology in the Neoliberal Era* (Seattle: University of Washington Press, 2008).

Corones, Anthony, and Hardy, Susan, 'En-gendered Surveillance: Women on the Edge of a Watched Cervix', *Surveillance & Society*, 6(4) (2009), 388–397.

Couturier-Storey, Françoise, and Jeffrey Storey, 'Re-Writing a Woman's Crime: Alias Grace and the Absence of Truth', in Rédouane Abouddahab and Josiane Paccaud-Huguet eds., *Fiction, Crime, and the Feminine* (Newcastle upon Tyne, England: Cambridge Scholars Publishing, 2011), 49–61.

Davey, Frank, *Margaret Atwood: A Feminist Poetics*, The New Canadian Criticism Series (Toronto: Talonbooks, 1984).

Davies, Madeleine, 'Margaret Atwood's Female Bodies', in Coral Ann Howells, ed., *Cambridge Companion to Margaret Atwood* (Cambridge: Cambridge University Press, 2006), 58–71.

Däwes, Birgit, 'Molecular Mimicry, Realism, and the Collective Memory of Pandemics. Narrative Strategies of COVID-19 Fiction', *DIEGESIS. Interdisciplinary E-Journal for Narrative Research / E-Journal für Erzählforschung*, 11(1) (2022), 1–24.

Debord, Guy, *Society of Spectacle* (New York: Zone Books, 1994).

Defalco, Amelia, 'MaddAddam, Biocapitalism and Affective Things', *Contemporary Women's Writing*, 11(3) (2017), 432–451, repository copy in *White Rose Research Online*, <https://eprints.whiterose.ac.uk/114550/>, accessed 20 June 2021.

De Beauvoir, Simone, *The Second Sex*. Trans. Constance Borde and Sheila Malovany-Chevallier (London: Vintage, 1949/2010).

de la Bellacasa, Maria Puig, 'Limitless Life and Devastated Living', *Biosocieties*, 4(2–3) (2009), 321–325.

De la Rochère, Martine Hennard Dutheil, 'From Griselda's Patience to Feminist Grit: Angela Carter's 'The Patience of Grizelda' as a Hidden Intertext to 'The Bloody Chamber' and 'The Tiger's Bride'', in Charlotte Crofts and Marie Mulvey-Roberts, eds., *Angela Carter's Pyrotechnics: A Union of Contraries* (London: Bloomsbury, 2022), 71–94.

Deleuze, Gilles, 'Postscript on the Societies of Control', *October*, 59 (1992), 3–7.

D'Ignazio, Catherine., and Klein, Lauren. *Data Feminism* (Massachusetts: Massachusetts Institute of Technology, 2020).

Domville, Eric, 'The Handmaid's Detail: Notes on the Novel and Opera', *University of Toronto Quarterly*, 75(3) (2006), 869–882.

Dubrofsky, R. E., and Magnet, S. A., eds., *Feminist Surveillance Studies* (Durham. N.C.USA: Duke University Press, 2015).

Dvořák, Marta, 'Atwood's *Hag-Seed* and *The Heart Goes Last*, a Generic Romp', in Shannon Wells-Lassagne and Fiona McMahon, eds., *Adapting Margaret Atwood* (New York: Springer 2021), 15–33.

Edwards, Gail and Judith Saltman, 'The 1970s: Developing a Children's Publishing Industry', in Gail Edwards and Judith Saltman, eds., *Picturing Canada: A History of Canadian Children's Illustrated Books and Publishing* (Toronto: University of Toronto Press, 2010), 69–98.

Eisler, Riane, and Douglas P. Fry, *Nurturing Our Humanity: How Domination and Partnership Shape Our Brains, Lives, and Future* (Oxford: Oxford University Press, 2019).

Eliot, T. S., 'Burnt Norton', in *Collected Poems 1909–1935* (New York: Harcourt, Brace and Co., 1936)

Elliott, Robin, 'Margaret Atwood and Music', *University of Toronto Quarterly*, 75(3) (2006), 821–832.

Engles, Tim, *White Male Nostalgia in Contemporary North American Literature* (Cham: Springer, 2018).

Enright, Anne, '*The Testaments* by Margaret Atwood Review—A Dazzling Follow-up to *The Handmaid's Tale*', *The Guardian* (10 September 2019), <https://www.theguardian.com/books/2019/sep/10/the-testaments-by-margaret-atwood-review>, accessed 8 December 2020.

Epstein, Joseph, 'Is There a Doctor in the White House? Not If You Need an M.D.', Op-ed, *Wall Street Journal* (11 December 2020).

Erikson, Erik, *Life and the Historical Moment* (New York: W.W. Norton, 1975).

Evans, Shari, 'Not Unmarked: From Themed Space to a Feminist Ethics of Engagement in Atwood's *Oryx and Crake*', *Femspec: An Interdisciplinary Feminist Journal*, 10(2) (2010), 35–58.

Falk, Pasi, *The Consuming Body* (London: SAGE, 1994).

Federal Bureau of Intelligence, 'Number of Murder Offenders in the United States in 2021, by Gender', 5 October 2022, < https://wwwstatistacom.ezproxy.stthomas.edu/statistics/251886/murder-offenders-in-the-us-by-gender; https://crimeandjusticeresearchalliance.org/rsrch/gender-and-homicide/>, accessed 8 July 2023.

Fee, Margery, *The Fat Lady Dances: Margaret Atwood's* Lady Oracle (Toronto: ECW, 1993).

Feldman-Kołodziejuk, Ewelina, 'From Villainess to Gilead's Nemesis: The (Un) easy Rehabilitation of Aunt Lydia', *Canada and Beyond: A Journal of Canadian Literary and Cultural Studies*, 14 (2025), 85–103,

Fox, James, 'Gender and Homicide', Gender and Crime. Crime and Justice Research Alliance: National Criminal Justice Association (2020), <https://crimeandjusticeresearchalliance.org/rsrch/gender-and-homicide/>, accessed 3 July 2023.

Foucault, Michel, *The History of Sexuality Vol. I: An Introduction*, trans. Robert Hurley (New York: Pantheon Books, 1978).

Foucault, Michel, *Power/Knowledge: Selected Interviews and Other Writings 1972–1977*, ed. and trans. Colin Gordon et al. (Brighton: Harvester, 1980).

Freud, Sigmund, 'Mourning and Melancholia', in *The Standard Edition of the Complete Psychological Works of Sigmund Freud Volume XIV* (1914-1916): *On the History of the Psycho-Analytic Movement, Papers on Metaphysiology and Other Works*, trans. James Strachey (London: Vintage, 2001).

Freud, Sigmund, *Totem and Taboo* (London: Routledge,1991).

Freud, Sigmund, 'Repression', in Anna Freud, ed., *The Essentials of Psychoanalysis* (London: Penguin, 1991).

Friedan, Betty, *The Feminine Mystique* (London: Penguin, 2010 [1963]).

Fromm, Harold., 'From Transcendence to Obsolescence: A Route Map', in Cheryll. Glotfelty & Harold Fromm, eds., *The Ecocriticism Reader: Landmarks in Literary Ecology* (Athens, GA: University of Georgia Press) 30–39.

Gallagher, Paul, 'Interview: Margaret Atwood on new novel MaddAddam'. (archived: available at list.co.uk > news > interview-margaret-atwood-on-ne)

Gilbert, Sophie, '"Margaret Atwood Bears Witness": Review', *The Atlantic* (December 2019), <https://www.theatlantic.com/magazine/archive/2019/12/margaret-atwood-bears-witness/600796/>, accessed 17 May 2022.

Gill, Ian, *North of Caution: A Journey through the Conservation Economy on the Northwest Coast of British Columbia* (Ecotrust,Vancouver,Canada, 2001).

Given, Casey, 'The Handmaid's Tale is Profiting Off anti-Trump Hysteria', *Washington Examiner* (24 September 2019).

Goldberg, Jonathan, *Tempest in the Caribbean* (Minneapolis: University of Minnesota Press, 2004).

Gosetti-Ferencei, Jennifer Anna, *The Life of Imagination: Revealing and Making the World* (New York: Columbia University Press, 2018).

Grace, Sherrill E., *Violent Duality: A Study of Margaret Atwood* (Montréal: Véhicule, 1980).

Grace, Sherrill E., 'Margaret Atwood and the Politics of Duplicity', in Arnold Davidson and Cathy E. Davidson, eds., *The Art of Margaret Atwood: Essays in Criticism* (Toronto: Anansi, 1981), 55–68.

Green, Philippa, 'Lady Killers is Back for a Third Season', *The Open University* (8 January 2024), <https://ounews.co/arts-social-sciences/lady-killers-is-back-for-a-third-series/>, accessed July 8, 2023.

Greenhill, Pauline, and Leah Claire Allen, 'Animal Studies', in Pauline Greenhill, Jill Terry Rudy, Naomi Hamer, and Lauren Bosc, eds., *The Routledge Companion to Media and Fairy-Tale Cultures*, (New York: Routledge, 2018), 225–234.

Greer, Germaine, *The Female Eunuch* (London: MacGibbon and Kee, 1970).

Guth, Karen V., 'Moral Injury, Feminist and Womanist Ethics, and Tainted Legacies', *Journal of the Society of Christian Ethics*, 38 (2018), 167–186.

Haden, Roger, 'Taste in an Age of Convenience: From Frozen Food to Meals in *The Matrix*', in Carolyn Korsmeyer, ed., *The Taste Culture Reader: Experiencing Food and Drink*, (Oxford: Berg, 2005), 344–358.

Haraway, Donna, *Simians, Cyborgs and Women: The Reinvention of Nature* (New York: Routledge, 1991).

Haraway, Donna, *Modest_Witness@Second_Millennium.FemaleMan_Meets_OncoMouse: Feminism and Technoscience* (London: Routledge, 1997).

Haraway, Donna, *The Haraway Reader* (London: Routledge, 2004).

Haraway, Donna, *Staying With the Trouble: Making Kin in the Chthulucene* (Durham and London: Duke University Press, 2016), 1–8.

Harvey, David, *The Condition of Postmodernity: An Enquiry into the Origins of Cultural Change* (Oxford: Basil Blackwell, 1989).

Hayles, Katherine N., *How We Became Posthuman: Virtual Bodies in Cybernetics, Literature and Informatics* (Chicago: University of Chicago Press, 1999a).

Hayles, Katherine N., 'The Life Cycle of Cyborgs: Writing the Posthuman', in Jenny Wolmark, ed., *Cybersexualities: A Reader on Feminist Theory, Cyborgs and Cyberspace* (Edinburgh: Edinburgh University Press, 1999b), 157–173.

Haynes, Joanna, and Karin Murriss, 'Taking Age Out of Play: Children's Animistic Philosophizing Through a Picturebook', *Oxford Literary Review*, 41(2) (2019), 290–309.

Hesiod, 'Hymn to Hecate', *Theogony*, 8th-7th century BC.

Heyen, Robert, and Van der Meuleun, Emily, eds., *Expanding the Gaze: Gender and the Politics of Surveillance* (Toronto: University of Toronto Press, 2016).

Heyman, Michael, and Kevin Shortsleeve, 'Nonsense', in Philip Nel and Lissa Paul, eds., *Keywords for Children's Literature* (New York: New York University Press, 2011), 165–169.

Hinchliffe, Jade., 'Speculative Fiction, Sociology, and Surveillance Studies: Towards a Methodology of the Surveillance Imaginary', *Surveillance & Society*, 19(4) (2016), 414–424.

Hobgood, Jennifer, 'Anti-edibles: Capitalism and Schizophrenia in Margaret Atwood's *The Edible Woman*', *Style*, 36 (2002), 146–168.

Howells, Coral Ann, *Margaret Atwood* (London: Macmillan, 1996).

Howells, Coral Ann, 'Introduction', in Coral Ann Howells, ed., *The Cambridge Companion to Margaret Atwood* (Cambridge: Cambridge University Press, 2006), 1–11.

Howells, Coral Ann, 'Margaret Atwood's Dystopian Visions: *The Handmaid's Tale* and *Oryx and Crake*', in Carol Ann Howells, ed., *The Cambridge Companion to Margaret Atwood* (Cambridge: Cambridge University Press, 2006), 161–175.

Howells, Coral, 'True Trash: Genre Fiction Revisited in Margaret Atwood's *Stone Mattress, The Heart Goes Last*, and *Hag-Seed*', *Contemporary Women's Writing*, 11(3) (2017), 297–315.

Howells, Coral Ann, 'Margaret Atwood's Recent Dystopias', in *The Cambridge Companion to Margaret Atwood*, 2nd edn (Cambridge: Cambridge University Press, 2021), 171–188.

Husserl, Edmund, *Ideas Pertaining to a Pure Phenomenology and to a Phenomenological Philosophy – First Book: General Introduction to a Pure Phenomenology*, trans. F. Kersten (The Hague: Martinus Nijhoff, 1982 [1913]).

Hutcheon, Linda, *A Theory of Adaptation* (Abingdon: Routledge, 2006).

Hvidt, Eva, 'Tjenerindens dramatiske fortalling [The Handmaid's Dramatic Story]', *Kristeligt Dagblad* (1 March, 2000)

Jaeger, Cora, 'Animal', *Brock Education Journal*, 27(2) (2018), 188–222.

Jayendran, Nishevita, '"Set Me Free": Spaces and the Politics of Creativity in Margaret Atwood's *Hag-Seed* (2016)', *Journal of Language, Literature and Culture*, 67(1) (2020), 15–27.

Judge, Shelby, 'Dearly', *The Literary Encyclopedia*, <https://www.litencyc.com>, accessed 9 May 2023.

Kakutani, Michiko, 'The Handmaid's Thriller: In 'The Testaments,' There's a Spy in Gilead', *New York Times* (3 September 2019).

Kaminski, M., 'Preserving Mythologies', in E. G. Ingersoll, ed., *Margaret Atwood: Conversations* (London: Virago, 1992), 88–92.

Keats, John, 'Ode to a Nightingale' 1819.

Keightley, Emily, and Pickering, Michael, 'The Mnemonic Imagination', in *The Mnemonic Imagination*, Palgrave Macmillan Memory Studies (London: Palgrave Macmillan, 2012), 43–80.

Kowal, Ewa, 'Nostalgia, Kitsch and the Great Recession in Margaret Atwood's *The Heart Goes Last* and *Westworld* (Season 1)', *Brno Studies in English*, 45(1) (2019), 143–155.

Krashinsky Robertson, Susan, 'Inside the Weird and Wild Making of the MaddAddam Ballet', *Toronto Globe and Mail* (11 November 2022).

Langdon, Alison, 'The More Things Change: Maria Edgeworth's "The Modern Griselda"', *The Year's Work in Medievalism*, 28 (2012), 2–9.

Lecker, Robert, 'Janus through the Looking Glass: Atwood's First Three Novels', in Arnold Davidson and Cathy E. Davidson, eds., *The Art of Margaret Atwood: Essays in Criticism* (Toronto: Anansi, 1981), 177–203.

Magnet, Shoshana, Amielle. *When Biometrics Fail: Gender, Race, and the Technology of Identity* (London: Duke University Press, 2011).

Marcus Millicent, 'Reading *The Decameron* through the Lens of COVID: The Fallacy of "Literary Distancing"', *The Yale Review*, 108(2) (2020), <https://yalereview.org/article/reading-decameron-through-lens-covid-19>, accessed 29 September 2023.

Marks, Peter., *Imagining Surveillance: Eutopian and Dystopian Literature and Film* (Edinburgh: Edinburgh University Press, 2017).

Marquardt, Patricia A., 'A Portrait of Hecate', *The American Journal of Philology*, 102 (1981), 243–260.

Marsden, Jean I., *The Re-Imagined Text: Shakespeare, Adaptation, and Eighteenth-Century Literary Theory* (Lexington: University Press of Kentucky, 1995).

Maunther, Melanie, 'Distant Lives, Still Voices: Sistering in Family Sociology', *Sociology*, 39(4) (2005), 623–642.

Merleau-Ponty, Maurice., *Phenomenology of Perception* (London: Routledge, 1972 [1945])

Michael, Magali Cornier, 'Narrative Multiplicity and the Multi-Layered Self in *The Blind Assassin*', in J. Brooks and Sarah Graham, eds., *Margaret Atwood: The Robber Bride, The Blind Assassin, Oryx and Crake* (New York: Continuum, 2010), 88–102.

Miller, Bruce, *Hulu and MGM's The Handmaid's Tale*, 2017.

Mitchell, Juliet, *Siblings* (Cambridge: Polity Press, 2003).

Mohr, Dunja M., *Worlds Apart? Dualism and Transgression in Contemporary Female Dystopias* (Jefferson, NC: McFarland, 2005).

Moodie, Susanna, *Life in the Clearings versus the Bush* (Toronto: McClelland & Stewart, 1989).

Murai, Mayako, and Cardi, Luciana, eds., *Re-Orienting the Fairy Tale: Contemporary Adaptations across Cultures* (Detroit: Wayne State University Press, 2020).

Mycak, Sonia, *In Search of the Split Subject: Psychoanalysis, Phenomenology, and the Novels of Margaret Atwood* (Toronto: ECW, 1996).

Myerson, Julie, 'The Testaments by Margaret Atwood Review – Hints of a Happy Ending', *The Guardian*, 15 September 2019, <https://www.theguardian.com/books/2019/sep/15/the-testaments-margaret-atwood-review>, accessed 23 May 2022.

Napolitano, Marc, 'Musical Madness: Biofictional Performances of the Lizzie Borden Murders', in Marie-Luise Kohlke and Christian Gutleben, eds., *Neo-Victorian Biofiction: Reimagining Nineteenth-Century Historical Subjects* (Leiden, The Netherlands: Brill Rodopi, 2020), 354–374.

Nicholson, Colin, ed. *Margaret Atwood: Writing and Subjectivity: New Critical Essays* (Basingstoke: Palgrave Macmillan, 1994), 4–5.

Nischik, Reingard, *Engendering Genre: The Works of Margaret Atwood* (Ottawa: University of Ottawa Press, 2009).

Nodelman, Perry, 'Children's Literature as a Genre', in Perry Nodelman, ed., *The Hidden Adult: Defining Children's Literature* (Baltimore: Johns Hopkins University Press, 2008), 133–244.

Orwell, George, *Nineteen Eight-Four* (Ware, Wordsworth, 2021).

Ostad, Katrina, '"Alias Grace": Twenty Years in the Making, But On TV at the Right Time', *The New York Times* (29 October 2017), <https://login.ezproxy.stthomas.edu/login?url=https://www.proquest.com/newspapers/october-29-2017-page-1-ar/docview/1985363288/se-2>, accessed 3 July 2023.

Ostriker, Alicia, 'The Thieves of Language – Women Poets and Revisionist Mythmaking', in Elaine Showalter, ed., *The New Feminist Criticism – Essays on Women, Literature and Theory* (London: Virago, 1986), 316.

Parkin-Gounelas, Ruth, '"What Isn't There' in Margaret Atwood's *The Blind Assassin*: The Psychoanalysis of Duplicity', *Modern Fiction Studies*, 50(3) (2004), 681–700.

Percec, Dana, 'The Canadian *Tempest*: Margaret Atwood and Shakespeare Retold as *Hag-Seed*', *Caietele Echinox*, 34 (2018), 295–307.

Rabia, K. A., 'Deconstructing the Witch: As Etched on the Body', *Literary Herald*, 2 (2017).

Rasmussen, Per Erland, '*The Handmaid's Tale* (1996–98)', Chapter 15 in *Acoustical Canvases: The Music of Poul Ruders* (Denmark: DMT Publishing, 2007), 367–403.

Reed, Alison, 'Disembodied Hands: Structural Duplicity in Atwood's *The Blind Assassin*', *Margaret Atwood Studies*, 3(1) (2009), 18–25.

Reichenbächer, Helmut, 'Offred at the Opera: Dimensions of Adaptation in Poul Ruders and Paul Bentley's *The Handmaid's Tale*', in Shannon Wells-Lassagne and Fiona McMahon, eds., *Adapting Margaret Atwood:* The Handmaid's Tale *and Beyond* (London: Palgrave Macmillan, 2021), 177–209.

Relke, Diana M. A., 'Double Voice, Single Vision: A Feminist Reading of Margaret Atwood's *The Journals of Susanna Moodie*', *Atlantis*, 9(1) (1983), 35–48.

Rine, Abigail, *Irigaray, Incarnation and Contemporary Women's Fiction* (London: Bloomsbury, 2015).

Rountree, Kathryn, 'The Politics of the Goddess: Feminist Spirituality and the Essentialism Debate', *The International Journal of Anthropology*, 43 (1999), 138–165.

Roupenian, Kristen, 'The Uneasy Uplift of *The Testaments*', *The New Republic* (5 December 2019), <https://newrepublic.com/article/155690/uneasy-uplift-margaret-atwood-testaments-book-review>, accessed 8 December 2020.

Rye, Matthew, 'A Topical Tale: Gilead Returns to the Coliseum Stage', *Bachtrack* (April 2022), <https://bachtrack.com/review-handmaids-tale-miskimmon-lindsey-bell-amereau-english-national-opera-april-2022>, accessed 23 August 2023.

Sabo, Peter, and Rhiannon Graybill, 'Testifying Bodies: The Bible and Margaret Atwood's *The Testaments*', *Journal of Feminist Studies in Religion*, 38(1) (2022), 131–147. *Project MUSE*, <https://dx.doi.org/10.2979/jfemistudreli.38.1.24>

Sandler, Linda, 'Interview with Margaret Atwood', *Malahat Review*, 41 (1977), 7–27.

Sartre, Jean Paul, *Being and Nothingness* (New York: Simon and Schuster/Pocket Books, 1972 [1943]).

Sceats, Sarah, *Food, Consumption and the Body in Contemporary Women's Fiction* (Cambridge: Cambridge University Press, 2004).

Scholes, Robert, *Fabulation and Metafiction* (Urbana: University of Illinois Press, 1979).

Schwan, Anne, *Convict Voices: Women, Class, and Writing about Prison in Nineteenth-Century England* (Durham: University of New Hampshire Press, 2014).

Sentov, Ana, 'Changing the Pattern: Reclaiming History, Constructing Herstory in Margaret Atwood's *Alias Grace*', *Folia Linguistica et Litteraria*, 26 (2019), 109–125.

Shah, Bina, *Before She Sleeps* (Encino: Delphinium, 2019).

Shakespeare, William, '*The Tempest* [1611]', in Stephen Greenblatt, Walter Cohen and Jean E. Howard, eds., *The Norton Shakespeare*, 3rd edn (New York: W.W. Norton, 2016).

Shamas, Laura, *We Three: The Mythology of Shakespeare's Weird Sisters* (New York: Peter Lang Publishing, 2007).

Shead, Jackie, *Margaret Atwood: Crime Fiction Writer: The Reworking of a Popular Genre* (London: Routledge, 2016).

Shephard, Nicole, 'Big Data and Sexual Surveillance', *Association for Progressive Communications*, (2016), 1–18.

Silverstein, Brett, *Cost of Competence: Why Inequality Causes Depression, Eating Disorders and Illness in Women* (New York: Oxford University Press, 1995).

Smarr, Janet Levarie, 'Women Rewrite Griselda: From Christine de Pizan to Julia Voznesenskaya', *Heliotropia*, 15 (2018), 205–229.

Smith, Ali, 'Atwood at 80: How Her Work Shaped the Lives of Authors and Activists', Features, Penguin (18 November 2019), <https://www.penguin.co.uk/articles/2019/11/authors-activists-celebrate-margaret-atwood-80th-birthday>

Smith, Andrew and William Hughes, eds., *EcoGothic* (Manchester: Manchester University Press, 2013).

Smith, Laurajane and Campbell, Gary, "Nostalgia for the Future': Memory, Nostalgia and the Politics of Class', *International Journal of Heritage Studies*, 23(7) (2017), 612–627 < https://doi-org.ezproxy.lancs.ac.uk/10.1080/1352725 8.2017.1321034>.

Snyder, Katherine V., '"Time to Go": The Post-Apocalyptic and the Post-Traumatic in Margaret Atwood's *Oryx and Crake*', *Studies in the Novel*, 43(4) (2011), 470–479.

Stern, Tiffany, '"A small-beer health to his second day": Playwrights, Prologues, and First Performances in the Early Modern Theater', *Studies in Philology*, 101(2) (2004), 172–199.

Stoeber, Orville, *Hymns of the God's Gardeners* (CD Baby B002OJGGJY, 2009), compact disc.

Stovel, Nora Foster, 'Reflections on Mirror Images: Double and Identity in the Novels of Margaret Atwood', *Essays on Canadian Writing*, 33 (1986), 50–67.

Su, John J., *Ethics and Nostalgia in the Contemporary Novel* (Cambridge: Cambridge University Press, 2005).

Tatar, Maria, 'Why Fairy Tales Matter: The Performative and the Transformative', *Western Folklore*, 69(1) (2010), 55–64.

Tatar, Yağmur, '"Spirits to Enforce, Art to Enchant": Metatheatricality and Art in *The Tempest* and *Hag-Seed*', *British and American Studies; Timisoara*, 26 (2020): 93–100, 271.

Tate, Andrew, *Apocalyptic Fiction* (London: Bloomsbury Academic, 2017)

Tenorio, Juanita Marie, 'Immigrant, Slave, and Prostitute: Murderous Gothic Heroines in Neo- Victorian Screen Adaptations', ProQuest Dissertations Publishing, 2021.

Terauds, John, 'Margaret Atwood's long-lost Canadian Opera Company work turns up in Vancouver with new composer', *Ludwig van Toronto*, 28 February 2013. <https://www.ludwig-van.com/toronto/2013/02/28/margaret-atwoods-long-lost-canadian-opera-company-work-turns-up-in-vancouver-with-new-compsoer/>, accessed 17 August 2025.

Teverson, Andrew, *Fairy Tale* (London: Routledge, 2013).

Tolan, Fiona, 'Margaret Atwood's Revisions of Classic Texts' *The Cambridge Companion to Margaret Atwood* (Cambridge: Cambridge University Press, 2021a), 109–123.

Tolan, Fiona, 'Twenty-first-century Gileads: Feminist Dystopian Fiction After Atwood—The Handmaid's Tale, The Natural Way of Things, The Water Cure, and The Testaments', in Kataryzyna Ostalska and Tomasz Fisiak, eds., *The Postworld In-Between Utopia and Dystopia: Intersectional, Feminist, and Non-Binary Approaches in 21st-Century Speculative Literature and Culture* (London: Routledge, 2021b), 155–167.

Tolan, Fiona, *The Fiction of Margaret Atwood* (London and New York: Bloomsbury Academic, 2023).

Trumpener, Katie, 'Picture-book Worlds and Ways of Seeing', in M. O. Grenby and Andrea Immel, eds., *Cambridge Companion to Children's Literature* (Cambridge: Cambridge University Press, 2009), 55–75.

Van Luyn, Ariella, '(In)Famous Subjects: Representing Women's Criminality and Violence in Historical Biofictions', *New Writing: The International Journal for the Practice and Theory of Creative Writing*, 16(1) (March 2019), 67–76.

VanSpanckeren, Kathryn, 'Atwood's Space Crone: Alchemical Vison and Revision in Morning in the Burned House', in Phyllis Sternberg Perrakis, ed., *Adventures of the Spirit: The Older Woman in the Works of Doris Lessing, Margaret Atwood, and Other Contemporary Women Writers* (Columbus: Ohio State University Press, 2007).

Vevaina, Coomi S., 'Margaret Atwood and History', in Coral Ann Howells ed., *The Cambridge Companion to Margaret Atwood* (Cambridge: Cambridge University Press, 2006), 86–99.

Vint, Sherryl, *Bodies of Tomorrow: Technology, Subjectivity, Science Fiction* (Toronto: University of Toronto Press, 2007).

Wagner-Martin, Linda, '"Giving Way to Bedrock" – Atwood's Later Poems', in L. M. York, ed., *Various Atwoods – Essays on the Later Poems, Short Fiction, and Novels* (Ontario: Anansi, 1995), 81.

Walton, Heather, *Literature, Theology and Feminism* (Manchester: Manchester University Press, 2007).

Ward, David, 'Surfacing: Separation, Transition, Incorporation', in Colin Nicholson, ed., *Margaret Atwood: Writing and Subjectivity: New Critical Essays* (Toronto: Macmillan, 1994), 94–118.

Warner, Marina, *Once Upon a Time: A Short History of Fairy Tale* (Oxford: Oxford University Press, 2016).

Warner, Marina, *Fairy Tale: A Very Short Introduction* (Oxford: Oxford University Press, 2018).

Warner, Marina, 'The Truth in Stories', *History Workshop* (5 February 2018), <https://www.historyworkshop.org.uk/the-truth-in-stories/>

Watkins, Susan, 'Review: *The Testaments* – Margaret Atwood's Sequel to *The Handmaid's Tale*', *The Conversation* (12 September 2019), <https://theconversation.com/review-the-testaments-margaret-atwoods-sequel-to-the-handmaids-tale-123465>

Watkins, Susan. *Contemporary Women's Post-Apocalyptic Fiction* (London: Bloomsbury, 2020).

Weaver, Robert, ed. *Poems for Voices* (Toronto: Canadian Broadcasting Corporation, 1970).

Wilde, Oscar, 'A Preface to "Dorian Gray', *Fortnightly Review*, 49(291) (1891), 480–481.

Williams, Holly, 'The Testaments Review: Margaret Atwood's Overly Neat Handmaid's Tale Sequel is Surprisingly Fun', *The Independent* (6 September 2019), <https://www.independent.co.uk/arts-entertainment/books/reviews/testaments-review-margaret-atwood-handmaids-tale-sequel-aunt-lydia-offred-book-a9094336.html>, accessed 23 May 2022.

Wilson, Sharon Rose, ed., *Margaret Atwood's Textual Assassinations: Recent Poetry and Fiction* (Columbus: Ohio State University Press, 2004).

Wilson, Sharon Rose, *Myths and Fairy Tales in Contemporary Women's Fiction: From Atwood to Morrison* (New York: Palgrave, 2008).

Wilson, Sharon Rose, *Margaret Atwood's Fairy-Tale Sexual Politics* (Jackson: University Press Mississippi, 2010).

Wisker, Gina, 'Margaret Atwood and History', in Coral Ann Howells ed., *The Cambridge Companion to Margaret Atwood* (Cambridge: Cambridge University Press, 2006), 92–108.

Wisker, Gina, *Atwood's The Handmaid's Tale:* Reader's Guide (London: Bloomsbury, 2010).

Wisker, Gina, 'Imagining beyond Extinctathon: Indigenous Knowledge, Survival, Speculation – Margaret Atwood's and Ann Patchett's Eco-Gothic', *Contemporary Women's Writing,* 11(3), (November 2017), 412–431.

Woolf, Virginia, *To the Lighthouse* (London: Hogarth Press, 1927).

Wordsworth, William, and Samuel Taylor Coleridge, *Lyrical Ballads* (London: 1798)

Worsley, Lucy, 'Jane and Ann Boyd—Secret Baby', *Lady Killers with Lucy Worsley*. A StoryHunter Production for BBC Radio 4 (24 January 2022).

Wrobel, Claire., 'Negotiating Dataveillance in the Near Future: Margaret Atwood's Dystopias', *Commonwealth Essays and Studies,* 43(2) (2021).

Yorke, Liz, *Impertinent Voices-Subversive Strategies in Contemporary Women's Poetry* (London: Routledge, 1991).

Zajac, Paul Joseph, 'Prisoners of Shakespeare: Trauma and Adaptation in Atwood's *Hag-Seed*', *Studies in the Novel,* 52(3) (2020), 324–343.

Zapf, Hubert, *Literature as Cultural Ecology: Sustainable Texts* (London: Bloomsbury, 2016).

Zipes, Jack, 'Cross-Cultural Connections and the Contamination of the Classical Fairy Tale', in Jack Zipes, ed., *The Great Fairy Tale Tradition: From Straparola and Basile to the Brothers Grimm* (New York: Norton, 2001), 845–869.

Zipes, Jack, 'Introduction', in Jack Zipes, ed., *The Great Fairy Tale Tradition: From Straparola and Basile to the Brothers Grimm* (New York: Norton, 2001), xi–xiv.

Zipes, Jack, *The Irresistible Fairy Tale: The Cultural and Social History of Genre* (Princeton: Princeton University Press, 2012).

Zipes, Jack, *The Oxford Companion to Fairy Tales* (Oxford: Oxford University Press, 2015).

Zipes, Jack, *Buried Treasures: The Power of Political Fairy Tales* (Princeton: Princeton University Press, 2023).

Zumas, Leni, *Red Clocks* (London: Harper Collins, 2019).

Audio Books

Atwood, Margaret, *The Handmaid's Tale*, narrated by Claire Danes et al. (Audible, 2017).

TV

Alias Grace, CBC/Netflix, 2017.

The Handmaid's Tale, Hulu, 2017–present.

Websites

<https://essaygpt.hix.ai/essay/analysis-of-morning-in-the-burned-house-6c1356>, accessed 2 June 2923

<https://podcasts.apple.com/us/podcast/23janeandannboydsecretbaby/id1620155570?i=1000640956754>, accessed 2 June 2023.

The List online (2022), <https://list.co.uk/news/16759/interview-margaret-atwood-on-new-novel-maddaddam>, accessed 22 August 2023.

'2022 Deadliest Year of the Decade for Women and Children,' *Safe Ireland: Creating Safety for Women and Children,* 2022. <https://www.safeireland.ie/2022-deadliest-year-of-thedecadeforwomenandchildren/#:~:text=According%20to%20Garda%20statistics%20published,have%20been%20victims%20of%20femicide>, accessed 3 July 2023.

Notes on Contributors

LAURA-JANE DEVANNY is currently Senior Lecturer with the University of Northampton (Education Department). She returned to study in 2012 through a fully funded AHRC award and earned a PhD at De Montfort University (UK) in 2017. Following the completion of her doctoral studies with a thesis titled 'Speculative Fiction by Twenty-First Century Women Writers', she returned to a previous successful career in international secondary English teaching (Thailand and Bali), before returning to teach in the UK. Her research interest lies within contemporary feminisms and literary representations of the future female, with a particular focus on the female body as the locus of choice. She has previously published on science fiction and prize culture and her most recent publication centred around cloning and reproductive choice. She is currently working on a monograph charting the works of contemporary UK women writers of speculative fiction.

ROBIN ELLIOTT has devoted his career to furthering the cause of scholarly research in the field of Canadian music studies. In this field he has published over a dozen books or editions of music as author, editor, or co-editor, and has written dozens of peer-reviewed articles in edited collections and scholarly journals. As a professor of musicology and Jean A. Chalmers Chair in Canadian Music at the University of Toronto, he invests a great deal of energy in educating and mentoring young Canadian music scholars; many of his former graduate student advisees hold academic positions in Canada and abroad. His current major research project, titled 'European Refugee Musicians in Canada, 1937–1950', examines the life stories and career experiences of over 100 artists, the majority of them Jewish, who fled from Nazi-occupied Europe to Canada.

JESSICA GILDERSLEEVE is Professor of English Literature and Associate Head of School (Research) at the University of Southern Queensland.

Her research explores literary and cultural trauma throughout the twentieth and twenty-first centuries. She is the author and editor of several books, including most recently *Screening the Gothic in Australia and New Zealand: Contemporary Antipodean Film and Television* (2022) and *The Routledge Companion to Australian Literature* (2021).

BLANKA GRZEGORCZYK teaches at the University of Cambridge and Manchester Metropolitan University and is the author of *Discourses of Postcolonialism in Contemporary British Children's Literature* (2015), *Terror and Counter-Terror in Contemporary British Children's Literature* (2020) and *Reading Across Worlds: Postcolonial Intersectionality in Contemporary Children's Literature* (forthcoming in 2026). Her main research interests are in the literature and culture of twentieth and twenty-first centuries, with a particular interest in colonial, postcolonial and 'wars around terror' literatures in English; knowledges and writing from below; post-war and contemporary fiction; arts, creativities and literature; and writing for and about the young.

JADE HINCHLIFFE specialises in surveillance studies and speculative fiction and has a PhD in Sociology from The University of Hull. She has a BA (Hons) in English Literature and a MRes in English Literature, both from The University of Huddersfield. Jade was awarded the Surveillance Studies Network's Early Career Researcher Prize for her article in *Surveillance & Society* published in 2021. Jade works in the charity sector and is currently Centre Leader at IntoUniversity Hull East.

CORAL ANN HOWELLS is Professor Emerita, University of Reading and Senior Research Fellow, Institute of English Studies, University of London. She has published widely on contemporary Canadian fiction, especially writing by women. Her publications include *Private and Fictional Words: Canadian Women Novelists of the 1970s and 80s* (1987), *Margaret Atwood* (1996, 2005), *Alice Munro* (1998) and *Contemporary Canadian Women's Fiction: Refiguring Identities* (2003). She edited the *Cambridge Companion to Margaret Atwood* (2006) and the *Cambridge Companion to Margaret Atwood, 2nd edition* (2021). She co-edited with

Eva-Marie Kroller *The Cambridge History of Canadian Literature* (2009) and is co-editor with Gerry Turcotte and Paul Sharrad of the final volume of the *Oxford History of the Novel in English* (2017). She is a Fellow of the Royal Society of Canada.

LAURIE JOHNSON is Professor of English and Cultural Studies at the University of Southern Queensland and a Fellow of both the Society of Antiquaries of London and the Royal Historical Society. His books include *Leicester's Men and their Plays: An Early Elizabethan Playing Company and its Legacy* (2023), *Shakespeare's Lost Playhouse: Eleven Days at Newington Butts* (2018), *The Tain of Hamlet* (2013) and *The Wolf Man's Burden* (2001), as well as edited books, *Embodied Cognition and Shakespeare's Theatre: The Early Modern Body-Mind* (with John Sutton and Evelyn Tribble, 2014) and *Rapt in Secret Studies: Emerging Shakespeares* (with Darryl Chalk, 2010).

SALLY MCLUCKIE is a self-employed Secondary English tutor. She has recently submitted her doctoral thesis looking at moral injury, moral agency and moral repair in the work of Margaret Atwood and Carol Ann Duffy. She is currently awaiting confirmation on a proposal for her first monograph and in the meantime continuing research in the areas of gender studies, feminisms, spiritual feminisms, literature and theology. Sally is also an English Language examiner.

DUNJA M. MOHR is the Vice President of the Margaret Atwood Society and the Society's European Representative. She acts as Head of the Women, Gender, and Diversity Studies Section of the Association for Canadian Studies in German-speaking Countries and serves on the Advisory Boards of *Utopian Studies* and *Margaret Atwood Studies*. Together with Kirsten Sandrock, she organized the international confer- ence 'Artpolitical: Margaret Atwood's Aesthetics' in 2021 and co-edited a special issue on 'Politics and Literature in Margaret Atwood's Oeuvre' for *Margaret Atwood Studies* (2024). She is the author of the award-winning monograph *Worlds Apart? Dualism and Transgression in Contemporary Female Dystopias* and has (co-)edited several volumes. Currently, she is editing a collection on Atwood and the Artpolitical and working on a monograph on *Frankenstein Adaptations*.

LORNA PIATTI-FARNELL is Academic Dean at SAE Creative Media Institute, New Zealand. She is the Director of the Australasian Horror Studies Network (AHSN). Her research sits at the intersection between screen media, popular culture, and cultural history, with a particular focus on transmedia storytelling, eco-narratives, digital technologies, food cultures, and popular iconographies, and a long-standing interest in Gothic horror and fantasy. She has published widely in these areas, including volumes such as *The Routledge Companion to Literature and Food* (2018), *Consuming Gothic: Food and Horror in Film* (Palgrave, 2017), and *Poison and the Popular Imagination: Representations, Iconographies, and Meanings* (Bloomsbury, 2026). Professor Piatti-Farnell is the sole editor the *Routlege Advances in Popular Culture Studies* and Bloomsbury's *Research in Horror Studies* book series.

SHANNON SCOTT is Adjunct Professor of English and film at the University of St. Thomas. She has contributed essays to collections published by Manchester University Press, Routledge, Palgrave and Bloomsbury. In addition, she has published short fiction in *Nightmare Magazine*, *Nightscript*, *The Other Stories* and *Water~Stone*. She has created two lecture series on the horror genre for Audible and is co-editor, along with Alexis Easley, of *Terrifying Transformations: An Anthology of Victorian Werewolf Fiction, 1838–1896*.

HELENE STAVELEY has specialised in teaching contemporary Canadian fiction and children's literature in undergraduate courses in the English Department at Memorial University of Newfoundland and Labrador. Her research interests include the literary production of Margaret Atwood and Thomas King in particular, along with representations of play and game in fiction, children's literature, film and graphic narrative. She is currently researching how Atlantic Canadian books for children and young adults present scenes of play and game, and lives in St. John's, Newfoundland and Labrador, Canada.

FIONA TOLAN is Reader in Contemporary Women's Writing at Liverpool John Moores University, UK. She is author of *The Fiction of Margaret Atwood* (2023) and *Margaret Atwood: Feminism and Fiction* (2007), both of which were awarded 'Book of the Year' by the Margaret Atwood Society. As well as numerous articles and chapters on Atwood, she is co-editor of *The Routledge Companion to Literature and Feminism* (2023) and *Jackie Kay: Critical Essays* (forthcoming). She is currently writing a monograph, *The Politics of Cleaning in Post-War Women's Writing*.

SARAH WAGSTAFFE holds a PhD in English Literature from Lancaster University, where she also worked as an Associate Lecturer in the English Literature and Creative Writing, History and Sociology departments. Her current research analyses contemporary literature and media with a focus on gender, psychology and politics, with an ongoing interest in speculative fiction and modern representations of the apocalypse. Her research spans literature and new media, having published work on novels, television and video games. Her first monograph, *Nostalgia, Identity and Fear in Contemporary American Women's Speculative Fiction: Encroaching Pasts, Uncertain Futures*, is currently in the publication process.

GINA WISKER is a professor and doctoral supervisor at the University of Bath, professor emeritus at the University of Brighton and lecturer in literature at Open University. She is also a Visiting Research Associate at the Universities of Gibraltar, Johannesberg and Stellenbosch. She is a long-established practising teacher of literature (women's writing, the Gothic) contributing to MA literature, creative writing and humanities research methods. She has been Chief Editor of IETI (*Innovations in Education and Teaching International*) since 1987 and in 2006 founded and coedits online horror and dark fantasy journal *Dissections*. Her books include *Margaret Atwood, an Introduction to Critical Views of Her Fiction* (2007), *Contemporary Women's Gothic Fiction* (2012), *Contemporary Women's Ghost stories: Spectres, revenants and deadly returns* (2016) and *Postcolonial and African American women's writing* (2022), amongst many others.

SARAH WORGAN completed her PhD at Kingston University, with the support of TECHNE. The chapter in this collection was born out of ideas from her thesis, which explored the connection between monstrosity and a politics of life. She has a particular interest in conceptions of power and how art is able to form a resistance. She is a member of the International Gothic Association and IN-CSA.

Index

Genre Fiction and Film Companions

Series Editor: Simon Bacon

The *Genre Fiction and Film Companions* provide accessible introductions to key texts within the most popular genres of our time. Written by leading scholars in the field, brief essays on individual texts offer innovative ways of understanding, interpreting and reading the topics in question. Invaluable for students, teachers and fans alike, these surveys offer new insights into the most important literary works, films, music, events and more within genre fiction and film.

We welcome proposals for edited collections on new genres and topics. Please contact baconetti@googlemail.com or oxford@ peterlang.com.

Published Volumes

The Gothic
Edited by Simon Bacon

Cli-Fi
Edited by Axel Goodbody and Adeline Johns-Putra

Horror
Edited by Simon Bacon

Sci-Fi
Edited by Jack Fennell

Monsters
Edited by Simon Bacon

Transmedia Cultures
Edited by Simon Bacon

Shirley Jackson
Edited by Kristopher Woofter

Toxic Cultures
Edited by Simon Bacon

Magic
Edited by Katharina Rein

The Undead in the 21st Century
Edited by Simon Bacon

The Deep
Edited by Marko Teodorski and Simon Bacon

Death in the 21st Century
Edited by Katarzyna Bronk-Bacon and Simon Bacon

Alice Through the Looking-Glass
Edited by Franziska E. Kohlt and Justine Houyaux

The Weird
Edited by Carl H. Sederholm and Kristopher Woofter

Aliens
Edited by Elana Gomel and Simon Bacon

IndigePop
Edited by Svetlana Seibel and Kati Dlaske

Fairies
Edited by Lorna Piatti-Farnell and Simon Bacon

Margaret Atwood
Edited by Gina Wisker